New Developments in Economic Education

To Darlene, Trey and Sparks, for their love and support, and for Uncle Hugh, who is missed each and every day.

Franklin G. Mixon, Jr

To my wife, Gigi Alexander, and to my grandsons, Jeffrey, Richard, Ryan and Zachary, and to Lilly.

Richard J. Cebula

New Developments in Economic Education

Edited by

Franklin G. Mixon, Jr

Columbus State University, USA

Richard J. Cebula

Jacksonville University, USA

Edward Elgar

Cheltenham, UK • Northampton, MA, USA

Published by
Edward Elgar Publishing Limited
The Lypiatts
15 Lansdown Road
Cheltenham
Glos GL50 2JA
UK

Edward Elgar Publishing, Inc.
William Pratt House
9 Dewey Court
Northampton
Massachusetts 01060
USA

A catalogue record for this book
is available from the British Library

Library of Congress Control Number: 2013949882

This book is available electronically in the ElgarOnline.com Economics Subject Collection, E-ISBN 978 1 78254 972 7

MIX
Paper from
responsible sources
FSC® C013056

ISBN 978 1 78254 971 0

Typeset by Columns Design XML Ltd, Reading
Printed and bound in Great Britain by T.J. International Ltd, Padstow

Contents

Contributors

Carlos J. Asarta is Director of the Center for Economic Education and Entrepreneurship and Associate Professor in the Department of Economics at the University of Delaware. He holds Master's and PhD degrees in economics from the University of Nebraska-Lincoln. His work focuses on the areas of economic education, assessment and economic/financial literacy. His research has been published in academic journals such as the *Journal of Economic Education* and the *Decision Sciences Journal of Innovative Education*. Asarta is the recipient of several teaching, service and research awards including the 2013 Association of Students of the University of Nebraska Outstanding Educator of the Year Award, the 2012 Rising Star Award from the Council for Economic Education and the 2011 Phillip Saunders Best Research Paper Award from the National Association of Economic Educators.

Yoram Bauman, 'the world's first and only stand-up economist,' performs regularly at colleges and corporate events, sharing the stage with everyone from Robin Williams to Paul Krugman. He has appeared in *Time* and on PBS and NPR, and is the co-author of the two-volume *Cartoon Introduction to Economics*. He is the organizer of the humor session at the annual meeting of the American Economic Association. Bauman founded Non-Profit Comedy in Seattle, providing a series of benefit shows to raise money for local non-profits. He has a BA in mathematics from Reed College and a PhD in economics from the University of Washington. He is a fellow at Sightline Institute in Seattle, and in 2011 spent five months in Beijing as a visiting scholar at the University of International Business and Economics. His website is http://www.standupeconomist.com.

Scott A. Beaulier is the Adams-Bibby Chair of Free Enterprise and the Executive Director of the Manuel H. Johnson Center for Political Economy, both at Troy University in Alabama. Beaulier is the recipient of awards such as the William P. Snavely Award for Outstanding Achievement in Graduate Studies in Economics (George Mason University, 2004), the Israel M. Kirzner Award for Outstanding Dissertation in Austrian Economics (George Mason University, 2004) and the Professor of the Month Award (Mercer University, April 2005). Beaulier's research in economic education has appeared in the *Journal of Economic Education* and the *Journal of Economics and Economic Education Research*. He is the author of *The Making of an African Exception: How Botswana Escaped the African Tragedy (and How Other African Countries Could Do the Same)* (Edward Elgar, 2009). His work outside economic education has appeared in the *Journal of Sports Economics*, *Kyklos*, *Constitutional Political Economy* and the *Eastern Economic Journal*, among others.

Calvin Blackwell is Associate Professor of Economics at the College of Charleston in South Carolina. Blackwell's work in the area of economic education has been published in the *Journal of Economic Education*, *Journal of Economics and Finance Education*, *Classroom Expernomics* and the *Journal for Economic Educators*. His research in other areas has appeared in the *Journal of Economic Behavior and Organization*, *Kyklos*, the *National Tax Journal* and *Public Finance Review*, among others.

William D. Bosshardt is Associate Professor of Economics and Director of the Center for Economic Education at Florida Atlantic University. He is Associate Editor of *The International Review of Economic Education* and Associate Editor of *The American Economist*. His research has appeared in a number of journals, including *American Economic Review*, *Review of Economics and Statistics*, *Economic Inquiry* and *Journal of Economic Education*. Bosshardt is a past president of the National Association of Economic Educators.

Roger B. Butters is Assistant Professor of Economics at the University of Nebraska-Lincoln and President of the Nebraska Council on Economic Education. An active researcher and author, Butters has been invited to teach seminars on economics and international finance at universities around the United States, Europe and China. He teaches seminars for K-12 students and teachers and frequently appears on local television and radio as an advocate for economic literacy. His primary research interests are in the fields of economic education, international finance and growth. Butters is a contributor and evaluator of the 'Is Capitalism Good for the Poor?' curriculum, a recipient of the Lincoln Business Journal's 40 under 40 Award, a Paul Harris Fellow and was recognized by the National Association of Economic Educators as the inaugural recipient of the 'Rising Star' award.

Art Carden is Assistant Professor of Economics at Samford University in Alabama. Carden's research has appeared in the *Journal of Urban*

Economics, *Public Choice*, *Contemporary Economic Policy* and the *American Review of Political Economy*, among others.

Richard J. Cebula holds the Walker/Wells Fargo Endowed Chair in Finance at Jacksonville University in Florida. Cebula is the Editor-in-Chief of the *Journal of Regional Analysis and Policy* and Senior Editor of the *Journal of Economics and Finance Education*, which he also co-founded in 2002. His research in economic education has appeared in the *Journal of Economics and Finance Education, Journal of Private Enterprise* and *International Advances in Economic Research*. Cebula was recognized for his teaching excellence by the Southern Economic Association when he was a recipient (Armstrong Atlantic State University, 2007) of the prestigious Kenneth G. Elzinga Distinguished Teaching Award. While on the faculty at Emory University, he received the Teacher of the Year Award on three occasions and he is a past winner of an NROTC Teaching Award (Armstrong Atlantic State University, 2007). He is author or co-author of 14 scholarly books. Cebula's research in areas outside economic education has been widely published, for example, in the *Quarterly Journal of Economics*, *Journal of the American Statistical Association*, *Land Economics*, *Industrial Relations* and *Economic Inquiry*, among others.

Emily Chamlee-Wright is Provost and Dean at Washington College in Maryland. She began her teaching career at Beloit College in 1993, and was awarded an endowed professorship, the Elbert H. Neese Professor of Economics, in 2007. Chamlee-Wright is the author of three books: *The Cultural and Political Economy of Recovery: Social Learning in a Post-disaster Environment* (2010), *Culture and Enterprise: The Development, Representation, and Morality of Business*, with Don Lavoie (2000) and *The Cultural Foundations of Economic Development* (1997). She is also co-editor of *The Political Economy of Hurricane Katrina and Community Development* (Edward Elgar, 2010).

Maggie Foley is Assistant Professor of Finance at Jacksonville University in Florida. Foley's research has appeared in the *Journal of Economics and Finance*, *International Research Journal of Applied Finance*, *Academy of Economics and Finance Journal*, *Eurasian Economic Review*, *International Journal in Finance and Accounting Studies* and *International Journal of Economics and Finance*, among others.

Wayne Geerling is Senior Lecturer in Economics at Pennsylvania State University in University Park in Pennsylvania. Prior to 2012, he worked at La Trobe University in Melbourne, Australia. Geerling has published articles on multimedia and Robert Frank's *Economic Naturalist* in the

International Review of Economics Education and is currently writing *The Ultimate Guide to Teaching Economics* (co-author Dirk Mateer). His dedication to teaching has been recognized with several awards including a La Trobe University Citation for Outstanding Contribution to Student Learning (March 2011) and the Dean's Teaching Award for Undergraduate Teaching, Faculty of Law and Management (April 2010). He received an Australian Learning and Teaching Council Citation for Outstanding Contribution to Student Learning in June 2011.

Trellis G. Green is Associate Professor of Economics at the University of Southern Mississippi. Green's research in economic education has appeared in the *Journal of Economics and Finance Education* and *Shaping the Learning Curve: Essays on Economic Education* (2005).

Paul W. Grimes is Professor of Economics and Dean of the Kelce College of Business at Pittsburg State University in Kansas and Professor Emeritus of Economics at Mississippi State University. He has a long record of service in the field of economic education – in terms of both research and program delivery. In 2005, Grimes was recognized for his economic education research with the Henry H. Villard Award presented by the National Council on Economic Education. In 2009, he served as President of the National Association of Economic Educators. He is Editor-in-Chief of *The American Economist.*

Joshua C. Hall is Associate Professor of Economics at West Virginia University. He earned his Bachelor's and Master's degrees in economics from Ohio University and his PhD from West Virginia University in 2007. Prior to returning to his alma mater, he was the Elbert H. Neese, Jr Professor of Economics at Beloit College. Formerly an economist for the Joint Economic Committee of the US Congress, he is a co-author of the widely cited *Economic Freedom of the World* reports. Hall is author of over 50 articles in journals such as *Contemporary Economic Policy*, *Journal of Economic Behavior and Organization*, *Journal of Economic Education* and *Journal of Labor Research*, among others. He is a two-time winner of the Best Educational Note award from the *Journal of Private Enterprise*.

Michael R. Hammock is Assistant Professor of Economics at Middle Tennessee State University. Hammock's research in economic education has been published in *The American Economist*. His work in other areas has appeared in *Policy and Internet*.

Denise Hazlett is Professor of Economics at Whitman College in Washington. Her academic interest is primarily in the design of classroom experiments of economics. Hazlett's classroom experiments appear in the *Journal of Economic Education*, *Economic Inquiry*, *International Review of Economics Education*, *Southern Economic Journal*, *Journal of Economics*, *Perspectives on Economic Education Research* and *Classroom Expernomics*. She works with students to design classroom experiments and has received several awards from Whitman College supporting these collaborative projects. Hazlett's work in economic education includes contributions to edited volumes, including the *International Handbook on Teaching and Learning Economics* (Edward Elgar, 2012), *Teaching Innovations in Economics: Strategies and Applications for Interactive Instruction* (Edward Elgar, 2010) and *Teaching Economics: More Alternatives to Chalk and Talk* (Edward Elgar, 2006). Her research in other areas has been published in journals such as *Economic Theory* and *Social Science Computer Review*.

G. Dirk Mateer is Senior Lecturer at the University of Kentucky. He is the author of two books, *Principles of Economics* (with Lee Coppock) and *Economics in the Movies*. Mateer is nationally recognized for his teaching. He was the winner of the inaugural Economic Communicator Contest sponsored by the Association of Private Enterprise Education and the Market Based Management Institute (2007), profiled in the 'Great Teachers in Economics' series of the Gus A. Stavros Center of Economic Education at Florida State University (2005). In addition, he has received numerous awards including the George W. Atherton Award from Penn State, the university's highest teaching award (2011), was named a member of the Faculty Homecoming Court (2008 and 2010) and was voted the Best Overall Teacher in the Smeal College of Business by the readers of *Critique Magazine* (2010).

Franklin G. Mixon, Jr is Professor of Economics and the Director of the Center for Economic Education at Columbus State University in Georgia. Mixon serves on the editorial board of the *Journal of Economics and Finance Education*, and he has authored teaching manuals and test banks for principles and intermediate economics textbooks. Mixon's research in economic education has appeared in the *Journal of Economic Education*, *International Review of Economics Education*, *Journal of Economics and Finance Education* and the *Journal of Economics and Economic Education Research*. He has published studies ranking economics departments on the basis of economic education research. These have appeared in the *Southern Economic Journal* and *Bulletin of Economic Research*. While on the faculty at the University of Southern

Mississippi, he won the Business Advisory Council Distinguished Faculty Award (2001) and was a university finalist for the Aubrey K. and Ella G. Lucas Endowment for Excellence in Teaching Award (2005). Mixon's research in areas outside economic education has been widely published, for example, in the *Oxford Bulletin of Economics and Statistics*, *Journal of Money, Credit, and Banking*, *Journal of Applied Econometrics* and *Public Choice*, among others.

Andrew Perumal joined the University of Massachusetts as Assistant Professor of Economics in 2011. He received his BS in economics and management from the London School of Economics and Political Science and his MA and PhD in economics from the University of Nebraska-Lincoln. Prior to beginning his graduate work, Perumal was Research Assistant at the Institute of Policy Studies in Sri Lanka. His research interests span the core contributors to success in the economics major, the nature of firm-level productivity in urban areas and the dynamics of household migration to metropolitan areas.

Joel M. Potter is Associate Professor of Economics at the University of North Georgia. Potter's research has appeared in the *Southern Economic Journal*, *European Journal of Political Economy*, *Defence and Peace Economics* and the *Economics Bulletin*, among others.

Kenneth C. Rebeck is Associate Professor of Economics at St Cloud State University in Minnesota and Research Associate at the National Center for Research in Economic Education. Rebeck's research focuses on K-12, college-level and adult understanding of and attitudes toward economics and personal finance, with studies published in the *Journal of Economic Education*, *American Economic Review* and the *Journal of Consumer Affairs*, among others. He is active in creating and revising standardized tests and examiner's manuals in economics and personal finance, including the *Basic Economics Test*, *Test of Economic Knowledge*, *Test of Economic Literacy*, *Test of Understanding College Economics* and the *Financial Fitness For Life* exams for grades 3–5, 6–8 and 9–12.

Kevin E. Rogers is Professor of Economics and Associate Dean of the College of Business at Mississippi State University. He holds a PhD in economics from the University of Georgia and his research has appeared in a number of journals such as the *Review of Financial Economics*, *Journal of Productivity Analysis*, *Economics of Education Review* and *Journal of Consumer Affairs*. Rogers currently serves as Associate Editor for *The American Economist*.

Philip J. Ruder is Professor of Economics at Pacific University, a liberal arts college in Oregon. Since receiving his PhD in economics from the University of Wisconsin in Madison in 1994, Ruder has conducted research projects in forestry economics, urban and regional planning and pedagogy. At Pacific University, he has twice won the Trombley Award, which is awarded annually by students in recognition of teaching excellence.

John L. Scott is Professor of Economics at the University of North Georgia. Scott's research in economic education has been published in the *Journal of Economics and Economic Education Research*. His work in other areas has appeared in the *American Journal of Economics and Sociology*, *Economics of Peace and Security Journal* and the *Journal of Economics*, among others.

Sarah E. Skwire is a Fellow at The Liberty Fund in Indianapolis. Skwire holds a PhD in English from the University of Chicago, and she is the author of the 2013 book *Writing a Thesis* (12th edition). Her research has been published in the *Journal of Economic Behavior and Organization*, *Review of English Studies*, *Queen: A Journal of Rhetoric and Power* and *Literature and Medicine*, among others. She is currently working on a book-length project about money in early modern poetry.

Len J. Treviño holds the Gerald N. Gaston Eminent Scholar Chair in International Business at Loyola University–New Orleans in Los Angeles. Treviño's research in business and economic education has appeared in the *Journal of Education for Business* and *Shaping the Learning Curve: Essays on Economic Education* (2005). His work in international business and management has appeared in the *Journal of International Business Studies*, *Management International Review*, *International Business Review*, *Journal of World Business* and *Business Horizons*, *Review of World Economics*, among others.

Michelle A. Vachris is Professor of Economics and the BB&T Professor for the Study of Capitalism at Christopher Newport University (CNU) in Virginia. Before joining CNU, Vachris was an economist with the Bureau of Labor Statistics. Her research in the area of economic education has been published in the *Journal of Economic Education*, and she is a contributor to *International Handbook on Teaching and Learning Economics* (Edward Elgar, 2012).

William B. Walstad is the John T. and Mable M. Hay Professor of Economics at the University of Nebraska-Lincoln. He is Editor of the *Journal of Economic Education*. From 2000–06, he served as the Chair of the American Economic Association's standing Committee on Economic Education. From 2004–10, he was the Principal Investigator with Michael Salemi for the Teaching Innovations Program in economics, funded by the National Science Foundation, with the results reported in *Teaching Innovations in Economics: Strategies and Applications for Interactive Instruction* (Edward Elgar, 2010). His research focuses on the evaluation of programs and coursework in economics and personal finance at all education levels and for all age groups.

Zenon X. Zygmont is Professor of Economics at Western Oregon University. His research interests are in the post-communist economies, regulation and antitrust, the economics of collegiate and professional sports and economic education. Zygmont is a co-author, with Randy Grant and John Leadley, of *The Economics of Intercollegiate Sports* (2008). His research in economic education has been published in the *Journal of Economic Education*, while his research in other areas has been published in the *International Journal of Sport Finance*, *Journal of Sports Economics*, *Journal of Sport Management* and *Canadian Public Policy*.

Preface

When I entered college, I had dreams of being a chemist or a mathematician. I struggled to earn a B in freshman chemistry; so much for that major! With hard work, I earned As in math. However, my other coursework in the humanities and life experiences made me want not simply to solve math problems but rather use math to solve 'people' problems.

Then along came Principles of Economics. I was fortunate to have a professor who was basically a teacher as opposed to a researcher, and he was a good teacher. This made economics easy to learn, but I still longed for something more rigorous. In my senior year, I took Intermediate Macroeconomics with Professor John J. Klein, a disciple of Milton Friedman. He introduced me to economic rigor and a more math-oriented way of looking at the discipline. Then I was taught graduate macroeconomics by Professor Jim Quirk, who raised the math content of economics exponentially. I learned myriad applications of mathematics in economics and even published my first half dozen peer-reviewed papers while still a graduate student in the PhD program.

What Professors Klein and Quirk both did was raise my interest not only in economics and the tools of economics but also their many fascinating applications to real human economic problems, such as economic growth, implications of tax policy, theories of consumer behavior and complex utility functions, investment behavior, migration, interest rate determination, theories of the firm and human capital and game theory. And so much more. How my professors both taught me to love my chosen field of study was through a combination of authoritatively taught lectures mixed with humor and seriousness, with the Socratic Method and often creative class participation. For example, I was the only student in my class to prove a simple problem in qualitative economics. They made learning economics fun as well as mind expanding.

This is the context and underlying spirit of the present book. To help provide professors teaching economics with a variety of means by which to engage students, to keep their interest, to allow them access to the folly of economics as well as the brute seriousness of economics, to grow their interest, and to challenge their minds to apply their knowledge and technical tools to an ever-expanding range of economics problems. We want to make economics more fun to learn and more fun to teach as well. The better professors can succeed in these endeavors, the more successfully we can improve the human condition.

The chapters in this book that are fundamentally true research endeavors involving economics in the classroom and the educational process serve to reinforce the goal of understanding how to put economics in the proper context for it to most effectively be taught and understood.

Hopefully, the chapters that follow will provide a variety of insights and ideas that will facilitate the enhancement of the quality of teaching economics and the degree of learning economics reasoning and how to assess problems, how to identify solutions thereto and how to choose the best of those solutions.

Richard J. Cebula

1. A spoonful of sugar helps the medicine go down: why good content is never enough

Wayne Geerling and G. Dirk Mateer*

1.1 INTRODUCTION

Human beings have a natural curiosity for how the world works. It is what led us out of the cave, over the mountain and across the seas. Economics is a discipline that attempts to explain the ways of the world and the people in it. So why is the joke, 'How do you make an accountant seem interesting? Should we put him next to an economist?' so common an issue. We believe that it has a lot to do with how economics is taught. This is why we decided to share our approach to teaching. It is our hope that you will decide to try one, or more, of these ideas the next time you teach an introductory course.

We share a common passion for teaching but this chapter is not about us. It is about what we have discovered through teaching 30,000 students over the past decade and across two continents. We wish to emphasize three lessons. First, economics is a fascinating and rewarding discipline. Second, introductory economics courses are typically comprised of non-majors and instructors need to cater for this reality. Third, passion and commitment are contagious.

We shall touch on each of these points briefly and then share the specific techniques we use to connect with our students in greater detail. Our hope is to inspire the reader to adopt our philosophy, to try some of our methods in their courses and to start being creative in how they teach.

Presumably, readers of this chapter already share our interest and enthusiasm for economics. But students also want to know the answers to the questions that economics seeks to address, even if in the same breath they describe economics as 'boring.' They are fascinated by the global financial crisis, debt crises and the implications these have for their future. They want to know more about globalization and why some countries are wealthy and others remain impoverished. Almost without exception, every student can recall loved ones who have experienced serious medical conditions and they want to learn more about how high-quality medical care can be delivered at a reasonable cost. Along the same lines, they want advice about how to save enough for retirement. More generally, they want to know more about personal finance questions that involve opportunity costs. For instance, should they buy or lease a car? Rent an apartment or purchase a house? How much life insurance is enough? And then there are the BIG questions about life. Like when to marry and the cost of having children. With a set of questions like that it is hard to imagine that economics could ever be seen as dry – but it is. There is a disconnect among students – and this disconnect is often a result of poor teaching (more on this later).

The challenge for lecturers is to bridge this disconnect. Economics tells us that self-interest is a prime motivator. A good instructor must be able to demonstrate the big picture by engaging students with material that is personally relevant to them now and then leverage that understanding to tackle the long-run issues.

Second, introductory economics is typically comprised largely of non-majors. This has implications for how the audience is engaged. We use multimedia, the economic naturalist writing assignment and interactive polling/response systems to develop intuitive skills, engage in formative assessment and improve student motivation. Too often, instructors emphasize the economist's tool kit, whereas we concentrate on imparting the 'big ideas' for everyday life (Adkins and Newsome, 2006; Salemi and Siegfried, 1999). Not surprisingly, most introductory students do not decide to take another economics course. Models, theories and problem solving play a crucial role in understanding economics, but for a non-major it is arguably more important to provide exposure to the ideas and concepts that frame economic decision making.

Third, effective teaching requires passion and dedication. We cannot emphasize this point enough. Students want to learn and they will follow your lead when they see that you care – about economics, about teaching and about them. Our approach goes beyond simple chalk and talk or churning through PowerPoint slides to help you connect with your students.

1.2 MAKING THE STUDY OF ECONOMICS MORE INCLUSIVE

How does one go about making economics more inclusive? The first step is to recall the advice that every good writer reflects upon – their audience. In this section, we examine the typical cohort that takes introductory economics and make a number of teaching suggestions based on these findings.

Many first-year university students are required to take a course in basic economics, yet few will go on to major, let alone undertake postgraduate study, in this field. In fact, a majority of students who take an introductory course in economics at university will have their first and last experience with economics in the same semester or year. Why, then, are most undergraduate economics programs designed with graduates and PhD students in mind, even though they make up a minuscule number of students studying economics?

It is hard to provide a coherent picture across universities given the diverse structure of offerings in economics. Some universities offer a separate Bachelor of Economics (BEc) or economics as part of a double degree,[1] but at most universities economics is one of several competing majors offered in a business-related degree.[2] These degrees usually – but not always – have a common first year that involves Introductory Macroeconomics and Microeconomics (or a combination of both), but few other economics electives. Moreover, economics programs face real competition for student enrollments from substitutes whose focus is on applications and real-world relevance and whose job market prospects are alluring (Round and Shanahan, 2010).

> Economists continue to lament the fall in popularity of their degree, but have done little to respond to the challenges posed by the market by changing their product, its method of delivery, or its appeal. This continues to be the case even in the face of the traditional compulsory role of economics in the core of the programs in business, commerce, management, and marketing being questioned, most notably in the first-year curriculum. (Round and Shanahan, 2010, p. 433)

Given the diverse structure of offerings in economics, in many cases bi-polar, with some students undertaking a BEc and the rest doing only one subject, any average of aggregated data would present a misleading view. The best we can do is cite a few different studies to illustrate the prevailing heterogeneity. According to Frank, only 2 percent of American students who take an introductory economics subject major in economics

(Frank, 2007, p. 5). In the UK, the comparable figure is as high as 60–70 percent at old universities, which offer economics as a single or joint degree, and as low as 0–20 percent for students at new or modern universities, which typically offer economics as part of a business degree (that is, in a non-economics program).[3] The figure Sloman cites for non-economics programs in the UK is similar to universities in Australasia, which offer no separate Bachelor of Economics: as a first or second major at Queensland University of Technology (QUT), the figure is 10 percent; for Waikato University, 13 percent.[4]

The heterogeneity of the student body will vary across universities, of course, but as universities seek to distinguish their 'brand' in a globalized, competitive market, the number of non-majors studying economics, whether they be mature-aged, full-time professionals or from lower socio-economic groups, is likely to rise. This fact alone should prompt a major rethink in how economics is taught at an introductory level, one that can embed threshold concepts (Davies and Mangan, 2008), in both students studying specialist economics degrees and non-specialists.

Research has shown that introductory economics classes have limited impact on economic understanding (Hansen et al., 2002; Walstad and Rebeck, 2002; Walstad and Rebeck, 2008). Part of this stems from the image of economics as a dry, uninspiring, abstract subject, known for its inaccurate and gloomy predictions. Economics, as a discipline, has been conservative in adopting innovative approaches to teaching (Becker, 2001, 2003; Becker and Watts, 2001, 2008). The traditional mode of 'chalk and talk' is still prevalent in many classrooms; technology, when used, often reinforces a teacher-centered, passive student learning environment. The worst example of this is colloquially known as 'PowerPoint karaoke,' 'Death by PowerPoint' or 'Killing me Microsoftly,' where a lecturer simply reads custom-made lecture slides (provided by a publisher) verbatim. The students can download the slides in their own time and memorize them – and may not even bother attending the lecture.

Another problem with introductory courses is that most try to cover too many concepts, with the result that insufficient time and attention is devoted to mastering the important threshold concepts (Frank, 2007). The idea that less is better in the teaching of economics is not new (Becker, 2004). Getting academics to agree on which threshold concepts should be mandatory in an introductory course is a different matter altogether (Frank, 2007). One approach, favored by Frank, is to begin with a well-articulated short list of principles and then illustrate and apply each principle in the context of simple examples drawn from familiar settings (Frank, 2006). We shall return to this theme in Section 1.5.

We aim to make economics relevant for first-time learners without changing the career trajectories of many introductory students. Instead, we argue that lecturers of these classes must keep their audience in mind. What is the best way to teach economics if the goal is to maximize what non-majors get out of these courses? That question rarely receives the attention it deserves.

The study of economics needs to become more inclusive (that is, help the non-majors), but not at the expense of the students majoring in economics. All students can benefit from an introductory course that is better designed. The teaching model in most courses attempts to develop the models and tool kits necessary for majors to succeed, with the view that the best students will go on to postgraduate study, ultimately a PhD, even though they only make up a minuscule number of any given year's intake.

Students who wish to major in economics certainly need exposure to the more rigorous principles of economics. Whether this is best served with another quantitative subject alongside an introductory course or saved for year two is a moot point. In this chapter, we argue that introductory subjects need less emphasis on abstract theory and mathematics. Instead, we want to inspire our students to discuss and share ideas, reflect on current events and consider life's larger and smaller questions, all in the context of straightforward models. If we succeed in motivating student learning, more students will explore intermediate and advanced theory, creating a positive externality in thc form of higher retention rates and a greater pool of economic graduates. The ultimate beneficiary is society, because students who develop an intuitive understanding of core economic principles make better economists, policy advisors and lecturers. Even those students who do not take another economics course will, at the very least, have a stronger grasp of how economics works and applies to their lives.

To summarize, an inclusive introductory economics class is very different from a traditional course that targets 'potential' majors. An inclusive class studies fewer topics, but covers them in greater depth and with more motivation. How is this done? By making each topic become alive through personal and real-world examples and by avoiding publishers' PowerPoint slides and the complex derivations of abstract concepts.

1.3 USING MEDIA IN TEACHING

One technique that is available to increase student engagement is the use of media, such as a short movie and television clips, to provide many useful examples of concepts found in introductory courses. We leverage the audience's interest in media to engage our students and to help make the ideas stick. In this section, we describe how we use media to create more engagement and a deeper cognitive learning experience. Media can be a useful learning device, so we also describe a number of best practices to help the reader accomplish their teaching objectives at the lowest possible cost.

One medium that is particularly useful is Starting Point: Teaching and Learning Economics, an online website designed to assist economists develop innovative teaching strategies and illustrate the benefits of using multimedia to reinvigorate the way we teach economics:

> The use of media to enhance teaching and learning complements traditional approaches to learning. Effective instruction builds bridges between students' knowledge and the learning objectives of the course. Using media engages students, aids student retention of knowledge, motivates interest in the subject matter, and illustrates the relevance of many concepts. (Mateer, 2011)

Economics has a (generally) well-deserved reputation for poor teaching and this has seeped into popular culture. Economists using 'chalk and talk' were immortalized in two films: *Ferris Bueller's Day Off* (1986) and *Back to School* (1986).[5] In *Ferris Bueller*, Ben Stein plays a high school economics teacher who famously puts his class to sleep while droning on about macroeconomics. Ben Stein ends up pleading for student input, repeatedly uttering, 'Anyone?' to try to get a response. In *Back to School*, Paxton Whitehead plays a college lecturer (Dr Phillip Barbay) who attempts to explain how firms operate by using a simplified model where widgets are sold. Then, an adult learner (Thornton Melon), played by Rodney Dangerfield, interrupts him pointing out that the lecturer's example is not very realistic:

> *Thornton Melon*: Oh, you left out a bunch of stuff.
>
> *Dr. Phillip Barbay*: Oh really? Like what for instance?
>
> *Thornton Melon*: First of all you're going to have to grease the local politicians for the sudden zoning problems that always come up. Then there's the kickbacks to the carpenters and if you plan on using any cement in this building I'm sure the Teamsters would like to have a little chat with ya and that'll cost ya. Oh and don't forget a little something for the building inspectors. Then there's long-term costs such as waste disposal. I don't know if you're familiar with who runs that business but I assure you it's not the Boy Scouts.

Dr. Phillip Barbay: That will be quite enough, Mr. Melon! Maybe bribes, kickbacks and Mafia payoffs are how YOU do business! But they are NOT part of the legitimate business world! And they are certainly not part of anything I am doing in this class. Do I make myself clear, Mr. Melon!

The disconnect between the way economists model decision making and the way the world actually works limits the effectiveness of traditional approaches to lecturing in reaching students.

More broadly, economists are seen as being painfully dry, if not humorless. This perception was reinforced in a 2009 US television commercial for T-mobile starring Catherine Zeta-Jones.[6] At the beginning, a group of economists in suits goes door-to-door trying to sell new mobile phone coverage. People hide, squirt them with garden hoses and slam the door in their faces. Then, we see Zeta-Jones approach a door and ask the homeowner if he would like a 'mobile makeover.' Startled by his good fortune, he responds, 'I believe I do.' We like to think of our approach as a classroom makeover. Students have low expectations when they take economics for the first time. Incorporating media into the classroom experience is one way to add value and also dispel the notion that economics is boring.

Media can be used in almost any discipline to create an interactive learning environment and improve student learning. This can occur in-class through lectures, tutorials and workshops; and out-of-class with homework, assignments, essays and projects. Research shows that the use of multimedia or popular culture can stimulate discussion in introductory classes (Becker, 2004), illustrate basic concepts (Hall, 2005; Hall and Lawson, 2008; Hammock et al., 2011) and explain abstract concepts like game theory (Dixit, 2005) or option value (Dixit, 2012) at an advanced level.

Students have different learning preferences. While those with a background in science or mathematics may have a comparative advantage in understanding the quantitative aspects of economics, other students learn abstract, new and novel concepts more easily when they are presented in both verbal and visual forms (Salomon, 1979). Visual media also make concepts more accessible to a person than text alone, promote deep learning rather than rote learning and help with later recall (Cowen, 1984; Willingham, 2009).

A genuine interactive learning environment prompts two-way discussion between the lecturer and students, allowing students to take greater control over the direction of their learning (Bransford et al., 2000). Media sources are usually more effective than traditional modes of teaching in illustrating complex ideas in a short period of time (Crisp and Mixon,

2012), connecting learners with events that are culturally relevant and theories taught in the classroom with real-world events and policies (Mixon, 2010; Mateer, 2011).

Before moving on to specific examples from our teaching, we provide a number of concrete answers to a number of questions you are likely to have about this method.

1.3.1 What to Use

Before using audiovisual materials in teaching, one should have an understanding of copyright, which, by default applies to materials found on the web.[7] 'Creative Commons' (UK) and 'Fair Use' (USA) provide guidelines for lecturers, which usually equate to 'for educational purposes, not for profit.'[8] The biggest hurdle in using audiovisual materials – aside from a willingness to do so – is the workload involved and the skill in recognizing content that will enhance learning, instead of becoming a distraction (Mateer, 2011).

1.3.2 When to Use It

Audiovisual material can be used: (1) at the beginning of class; (2) after a brief introduction but before learning the concept; (3) after learning the concept; (4) before and after. Alternatively, it can be set as a homework assignment (Mateer, 2011). Lecturers should consider the following before using audiovisual material in teaching:

1. Is there a clear link between learning and the media?
2. Is the context clear? Will students understand why the material is being shown? Are there concepts or background material that need to be explained in advance?
3. Will student learning be evaluated? This could take the form of a think-pair-share activity, where students discuss the question, work out an answer, then share it with their neighbor (Lyman, 1987). Other options include lecturer/student-led classroom discussion or homework assignments.
4. Think about how the audiovisual materials will be presented, for example, via the internet, embedded into a PowerPoint presentation, run from a hard drive, USB stick or DVD.

1.3.3 How to Use It

Audiovisual clips can be used as an 'ice breaker' at the beginning of the lecture. If the lecturer wishes to assess the students directly, then a general discussion might be needed to provide context, tying in with the economic concepts to be illustrated: either as a think-pair-share exercise or in a general class discussion. Students should be able to identify the concepts involved and provide written or verbal examples from the material.

Students can usually provide examples in 'layman's terms' but are often not aware of the theoretical underpinnings or concepts involved. If the audiovisual material requires a level of understanding more advanced than the material already covered in the course, then the lecturer might need to briefly explain the concepts involved before showing the clip to help students make the link between theory and reality. If the material is reinforcing concepts learned earlier in the subject or from a previous subject, this would be superfluous.

The use of YouTube throws up one interesting extension of this medium: filming classroom experiments and/or getting students to make their own clips. After all, most students belong to Generation Y, so they are familiar with its use. This can be used to give students 'ownership' of their individual learning and extend the two-way discussion highlighted above. The following section draws on material from our own teaching.

1.4 EXAMPLES FROM OUR TEACHING

One way of increasing student engagement is to actively involve students in the creation of economic content. In this section, we provide two examples of student media projects that showcase student learning and mastery of the material.

1.4.1 Example 1: Car Parking at La Trobe University: Is This a Case of Market Failure?

In 'Economics of Everyday Life,' four self-described student economists set out to determine whether the shortage of car parking places is the symptom of market failure or a transitory adjustment in the market.[9] Titled *Car Parking at La Trobe University: Is this a Case of Market Failure?*, the film draws on themes taught at the beginning of Introductory Macroeconomics and Microeconomics (scarcity, opportunity cost, tradeoffs, thinking at the margin), plus more general microeconomic concepts: free riding, externalities, market failure and government remedies. This film clip is suitable for an introductory course, a subject that requires students to apply theory to practical or real-life events or to reinforce knowledge of previously taught material.

> The student film project gave our group a chance to articulate what we had learned during the semester through a different medium. In many ways this was more challenging than a conventional assessment, as the logistical and collaborative issues associated with a group film project required higher developed time management skills (shooting the film, editing, brainstorming, etc.,) as well as teamwork. The fundamental difference between this project and writing an essay or doing an exam, is that it gave us great insight into working with technology and software and using such tools to convey the topics covered in a concise and entertaining way. If anything this is what economics lacks! Although the formal areas of economics are necessary and fundamental to the discipline it does tend to make this school of thought quite inaccessible to those whom economics affects the most – the everyday person. (Subject evaluation, student 1)[10]

Market failure is an important concept in economics, yet is often misunderstood by many students. The central issues are: (1) the market fails to allocate resources efficiently and (2) there is no market solution: in this case the market is the problem. A lecturer should ask students to consider whether the car parking problem is self-correcting (transitory) and identify instances of market failure in society. What is the appropriate role of the university in dealing with market failure? This question ties in with broader debates among economists about the appropriate level of government intervention in the economy. EconStories.tv has recently brought John Maynard Keynes and Friedrich Hayek back to life in a series of raps that trace the debate between government intervention and market forces over the twentieth century, up to and including the recent Global Financial Crisis: *Fear the Boom and Bust* and *Fight of the Century*.[11]

1.4.2 Example 2: I've Got 99 Problems, Economics Ain't One[12]

This student-created video for introductory microeconomics is based on Jay-Z's *99 Problems*. The student group wrote the lyrics, raps, then filmed and edited the video. Here is a sample of the lyrics:

> If you're having cash problems I feel bad for you son,
> I got 99 problems Economics ain't one.
> Supply is the curve that looks like y = x

Demand goes the other way, forget the rest
Quantity on the x axis, price on the y
If price is low, you know quantity is high
Now we all know that money makes the world go round
Income goes up, demand for inferior goods goes down
I'm spendin money like it don't mean nothin
Going on a spree – I'm sure I'll find somethin
Price for polos goes up, instead I'll buy a sweater
Ain't no big deal, I guarantee it's better
That's what we call a substitute
If it gets too expensive, we can give it the boot
Complements work the other way
If it gets too expensive, this is what I say
I'm not buyin the complement, no, I'm done
I got 99 problems economics ain't one

The typical group project is turned in directly to the lecturer, who provides feedback to the group. The group benefits from the learning experience but other students in the course do not. This video project allows other students to gain additional understanding by observing the work of others. Moreover, video group assignments can outlive the life of the courses they were created in, be seen by friends outside of the class, as well as family members, and when done really well can be sent to employers as part of a digital job application. This student-created video has been seen over 2000 times on YouTube.

More importantly, projects like the two examples described above show that students are learning how to apply the concepts we are teaching in situations that are personally relevant to them. In the next section, we describe a writing assignment that also engages and motivates student learning.

1.5 THE ECONOMIC NATURALIST

Our belief in the economic naturalist writing assignment comes from Bob Frank, who developed the idea. Frank uses the economic naturalist writing assignment in his Introductory Microeconomics course. Students come up with their own question based on a real-life observation and are encouraged to write free of algebra, graphs and jargon in a manner that would pass the so-called Grandma test: understandable by a relative who has never studied economics (Frank, 2007; Bray and Leape, 2008; Cowen, 2008a).

The term 'economic naturalist' derives from an analogy Frank makes with someone who has taken an introductory course in biology. Learning a little evolutionary theory helps you see things you didn't notice before, such as natural selection. What types of questions would a student then be able to answer afterwards (Frank, 2007)?

Research has shown that individual students have different learning preferences (Pashler et al., 2008). Frank's writing assignment builds on the 'narrative theory of learning,' which finds that the human brain absorbs information in narrative (storytelling) form easier than in abstract form (mathematical equations, graphs and theory). The evolution of our species as storytellers and the importance of narrative in a child's learning experience is testament to this theory of learning (Carter, 1993; Carter and Doyle, 1996; Doyle, 1997). Frank's writing assignment is a practical application of this approach to learning. Coming up with an interesting question, having fun and devoting energy to it, then discussing this with others, reinforces the practical aspects of learning and internalizes the knowledge.

It is well established in the academic literature that writing assignments improve student learning of economic principles: 'writing is a tool of discovery, a way of working through ideas that you don't fully understand. In other words, writing is a positive-sum game. When you write, you don't merely put down what you already know; rather you end up knowing more' (Greenlaw, 2003, p. 61). Regular, structured writing assignments are important in developing the skills needed for self-directed learning (Dynan et al., 2008). Furthermore, giving students more responsibility for framing questions is a key attribute of thinking like an economist and developing higher-order learning skills in line with Bloom's (1956) taxonomy. This is a prerequisite for self-directed learning.

All students who took 'Economics of Everyday Life' were required to write at least one economic naturalist piece for the semester in accordance with the guidelines set by Frank. Getting students to come up with an interesting question is difficult for most at the beginning of the subject. One way of dealing with this is to ask students to submit an essay proposal to check that they are on the right path: develop an appropriate question, understand the concepts involved and so on, but this is time-consuming and may lead to an over-reliance on the lecturer. This has the potential to create a lot of administrative work for the academic and it might be preferable to limit the lecturer's input to validating the question and consider adopting SWoRD, a web-based peer review system, which randomly assigns students within groups and creates the correct incentives for serious peer review of essays (Cho et al., 2006).

The most immediate benefit from this writing assignment is that students see the relevance of studying economics. 'The essays allowed me to make real-life connections between daily problems and economics' (Subject evaluation, student 2). When students draw on personal experience, they learn instinctively and naturally, a process that promotes critical thinking skills and deeper learning. 'The essay contributed to my learning in that I was able to independently research and apply economic concepts to real world observed situations. This enabled me to use my individual economic thought to try and decipher human behavior in given circumstances' (Subject evaluation, student 3).

Writing assignments are rarely used as a means of assessment in an economics subject. The tendency to rely on formalism often encourages rote learning of key concepts.

> I found essay writing to be a particularly effective way for me to convey economic concepts. Using mathematics and formulas is effective to an extent. However, having the opportunity to describe and critically analyze economic concepts in conjunction with real world scenarios extends the study of economics to a whole new level. (Subject evaluation, student 4)

It is difficult to teach students to consider various hypotheses and to apply economic principles in a consistent, logical and rational manner to arrive at the most plausible answer. They usually think in terms of simple black and white dichotomies, as this is the prevailing mode of teaching in most subjects. The best questions, to paraphrase the subtitle of *Freakonomics* (Dubner and Levitt, 2005), explore the 'hidden side of everything' (that is, contain an element of counter-intuition).

1.5.1 Examples from the Classroom

In line with the criteria set by Frank, 'all that matters is that the question posed be interesting and that the proposed answer to it rest on plausible economic reasoning' (Frank, 2006, p. 62). Therefore, the existence of a plausible explanation or intelligent hypothesis is more important than whether the answer is right or wrong, a belief that is necessary to encourage students to pose and tackle problems from different perspectives. Remember: these are essays from undergraduate students, not PhD students (their arguments have been paraphrased).

1.5.2 The Market is Amoral: Should You Buy the Last Can of Coke on the Shelf? (Student 1)

This is one of our favorite questions. On the surface, it represents a simple dilemma that can be answered by any audience: act according to altruism or through self-interest? Self-interest is, of course, one of the central aspects of Adam Smith's 'Invisible Hand,' which lies at the heart of our understanding of how free markets function. This question can be used to teach students the water/diamond paradox and answer the question of 'who feeds Paris?' – or how markets actually work in a decentralized economy (Wheelan, 2002).

The question of who actually takes the last can of Coke in a free market is determined by the marginal willingness to pay of the two parties. Student 1 then throws up an interesting hypothetical scenario. Assume that both parties vying for the can of coke decide to act altruistically (that is, sacrifice their own want), making it available to the other. Would this lead to an efficient outcome? If both consumers signal their willingness to pay, then the issue is resolved: the party with the highest willingness to pay gets the can. But if, for whatever reason, this information is not received (misinterpreted or poorly sent), we have what is known as a 'separating equilibrium.' A negative externality is imposed on the seller (the can remains unsold) and all parties lose, including the two customers, who have incurred an opportunity cost (alternative use of time forgone). The two customers are like fielders in a game of baseball who run to take a catch, stop, look at each other, then leave the ball for the other. Nobody takes the catch. If you extrapolate this result across the economy, the results are dire: market failure.

This is a very simplistic example of how an altruistic market would operate but the lesson is clear: the issue of information asymmetry must be resolved to ensure markets operate efficiently and clearly. So the next time you are at the shop and staring at the last can of Coke on the shelf, just buy it. Unless, of course, you derive more benefit from allowing a nice young lady, or large under-caffeinated fridge with a head, to purchase it.

1.5.3 Why are Designer Denim Shorts So Expensive? (Student 2)

Student 2 performs the role of an 'Undercover Economist' in the mold of Tim Harford to ascertain the reasons why denim shorts are expensive vis-à-vis denim jeans. A pair of denim shorts in Australia retails for $150–$250, which is actually more expensive than a standard pair of jeans. The student begins with the obvious answers: (1) prestige and exclusivity; (2) better fit; (3) quality of the materials; and (4) innovation and designing process. But this is incomplete.

Market structure is an important piece of this puzzle. The designer firms seek to maximize profits by charging consumers the highest price they are willing to pay. And if consumers are willing to pay more for a pair of shorts than a pair of jeans, the issue (at least in part) relates to what utility consumers derive from designer shorts. Why is their marginal willingness to pay so high?

Three main factors are presented, each of which is persuasive. First, appearance and being fashionable. One might argue that wearing more expensive, designer clothing improves a man's appearance and therefore signals a higher 'value.' I am wealthy and fashionable. Women generally regard men with higher incomes and social status as more desirable marriage partners (Frank, 2007). As a result, men's marginal willingness to pay for designer shorts rises.

Second, the pursuit of happiness. Being rich does not necessarily make one happier in life, as our expectations and aspirations adjust over time (Frank, 1999). Nevertheless, having certain positional goods does give many consumers a general sense of self-value and contentment. Relative position is often more important to consumers than absolute position, but this is a zero sum game: one can only win when somebody else falls behind. And one must remain on this hedonic treadmill to stay ahead.

Finally, the perception of scarcity: designer companies try to create an image of scarcity in the minds of consumers by differentiating themselves through price, design, image and the quality of their products. These markets are not perfectly competitive: firms can only set and keep prices above marginal cost and derive above-normal economic profits by creating the ideal of a heterogeneous product in the minds of consumers, creating an artificial barrier to entry. If consumers believed all denim shorts were essentially the same, a bidding war would drive the price down to where price equals marginal cost (that is, there would be no economic profits in the long run).

Ultimately, it is the branding that creates the perception of premium in the mind of the consumer: 'Brand X is worth much more than the next best alternative.' Demand for the designer products becomes inelastic for consumers, allowing designer companies to capitalize on this by reaping above-normal economic profits.

The economic naturalist assignment develops deeper thinking that forces students to synthesize many topics into a coherent story. Another technique, the use of response systems, also encourages students and instructors to interact at a deeper level. In the next section, we explain why we believe that response systems should play a central role in getting students to think critically about what they are learning while they are in class.

1.6 RESPONSE SYSTEMS

There are many different response systems on the market. They all have slightly different features and price points. We advocate the use of web-based mobile phone systems because they are substantially cheaper for students and the data can be collected outside the classroom as well. For example, Poll Everywhere[13] is a classroom response system, which enables an instructor to ask questions during class and receive electronic answers from all students. The results can be saved for generating grades at a later time or used solely for formative assessment. Students submit their answers via the system, which subsequently generates a histogram displaying the distribution of answers for the entire class or shows individual responses. Both the instructor and individual student receive immediate feedback on the extent of concept comprehension in the form of a visual summary. The instructor can leverage the question and answers to ensure that topics are fully understood before proceeding on in the course. Questions can be embedded into a PowerPoint presentation or asked as stand-alone questions posed throughout the class period.

This technology can be used in conjunction with other learning strategies to enhance student learning. However, simply inserting questions facilitated by using a personal response system into an economics lecture is not likely to produce the desired results in isolation. The tool must be carefully combined with an overall pedagogical strategy. Personal response devices are most effective when viewed as a way of teaching, not just a new technology to add to a class. We combine personal response devices with other teaching pedagogies including cooperative learning and the use of media to appeal to a variety of learning styles.

Salemi (2009) reports results based on a survey conducted over several semesters of his introductory economics class. He finds that 'Nearly 90 percent of students recommend the continued use of personal response devices.' Our personal survey indicates even stronger results with 75 percent of students reporting that they 'love' using their mobile phones to answer questions, 19 percent indicating that they 'like' the system, while only 6 percent indicated that the approach was just 'OK' (Salemi, 2009, p. 400).

Personal response systems can change the culture of the classroom. Trees and Jackson suggest 'the final effectiveness of the clicker will rest with each student accepting the potential of these systems to positively affect their learning. The success of these devices is in many ways dependent on social, not technological, factors. Instructors must work to facilitate student acceptance and to frame student perceptions of the technology' (Trees and Jackson, 2007, p. 38).

Determining the role a personal response system will play in the classroom environment is a critical decision for instructors. A formal or informal style may be adopted: the technology can be mandatory or optional, and it can be implemented in many different ways. Salemi (2009) proposes the following clicker strategies for the introductory course: (1) sampling student opinion; (2) asking 'Are you with me?' questions; (3) acquiring economic data from students; (4) peer instruction activities; and (5) games and simulations.

1.6.1 An Example: 'Are You With Me?' Questions

One of the most common points of confusion for economics students at the introductory level is the difference between demand and quantity demanded. After a careful presentation of these ideas, a lecturer may be inclined to ask, in some form or another, 'Does everybody understand the difference?' A question can be a more effective substitute if it requires students to demonstrate their understanding immediately. Consider the following question as an example:

1 When economists say the quantity demanded of a product has decreased, they mean the:
   A) demand curve has shifted to the left.
   B) demand curve has shifted to the right.
   C) price of the product has fallen and consequently, consumers are buying more of it.
   D) price of the product has risen and consequently, consumers are buying less of it.

When the distribution of answers is revealed in the histogram, the instructor will know if the students have understood the concept and the students themselves can track their learning. High incorrect response rates suggest that students don't know the difference as well as they should – information that is valuable for the instructor in determining whether to move on to the next topic or engage students in additional reviews of demand and quantity demanded concepts.

Poll Everywhere also allows students to submit open-ended questions or responses. This feature facilitates a two-way exchange of information between the lecturer and student. For example, if you are covering the economics of crime, you could ask how many students have ever exceeded the posted highway speed limit? Predictably, you will get a 'response' near 100 percent. But with an open-ended question like, 'What is the fastest speed you have driven on the highway?,' the breadth of the responses will be much more illuminating. Now you will get a wide range of answers, reflecting how fast students actually drive. This makes your class more engaged because they are finding out something about each other. In addition, you can post an open-ended poll question to solicit feedback about any part of the lecture. This serves as a back channel where students post questions and lecturers can periodically check to see if students comprehend the material during class.

An alternative to Poll Everywhere is Live Question,[14] a free resource that allows an instructor to solicit anonymous feedback from students, by logging into an administrative interface that allows students to post questions in real-time during class using a smart device. Student users can then vote on their favorite questions, with those receiving the most votes rising to the top of a queue. Once a particular question is answered, it can be hidden or deleted so that remaining questions are prominently displayed. Live Question is a technology that facilitates horizontal information flow from one student to another instead of the more common student–lecturer interaction.

Live Question can be used as a tool to organize interactive review sessions where the material that is covered is determined by the questions and votes that are received. Live Question can also be used during any particular class period to uncover questions about material in a timely manner. In both cases, lecturers should be careful to quickly review the posted content before projecting the questions to the entire class. Live Question is more structured than other social media (such as Twitter and Facebook).

This tool is especially effective in large classes where some students are reluctant to ask questions and participate in front of their peers. Large classes also provide the scale necessary to create traction for use. While smart technology is becoming more pervasive, it is not ubiquitous so at least for now smaller classes may not have enough students with smart devices to create a representative sample of student questions.

Response systems, when used to enhance teaching – and not just to take attendance – provide immediate feedback on student learning. They also provide the opportunity for the instructor to address any deficiencies on the spot. This makes learning personally relevant and more interactive and less tied to an outline (or set of PowerPoints). The end result is that the classroom is inverted, with the lecturer taking his or her cue for what to cover next from how well the students understand the material.

1.7 CONCLUSION

The approaches we have described, that is, the use of media, the economic naturalist approach and personal response devices, are effective because they appeal to students' regular lifestyles of watching videos, observing their environment and texting. Our approach changes the culture of their classrooms by making them more interactive, interesting and fun. However, this chapter is not about making economics fun; it is ultimately about finding a way to engage a cohort of learners that may never take another economics course. We believe that engagement can be achieved by the methods we have mentioned without changing the core learning objectives of our classes and these techniques can be used to supplement or augment the material that is already being covered. After gaining some experience, instructors will find they have to only give up a small amount of class time to implement these methods. The opportunity cost is small compared to the increased benefits of learning and understanding that students will achieve.

NOTES

* The authors would like to thank the following for comments and feedback: David Addison, Gary Magee and Michael Smiddy. Thanks also to Laura Moate for her brilliant proofreading skills. Finally, a big thank you to the following people whose creativity, hard work and talent deserve to be acknowledged: Amy Young, Anthony Bertuzzi, Brenton Norman, Cameron Thomas, Chris Gerendasi, Hans Christian Pedersen, Heath Webb, Helena Knapik, Laura Bulluss, Martin Przybyszewski, Maximilian Krahn, Naushad Ilahee, Neyat Sabedinovski, Sebastian Poulsen, Trevor Wright and Volkan Kaman.

1. In 2011, La Trobe University offered the following: Bachelor of Economics, Bachelor of Accounting/Bachelor of Economics, Bachelor of Arts/Bachelor of Economics, Bachelor of Laws/Bachelor of Economics, Bachelor of Politics, Philosophy and Economics.
2. Examples include Accounting/Commerce, Business, Finance, International Business, Management and Marketing. Queensland University of Technology, for example, does not offer a separate economics degree. Economics is one of nine majors offered in their business degree.
3. From personal correspondence with Professor John Sloman, Director of the Economics Network in Bristol, UK in May 2011. 'Old universities' refer to universities established before 1992 (aka sandstone universities). 'New' or 'modern' universities are usually former polytechnic institutions.
4. The data for QUT (2008–09) was presented to the School Advisory Committee meeting on 17 May 2011 and was obtained in personal correspondence with Dr Tommy Tang. The data for Waikato University (2006–10) came from Dr Michael Cameron (Waikato).

5. The scenes are available at http://www.youtube.com/watch?v=dxPVyieptwA (*Ferris Bueller's Day Off*) and http://www.youtube.com/dmateer#p/f/7/YlVDGmjz7eM (*Back to School*) (accessed 15 March 2013).
6. The 'T-Mobile Commercial' is available at http://blogs.wsj.com/digits/2009/05/20/t-mobile-brings-catherine-zeta-jones-back/ (accessed 15 March 2013).
7. The Economics Network's *The Handbook for Economics Lecturers* provides useful instructions on this issue. This is available at http://www.economicsnetwork.ac.uk/handbook/web/33.htm (accessed 15 March 2013).
8. Permission to use these materials may be requested directly, or granted in advance using a licence such as Creative Commons (Poulter, 2010). While permission laws vary across jurisdictions, 'fair use' (as defined in the USA) was liberalized in 2010. Under the new guidelines, lecturers are able to use copyrighted material inside the classroom as long as the content is solely for educational purposes and the faculty member does not profit from its use.
9. The clip is available at http://www.youtube.com/watch?v=umUzJGNt8UM.
10. The student evaluations were taken from 'Economics of Everyday Life' in November 2010.
11. Both clips can be found on the EconStories.tv website: http://econstories.tv/category/videos/.
12. The clip is available at http://www.youtube.com/dmateer#p/f/29/aaz7mWe639A.
13. See http://www.polleverywhere.com (accessed 15 March 2013).
14. See http://cyber.law.harvard.edu/questions/chooser.php (accessed 15 March 2013).

2. A classroom federal funds market experiment

Denise Hazlett*

2.1 INTRODUCTION

This chapter describes an experiment in which students demonstrate for themselves how the Federal Open Market Committee (FOMC) influences interest rates in the federal funds market. Most of the students in the class represent banks that borrow or lend in the federal funds market, using a double oral auction. The rest of the students operate the Federal Reserve Open Market Trading Desk. The instructor assumes the role of the FOMC, issuing directives to the trading desk. The students operating the trading desk must decide what quantity of open market sales or purchases to make, based on the interest rate target in the FOMC directive. These open market operations change the quantity of excess reserves in the banks, thereby shifting the equilibrium interest rate in the federal funds market. The experiment actively demonstrates how an open market sale or purchase changes the federal funds rate, making an otherwise abstract concept come alive and seem tangible. Participation reinforces the idea that the Federal Reserve (Fed) conducts monetary policy by targeting interest rates rather than monetary aggregates. The experiment gives students a concrete experience for later reference, as they consider how the Fed implements monetary policy, and why the Fed's injection or removal of liquidity changes short-term interest rates. As one intermediate macroeconomics student noted, the experiment 'helped clarify the role of the Fed that I really didn't understand before. It's hard to understand how buying/selling funds actually affects people.'

2.2 RUNNING THE EXPERIMENT

The experiment works well in a money and banking course or in a macroeconomics course at the intermediate or even introductory level. It can be run completely by hand, with the instructor recording loan contracts on a board in front of the room. Alternatively, the instructor can use a computer and projector to record and display the loan contracts. The experiment typically takes about 45 minutes to run in a class of 30 students. It takes longer in larger classes because of the time spent recording contracts. An assistant's help with recording speeds the process considerably. For access to all the materials needed to run the experiment in classes of 9–100 students, go to the website http://people.whitman.edu/~hazlett/econ/. Instructors can print out the materials they need for their class size and download an Excel spreadsheet for recording the loan contracts.

A previous reading assignment or class lecture on the Fed's monetary policy tools provides students with the basic background for participating in the experiment. On the day of the experiment, the instructor clears space in the classroom to use as the trading floor, making sure that students have enough room to move from the trading floor to the front of the room to report their results. As students enter the classroom, the instructor gives each one a private information slip establishing that person's role in the experiment. The instructor assigns most students to represent banks, creating an equal number of lending and borrowing banks. The instructor assigns two or three students to represent the Federal Reserve Trading Desk. It works best to have at least two students representing the trading desk, so they can consult with each other. However, in very small classes, a single student can represent the trading desk. The instructor next passes out the instructions and record-keeping sheets, and reads the instructions aloud, inviting student questions. Late-arriving students can be paired with a student running a bank or asked to join the students at the trading desk. See Appendices A and B for the instructions and record-keeping sheets.

Every bank in this experiment faces a reserve requirement, meaning that it must hold $100 million in reserve. Furthermore, each bank wants to hold excess reserves above and beyond the required reserves ('surplus excess reserves'). Holding surplus excess reserves makes a bank less likely to dip into its required reserves and therefore less likely to get penalized for not holding the required reserves. Banks have some flexibility in the amount of excess reserves they hold but generally want to hold about $10 million in excess reserves. In fact, no bank wants to hold less than $8 million or more than $12 million in excess reserves. A bank's private information slip specifies the amount of reserves with which it starts each period. All of the lending banks start every period with $112 million in reserves. All of the borrowing banks start every period with $108 million. Each lending bank can lend as much as

$3 million each period, and each borrowing bank can borrow as much as $3 million each period. A lender's private information slip specifies the minimum interest rate that bank will accept for each million dollars lent. Similarly, a borrower's private information slip specifies the maximum interest rate that bank will pay for each million dollars borrowed. Figure 2.1 shows example private information slips for a trading desk member, a lending bank and a borrowing bank. For the purpose of recording the experimental results, each bank gets a unique experimental ID. To prevent confusion, lending banks have numbers for their IDs, and borrowing banks have letters for their IDs.

You represent the Federal Reserve Trading Desk. For the first part of the experiment, you will observe.
You represent Bank 1. You are a potential lender in the Federal Funds Market. You currently have $112 million in reserve. You are willing to lend $1 million as long as you earn at least 4.6% interest on the $1 million. The $111 million you would have left in reserve would still provide a very good cushion against dipping into your required reserves. You would be willing to lend another $1 million as long as you earn at least 4.9% interest for that $1 million lent. The $110 million you would then have left in reserve would still provide a good cushion against dipping into your required reserves. You would be willing to lend yet another $1 million as long as you earn least 5.3% interest on that $1 million. The $109 million you would then have in reserve would still provide a fairly good cushion against dipping into your required reserves.
You represent Bank A. You are a potential borrower in the Federal Funds Market. You currently have $108 million in reserve. You are willing to pay at most 5.4% interest to borrow $1 million. The $109 million you would then have in reserve would provide a fairly good cushion against dipping into your required reserves. You would be willing to borrow another $1 million if you had to pay no more than 5.1% for this $1 million borrowed. The $110 million you would then have in reserve would provide an even better cushion against dipping into your required reserves. You would be willing to borrow yet another $1 million if you had to pay no more than 4.7% for this $1 million borrowed. The $111 million you would then have in reserve would provide a very good cushion against dipping into your required reserves.

Figure 2.1 Example private information slips

The experiment lasts several market periods, each of which exists independently of the others. Each period, the students representing banks use a double oral auction to arrange loans between them. They mingle, calling out offers to lend or offers to borrow at interest rates they specify. Loans must be in increments no smaller than $1 million dollars. Borrowing banks wish to pay as low an interest rate as possible, and lending banks wish to receive as high an interest rate as possible. Once a borrowing and lending bank have agreed on a loan contract, they come to the front of the room and report to the instructor their interest rate, the amount of the loan and their IDs. The instructor records this information for everyone to see, as in '4B $1m 5.1%,' which means that Bank 4 lent $1 million to Bank B at a 5.1 percent interest rate. After negotiating a loan contract, students record their gains from trade on their record-keeping sheets.[1]

Next, the borrowing and lending bank can each go back to the loan market to negotiate another loan contract, with each other or with other banks. Recall that each bank can borrow or lend at most $3 million in a period. Once banks have finished negotiating all of the loan contracts that would earn them profits, they take a seat at the edge of the trading floor to indicate that they have no further interest in negotiating during that period. Once all of the banks are so 'seated,' the instructor then begins the next period. None of these short-term loans carries over from one period to the next. Instead, each bank again starts with the amount of reserves shown on its private information slip. For simplicity, the experiment essentially starts anew each period.

This first phase of the experiment gives the federal funds market the chance to converge to equilibrium before the Fed begins intervening. So, in the first two or three periods, the members of the Federal Reserve Trading Desk simply observe. They get a feeling for what interest rate clears the federal funds market, absent Fed intervention. In fact, the supply and demand for excess reserves are such that in the periods without Fed intervention, the theoretical equilibrium federal funds rate is 5.0 percent.

After the instructor sees that interest rates have converged to the equilibrium rate (or reasonably close), the instructor begins the second phase of the experiment by handing out Part II of the instructions, as shown in Appendix C. From now on, before the beginning of each period, the members of the trading desk receive a directive from the FOMC. This directive specifies what interest rate the trading desk must achieve in the federal funds market that period. For instance, the instructor first issues a directive to achieve a federal funds rate target of

5.25 percent. A few periods later, the instructor issues a directive to achieve a target of 5.0 percent. Still later, the instructor issues a directive targeting 4.5 percent. The instructor announces each period's directive to the class as a whole, just as the real-world FOMC publicly announces its federal funds rate target immediately after each of its meetings.

After they hear this period's directive, trading desk members choose a quantity of Treasury bills (T-bills) to buy/sell to the public in order to add/subtract reserves from the banking system. The instructor takes the role of the public that sells the T-bills to the Fed (and then deposits the payment in the banks) or buys the T-bills from the Fed (by withdrawing deposits from the banks). Excess reserves in the banks thus rise as the Fed conducts an open market purchase or fall as the Fed conducts an open market sale. The interest rates banks negotiate in the federal funds market respond to the resulting shift in the supply or demand for excess reserves.

For example, consider the following scenario. From observation in the initial periods, students see that the federal funds market clears at 5 percent, absent Fed intervention. Before beginning the next period, the instructor announces a directive to achieve a federal funds rate target of 5.25 percent. So, the trading desk members know they need to take an action that raises the federal funds rate by 0.25 percent relative to the rate that prevails absent Fed intervention. They know from their reading assignment (or previous class lecture) that selling T-bills would raise the federal funds rate. However, they do not know how many T-bills they would have to sell to achieve the required increase. They take a guess, and see what happens. For instance, suppose the trading desk decides to sell $4 million dollars of T-bills. They announce their decision to the class as a whole. The instructor (representing the members of the public who bought the T-bills) announces to the class that customers who bank at Banks 1, 2, 3 and 4 bought the T-bills, and that these customers have withdrawn $1 million dollars of deposits from each of these banks in order to pay the Fed. The instructor explains that Banks 1, 2, 3 and 4 now have $111 million each in reserve, rather than the $112 million that they otherwise would have had. The instructor points out that each still has $2 million in reserves available to lend, once the federal funds market opens. However, in undertaking this lending, the lowest rates each would be willing to accept are the rates given on their private information slips for reducing to $110 and $109 million in reserves. They no longer find themselves willing to accept the lower rate for going down to $111 million because they already have gone down to that level of reserves. So, when Banks 1, 2, 3 and 4 consult their private information slips for their reservation values, they now skip the first line, the one that tells them the minimum they would be willing to accept for the $1 million dollar loan that leaves them with $111 million in reserves. Instead, they start with the next line, which tells them the minimum they would be willing to accept for the $1 million dollar loan that leaves them with $110 million in reserves.

Similarly, consider a later period in which the instructor has given the trading desk a directive to achieve a federal funds rate target of 4.5 percent. Here, the trading desk members know they need to take an action that will lower the federal funds rate by 0.5 percent relative to the rate that prevails absent Fed intervention. They know that buying T-bills would lower the federal funds rate. However, they do not know how many T-bills they would have to buy. So again, they take a guess. Suppose they decide to buy $7 million of T-bills from the public. The instructor (representing the members of the public who sold the T-bills) announces to the class that customers who bank at Banks A, B, C, D, E, F and G sold the T-bills, and that these customers have deposited $1 million dollars of payment from the Fed in each of these banks. The instructor explains that Banks A, B, C, D, E, F and G will each start the period with $109 million in reserves, rather than the $108 million with which they would otherwise have started. The instructor points out that each of these banks can borrow up to $2 million more, once the federal funds market opens. However, in undertaking this borrowing, the most they would be willing to pay are the rates given on their private information slips for reaching $110 and $111 million in reserves. They no longer find themselves willing to pay the higher rate for achieving $109 million, because they already have that level of reserves. So, when Banks A, B, C, D, E, F and G consult their private information slips for their reservation values, they now skip the first line, the one that tells them the most they would be willing to pay for a $1 million dollar loan taking them to $109 million in reserves. Instead, they start with the next line, which tells them the most they would be willing to pay for a $1 million dollar loan taking them to $110 million.

When people sell a T-bill to the Fed in the real world, they deposit the payment in whichever bank happens to be theirs, regardless of whether their bank is short on excess reserves or not. However, for convenience in the experiment, the instructor has the members of the public who receive payment from the Fed deposit that payment into banks that *are* short on excess reserves. The instructor thus avoids putting deposits into banks that already have $112 million in reserves. The instructor avoids those banks because their private information slips do not tell them their reservation interest rates for lending newly deposited funds. In contrast, the instructor explains to the other banks, the ones that have $108 million in reserves, how to read their private information slips so that they do know how to react to the newly deposited funds.

Similarly, the instructor has deposit withdrawals come only from banks that have too much in excess reserves. The instructor explains to these banks, the ones with $112 million in reserves, how to read their private information slips so they know how to react to the newly withdrawn funds. The instructor does not withdraw funds from banks with $108 million in reserves because their private information slips do not contain the information on reservation values they would need in order to react to newly withdrawn funds. Note that because the withdrawals come only from banks that are flush with reserves, the open market sales shift the supply curve for excess reserves leftward, but leave the demand curve unchanged. Similarly, because deposits go only into banks that are short on reserves, the open market purchases shift the demand curve for excess reserves leftwards, but leave the supply curve unchanged. If a student asks why the supply and demand curves do not both shift in both cases, the instructor explains that achieving the more general case of both curves shifting would require distributing new information on reservation values in the middle of the experiment, an unnecessary complication in that the trading desk's actions and the resulting change in the federal funds rate do not depend on which particular banks happen to receive the deposits or provide the withdrawals.

2.3 CLASS SIZE

The experiment has a slightly different version for smaller as opposed to larger classes. This chapter describes the version for small classes (that is, those with 27 or fewer students). The larger-class version is a straightforward simplification of the small-class version. The two versions differ in the amount that a bank can borrow or lend in any one period. The small-class version has each bank able to borrow or lend up to $3 million dollars per period in order to ensure enough transactions each period. In larger classes, each bank can borrow or lend at most $1million per period. The version for larger classes thus works like a typical double oral auction experiment, with each participant able to make at most one transaction per period. However, as is the case with the typical double oral auction experiment, some students in the large version will have reservation values that leave them unable to trade during most or even all of the periods. Their reservation values form the portions of the supply and demand curves to the right of equilibrium. The students with these values will become frustrated by their inability to trade. So, part-way through the experiment, the instructor has them switch roles with students who have more favorable reservation values.

2.4 EXPERIMENTAL RESULTS

This section of the chapter describes example experimental results from a session in a Principles of Economics course with 16 students, two of whom represented the Federal Reserve Trading Desk. The reservation values for the seven lending and seven borrowing banks appear in Table 2.1. After the experiment and before the follow-up analysis, the instructor would give students this information on reservation values. Students can then graph the supply and demand for excess reserves and find the theoretical equilibrium. The graph for the values in Table 2.1 would show the equilibrium interest rate to be 5.0 percent and the quantity lent either \$10 or \$11 million. That the equilibrium quantity could be either \$10 or \$11 million comes from trading in increments of \$1 million, which generates step-wise supply and demand curves.[2]

Table 2.1 Reservation values for a class with 14 banks

Lender ID	Minimum Interest Rate the Lender Will Accept (%)		
	First million lent, making reserves = \$111 million	Second million lent, making reserves = \$110 million	Third million lent, making reserves = \$109 million
Bank 1	4.6	4.9	5.3
Bank 2	4.4	4.8	5.2
Bank 3	4.3	4.7	5.0
Bank 4	4.5	5.1	5.4
Bank 5	4.2	5.5	5.8
Bank 6	4.1	5.6	5.9
Bank 7	4.0	5.7	6.0

Borrower ID	Maximum Interest Rate the Borrower Will Pay (%)		
	First million borrowed, making reserves = $109 million	Second million borrowed, making reserves = $110 million	Third million borrowed, making reserves = $111 million
Bank A	5.4	5.1	4.7
Bank B	5.6	5.2	4.8
Bank C	5.7	5.3	5.0
Bank D	5.5	4.9	4.6
Bank E	5.8	4.5	4.2
Bank F	5.9	4.4	4.1
Bank G	6.0	4.3	4.0

The summary of the results from this session, as well as the results predicted by economic theory, are shown in Table 2.2. In the first period, the average federal funds rate of 5.05 percent was quite close to the theoretical equilibrium rate. However, as is typical in the first period of a double oral auction experiment, rates were quite spread out, ranging from 4.5 percent to 5.5 percent. The results from countless classroom and research experiments show that replicating conditions in consecutive periods helps generate convergence to equilibrium (Roth, 1995). So, in the second period, I replicated the conditions of the first (that is, no Fed intervention), and we found that rates did indeed cluster closer to the theoretical equilibrium. Running more non-intervention periods would likely have clustered even closer to convergence. However, repetition that produces very small changes can bore students, thereby defeating the pedagogical goal of keeping them engaged and learning. In this particular session, the interest rates in Period 2 came close enough to equilibrium to give the trading desk a good feel for the rate that clears the federal funds market absent Fed intervention. Thus, in Period 3, I moved on to the second phase of the experiment by issuing the first FOMC directive. The trading desk responded to the 5.25 percent target by making a $3 million sale of T-bills. The resulting average federal funds rate of 5.16 percent convinced the trading desk that they had not acted aggressively enough. In Period 4, I again issued a 5.25 percent FOMC directive and this time the trading desk sold $7 million of T-bills. The resulting 5.27 percent average federal funds rate satisfied the trading desk. They declared victory.

In response to the 4.50 percent directive in Period 5, the trading desk bought $11 million of T-bills. The resulting federal funds rate did not go as low as they had hoped. However, rather than buying a larger amount in the next period, when they received the same directive, they decided to try an $11 million purchase again and see if the banks simply needed more experience with the new conditions caused by such a large open market purchase. In fact, the trading desk members were satisfied with the resulting 4.52 percent average rate. If they had not felt satisfied, I would have run another period with the 4.5 percent directive.[3]

Table 2.2 Theoretical predicted results and summary of actual results for an example session

Period	FOMC Directive (%)	Open Market Operation	Federal Funds Rate Predicted by Theory (%)	Average Actual Federal Funds Rate (%)	Range of Actual Federal Funds Rates (%)
1	None	NA	5.00	5.05	4.50–5.50
2	None	NA	5.00	5.06	5.00–5.10
3	5.25	$3 million sale	5.10–5.20	5.16	5.10–5.40
4	5.25	$7 million sale	5.30–5.40	5.26	5.20–5.50
5	4.50	$11 million purchase[a]	4.40–4.50	4.64	4.50–4.90
6	4.50	$11 million purchase	4.40–4.50	4.52	4.20–4.70

Note: [a] Of the $11 million that the Fed paid for these T-bills, I had $2 million deposited into each of Banks A, B, C and D, and $1 million into each of Banks E, F and G. Thus, Banks A, B, C and D each started the period with $110 million in reserves, and therefore wanted to borrow at most $1 million more. I had students skip to the last line of their private information slip, which told them the most they were willing to pay to borrow the $1 million that would take them to $111 million in reserves.

2.5 FOLLOW-UP ANALYSIS

In the follow-up, students analyse the experimental data. Questions to guide the student analysis, as part of a class discussion or as a writing assignment, appear in Appendix D. The questions in Appendix D refer to the results in the example session described in the previous section of this chapter. In addition to the analysis questions, the instructor gives students the experimental data, including a table showing the reservation values for all the banks, as in Table 2.1, and a list of all the trades conducted each period. In their analysis, students apply supply and demand tools to determine the theoretical equilibrium federal funds rate absent Fed intervention, to determine the theoretical equilibrium in each of the cases of Fed intervention and to determine the amount of open market sales or purchases necessary, in theory, to achieve each of the FOMC directives. The analysis questions also ask students to compare the experimental results to the theoretical predictions.

As part of their analysis, students graph the supply and demand for excess reserves that result when the Fed removes $3 million from banking reserves, as it did in Period 3. In that period, I had the public pay the Fed for the T-bills by writing checks on $1 million of deposits in each of Banks 2, 3 and 7. The supply curve thus shifts leftward by $3 million, relative to the non-intervention supply curve. Observing where the supply and demand curves overlap allows students to conclude that a $3 million sale generates a theoretical equilibrium federal funds rate range of 5.1 to 5.2 percent. Students note that our average federal funds rate of 5.16 percent fell within the equilibrium range. Similarly, when the Fed sells $7 million of T-bills in Period 4 (shifting the supply curve leftward by $7 million relative to the non-intervention supply curve), supply and demand analysis predicts an equilibrium range of 5.3 to 5.4 percent. Students note that our average rate of 5.27 percent in Period 4 was somewhat low compared to this theoretical prediction, but that this discrepancy is not surprising considering how much the trading desk and the banks had to learn as market conditions changed from one period to the next. Continuing with their analysis, students draw a supply and demand graph to show how many T-bills the trading desk would, in theory, have to sell to achieve the 5.25 percent directive. This graph would show that selling $5 million of T-bills (that is, shifting the supply curve leftward by $5 million) generates an equilibrium range of 5.2 to 5.3 percent.

The analysis of Periods 5 and 6 proceeds similarly. Students draw the supply and demand curves showing the predicted effects of the Fed's $11 million open market purchases. Note that the Fed bought $11 million in each of Periods 5 and 6, so the same graph works for both periods. The Fed's addition of $11 million of reserves shifts the demand curve leftward by $11 million, relative to the non-intervention demand curve. Observing where the supply and demand curves overlap allows students to determine that an $11 million purchase generates an equilibrium federal funds rate range of 4.4 to 4.5 percent. Students note that our average rates of 4.64 percent in Period 5 and 4.52 percent in Period 6 got progressively closer to the theoretical prediction. They conclude that the trading desk's decision to replicate its $11 million purchase helped participants gain experience, thereby moving the market towards equilibrium. Finally, students draw a supply and demand graph to show how many T-bills the trading desk would, in theory, have to purchase to achieve the 4.5 percent directive. This graph would show that buying $10 million of T-bills (that is, shifting the demand curve leftward by $10 million) generates an equilibrium rate of 4.5 percent.

2.6 CONCLUSION

From their participation in an experimental federal funds market, students come to better understand how a Fed injection of liquidity lowers interest rates and how a Fed removal of liquidity raises interest rates. This hands-on exercise allows students to see macroeconomic theory in action and to test its predictive power. Moreover, the learning-by-doing nature of the experiment and follow-up analysis creates an experience students remember.

NOTES

* Support for this work was provided by the National Science Foundation's Course, Curriculum and Laboratory Improvement Program under grant DUE-9950688. The author is grateful to the following people for beta-testing the experiment in their classes: Earl Adams of Allegheny College, Noelwah Netusil and Jeffrey Parker of Reed College, Jeffrey Johnson of Sullivan University, Richard Schiming of Minnesota State University, Gail Heyne Hafer of St Louis Community College at Meramec, Helen Roberts of the University of Illinois at Chicago, Nicole Simpson of Colgate University, Patricia Schneider of Mount Holyoke College and Xiaofen Chen of Truman State University. The author also thanks John Mountjoy and Peter Griffin for their assistance.

1. Some instructors use extra credit or candy payoffs for this experiment. The author uses hypothetical payoffs.
2. To download a program that allows easy creation of these step-wise graphs, see Murphy (2004).

3. In classes where achieving the 5.25 percent directive takes the trading desk several periods, I recommend running a subsequent period with a 5.0 percent directive before going on to the 4.5 percent directive. Also, the instructor could issue a directive of 4.75 percent instead of 4.5 percent. These smaller and more gradual changes help a market that is having problems achieving convergence.

APPENDIX A: INSTRUCTIONS FOR THE FEDERAL FUNDS MARKET EXPERIMENT

1. You are about to participate in an experiment in bank lending and borrowing. This experiment will last for several market periods. Most of you represent banks. The rest of you represent the Federal Reserve. Your private information slip tells you whether you represent a bank or the Fed. Those of you who represent the Fed will observe the experiment for the first few periods. In later periods, those of you representing the Fed will become active participants in the experiment.
2. Let's consider those of you who represent banks. Some of the banks in the experiment have too little cash in reserve, so these banks need to acquire more reserves. Other banks have so much in reserve that they would like to lend some of the excess in order to earn interest. The banks who want more reserves can borrow from the ones who have too much. Banks lend to each other in a market called the Federal Funds Market.
3. Every bank in this experiment faces a reserve requirement that means it **must** hold $100 million in reserve. Furthermore, each bank wants to hold excess reserves above and beyond the required reserves. Holding excess reserves makes a bank less likely to dip into its required reserves, and therefore less likely to get penalized for not holding the required reserves. Banks have some flexibility in the amount of excess reserves they hold, but most would like to hold about $10 million in excess reserves. In fact, no bank wants to hold less than $8 million or more than $12 million in excess reserves. Those of you who represent banks can tell how much you have in reserve by looking at your private information slip.
4. Let's consider those of you who want more reserves. You can borrow up to $3 million each period. Your private information slip tells you the highest interest rate you are willing to pay for each million borrowed. Borrowing banks have an upper-limit on the interest rate they are willing to pay to another bank, because they have alternative methods of raising reserves. For instance, they could sell some of their loans, or issue more deposits. Banks use these alternatives if the interest rate in the Federal Funds Market is too high.
5. Borrowing banks want to negotiate for the lowest possible interest rate on each loan. The lower the interest rate they pay, the higher are their profits.

6. Now let's consider those of you who would like to lend some of your excess reserves. You can lend up to $3 million each period. Your private information slip tells you the lowest interest rate you are willing to accept. Lending banks have a minimum interest rate they will accept, because they could keep the excess reserves as a cushion against dipping into their required reserves. Banks keep the excess reserves if the interest rate in the Federal Funds Market is too low.
7. Lending banks want to negotiate for the highest possible interest rate on each loan. The higher the interest rate they earn, the higher are their profits.
8. Banks lend to each other in the Federal Funds Market, using a double oral auction. Borrowing and lending banks mingle, calling out offers to borrow or offers to lend at interest rates they specify. For instance, a borrowing bank might offer to borrow $1 million at 3.24%. A lending bank might offer to lend $1 million at 9.35%. Loans must be in increments no smaller than one million dollars. Recall that a bank can borrow or lend at most $3 million each period. So, it's possible to lend or borrow either zero, one, two or three million dollars each period. Once a lending and borrowing bank have agreed on a loan, they will come to the front of the room and report to me the amount of the loan, the interest rate, and the names of their banks. I will record this information for everyone to see. The borrowing and lending bank can then each go back to the loan market to negotiate another loan contract, with each other or with other banks. Once you have finished negotiating all the loan contracts that would earn you profits, you should take a seat at the edge of the trading floor to indicate that you are no longer interested in negotiating.
9. Once banks have finished contracting for all of their loans, I will announce that the loan market is closed. That period of the experiment will end. We will then begin the next period, in which every bank again has all of the reserves indicated on its private information slip. Nothing carries over from one period to the next, so any borrowing or lending a bank did in the past does not affect its reserves in the current period.

APPENDIX B: RECORD-KEEPING SHEETS FOR LENDING AND BORROWING BANKS

Record-keeping Sheet for a Lending Bank

Your Bank ID Number: ___________

Your name: ____________________________

Please keep track of your gains from lending. If you made no loan, leave that space blank.

Period 1	The interest rate you received for lending your first $1 million	minus the interest rate you needed to receive to be willing to lend your first $1 million	equals your gain from lending your first $1 million
	–	=	
Period 1	The interest rate you received for lending your second $1 million	minus the interest rate you needed to receive to be willing to lend your second $1 million	equals your gain from lending your second $1 million
	–	=	
Period 1	The interest rate you received for lending your third $1 million	minus the interest rate you needed to receive to be willing to lend your third $1 million	equals your gain from lending your third $1 million
	–	=	
Period 2	The interest rate you received for lending your first $1 million	minus the interest rate you needed to receive to be willing to lend your first $1 million	equals your gain from lending your first $1 million
	–	=	
Period 2	The interest rate you received for lending your second $1 million	minus the interest rate you needed to receive to be willing to lend your second $1 million	equals your gain from lending your second $1 million
	–	=	
Period 2	The interest rate you received for lending your third $1 million	minus the interest rate you needed to receive to be willing to lend your third $1 million	equals your gain from lending your third $1 million
	–	=	

Record-keeping Sheet for a Borrowing Bank

Your Bank ID Letter: ____________

Your name: ____________________________

Please keep track of your gains from borrowing. If you did not borrow, leave that space blank.

Period 1	The interest rate you were willing to pay to borrow your first $1 million	minus the interest rate you actually did pay to borrow your first $1 million	equals your gain from borrowing your first $1 million
	–	=	
Period 1	The interest rate you were willing to pay to borrow your second $1 million	minus the interest rate you actually did pay to borrow your second $1 million	equals your gain from borrowing your second $1 million
	–	=	
Period 1	The interest rate you were willing to pay to borrow your third $1 million	minus the interest rate you actually did pay to borrow your third $1 million	equals your gain from borrowing your third $1 million
	–	=	
Period 2	The interest rate you were willing to pay to borrow your first $1 million	minus the interest rate you actually did pay to borrow your first $1 million	equals your gain from borrowing your first $1 million
	–	=	
Period 2	The interest rate you were willing to pay to borrow your second $1 million	minus the interest rate you actually did pay to borrow your second $1 million	equals your gain from borrowing your second $1 million
	–	=	
Period 2	The interest rate you were willing to pay to borrow your third $1 million	minus the interest rate you actually did pay to borrow your third $1 million	equals your gain from borrowing your third $1 million
	–	=	

APPENDIX C: INSTRUCTIONS FOR THE FEDERAL FUNDS MARKET EXPERIMENT, PART II

Those of you who do not represent banks instead work for the Federal Reserve. You represent members of the Federal Reserve Open Market Trading Desk. At the beginning of each period from now on, you will receive a directive from the Federal Open Market Committee telling you what interest rate the FOMC wants in the Federal Funds Market that period. You will then buy or sell Treasury Bills to achieve this interest rate. You must buy or sell T-bills in increments of $1 million. Each period, you will write down the dollar value of the T-bills you will buy or sell. I represent the public, which either purchases the T-bills you sell, or sells the T-bills you purchase.

Let's consider what happens when the Fed **sells** a T-bill to the public. As the purchaser paying for the T-bill, I will withdraw funds equal to the purchase price from my bank. This withdrawal reduces the amount of reserves in my bank. So, one of the banks in the experiment now has that much less in reserve.

Now let's consider what happens when the Fed **buys** a T-bill from the public. As the seller, I will deposit in my bank funds equal to the purchase price. This deposit increases the reserves at my bank. So, one of the banks in the experiment now has that much more in reserve.

Record-Keeping Sheet for the Federal Reserve Trading Desk

Period	Interest rate the FOMC directed the Trading Desk to achieve	Dollar Value of T-bills the Fed Will Buy or Sell (indicate whether the Fed is buying or selling)

APPENDIX D: FOLLOW-UP ANALYSIS QUESTIONS

The parts in bold are where instructors fill in the values from their own classes.

1. Consider the data on the minimum interest rates lenders are willing to accept. Use this data to draw the supply curve for loans that would prevail absent government intervention in the Federal Funds Market. Your graph should have the interest rate (called the Federal Funds Rate) on the vertical axis and the quantity of dollars lent (in millions) on the horizontal axis. As you draw the supply curve, remember that people cannot lend in increments smaller than $1 million. So, your supply curve will be a step graph. Now consider the data on the maximum interest rates borrowers are willing to pay. Use this data to draw (on the same graph as the supply curve) the demand curve for loans that would prevail absent government intervention in the Federal Funds Market. Again, because people cannot borrow in increments smaller than $1 million, your demand curve will be a step graph. What does theory predict would be the equilibrium Federal Funds Rate (FFR) and quantity of loans, when there is no government intervention? Now consider the results in the periods **(1 and 2)** when the Fed did not intervene in the Federal Funds Market. How close did our results come to your theoretical prediction?
2. Consider the periods **(3 and 4)** in which the Federal Open Market Trading Desk sold Treasury bills in order to comply with a directive from the Federal Open Market Committee to raise the FFR to 5.25%. Why is it that Fed sales of T-bills raise the FFR? In theory, exactly how many million dollars worth of T-bills would the Fed have to sell so that the interest rate in our experimental Federal Funds Market would go from its equilibrium level without government intervention to the 5.25% the Fed wants?
3. Consider **Period 3**, where the Fed sold **$3 million** of T-bills. What does theory predict would be the equilibrium Federal Funds Rate for this period, given the Fed's open market sales? How close did our results in **Period 3** come to this theoretical prediction? Consider **Period 4**, where the Fed sold **$7 million** of T-bills. What does theory predict would be the equilibrium Federal Funds Rate for this period, given the Fed's open market sales? How close did our results in **Period 4** come to this theoretical prediction?

4. Under what sort of real-world conditions would the Fed want to raise the FFR?
5. Consider the periods **(5 and 6),** in which the Federal Open Market Trading Desk bought Treasury bills in order to comply with a directive from the FOMC to lower the FFR to 4.5%. Why is it that Fed purchases of T-bills reduce the FFR? In theory, exactly how many million dollars worth of T-bills would the Fed have to buy so that the interest rate in our experimental Federal Funds Market would go from its equilibrium level without government intervention to the 4.5% the Fed wants?
6. What does theory predict would be the equilibrium Federal Funds Rate for **Periods 5 and 6**, given the Fed's **$11 million** of open market purchases? How close did the experimental results in **Periods 5 and 6** come to this theoretical prediction?
7. Under what sort of real-world conditions would the Fed want to lower the FFR?

3. An improved in-class bargaining demonstration

Calvin Blackwell

3.1 INTRODUCTION

In their excellent textbook, *Experiments with Economics Principles: Microeconomics*, Bergstrom and Miller (1999) include a chapter on bargaining. In this chapter, they outline a classroom demonstration intended to illustrate the way game theory is applied to bargaining, but that also brings up some of the empirical issues in this field. This bargaining demonstration as presented works well, but arguably it can be improved upon. In this chapter, I present a refined version of their demonstration, one that is simpler to implement and arguably more effective at generating thought and discussion among students.

3.2 THE DEMONSTRATION

Bergstrom and Miller (1999) present a bargaining environment that progresses from simple to complex. In the first part of the demonstration, students participate in an ultimatum game; in the second part, students participate in a two-stage bargain (in the first stage an offer is made whereas in the second stage a counter-offer can be made, which can then be rejected or accepted); finally, in the third part, students participate in a three-stage bargain. Although this demonstration is thorough, it typically requires extensive class time. For classes using the Bergstrom and Miller text, this high time cost is probably not a problem, but for instructors looking for a simple, quick demonstration of some of the basic results of bargaining research, their demonstration may be too time intensive. My version is much shorter, yet still allows for full coverage of bargaining research. This demonstration would be appropriate for classes in principles of microeconomics, intermediate microeconomics, law and economics, and game theory.

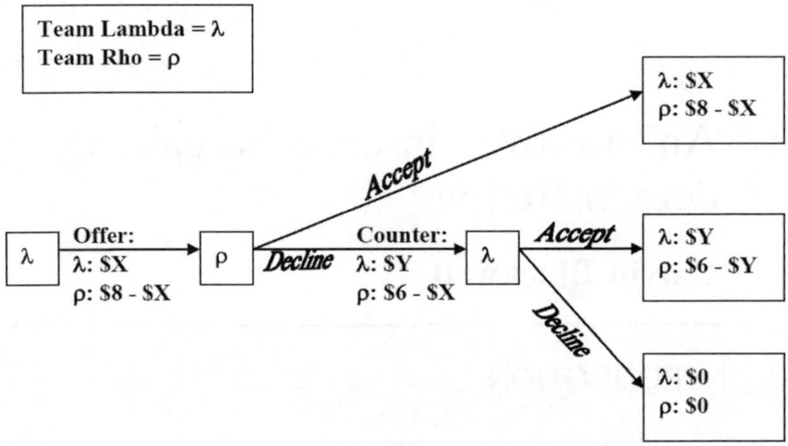

Figure 3.1 Three-stage bargaining demonstration game tree

In effect, I skip Bergstrom and Miller's first and second stages and move directly to the third stage. In addition, instead of having each individual student playing the role of either a proposer or acceptor, I put students into groups of 5 to 15 and have them make their decision as a group. The instructions are presented in the Appendix to this chapter. An illustration of the game tree is shown in Figure 3.1. The students are given the task of splitting \$8. Team Lambda is allowed to make an offer to Team Rho, which then has to decide either to accept the offer or to reject it. If the offer is rejected, Team Rho can make a take-it-or-leave-it counter-offer to split \$6. Team Lambda then must accept or reject the offer. The sub-game perfect equilibrium is for Team Lambda to offer \$6 (or \$5.50) to Team Rho and for Team Rho to accept this offer. This result is arrived at using backwards induction: in the final stage, Team Lambda should accept any offer, and so knowing this Team Rho would offer \$0.50 or nothing to Team Lambda, ensuring Team Rho of \$5.50 (or \$6). Because Team Rho is guaranteed \$5.50, Team Lambda will make the best offer it can in the first stage, and offer \$5.50 (or \$6).

3.3 DISCUSSION

I normally use this demonstration after presenting extensive form games and backwards induction, but before any specific coverage of bargaining. I find this ordering effective because it provides students with the optimal level of knowledge to make the experiment interesting. If students participate in an experiment after having attended a lecture on the topic, they tend to act far too much like game theory predicts. This result is undesirable because bargaining research has shown that experimental subjects act in much more complex ways than simple game theory can explain. This richness of incentives makes the subject fascinatingly complex, and in the role of instructor I do not want to lose that complexity. A little 'ignorance' in my students improves the demonstration.

Of course, the game is too difficult to analyse without some understanding of backwards induction. When students have been previously exposed to this idea, it speeds their understanding of my bargaining game. This background is what allows me to skip the first two parts of Bergstrom and Miller's original demonstration – the students already understand the ultimatum game (somewhat, at least), but they are often unable to apply backwards induction iteratively, as this game requires.

This combination of ignorance and knowledge generates fascinating discussions in the two student groups. Three approaches generally arise. First, with groups of five or more, there is almost always one student who can analyse the game correctly and find the sub-game perfect equilibrium. However, this student does not always succeed in convincing his or her fellow group members. Second, the desire simply to split 'the pot' in half is a powerful focal point that many groups use as the basis for their offers. In addition, a third group of students often (albeit incorrectly) believes that the initial proposer has the upper hand in the game. These three different understandings of the game suggest different offers and counter-offers,[1] generating a lively and interesting discussion for students in groups and afterwards when we discuss the demonstration as a class.[2]

3.4 CONCLUSION

I always look forward to covering game theory topics in my classes, particularly the application of game theory to bargaining. This application not only illustrates at least to some degree the power of game theory but also demonstrates the limitations of game theory, especially when issues of fairness are involved. This demonstration is fun for both students and instructor and may be a worthwhile undertaking in a variety of different microeconomics-oriented courses.

NOTES

1. The conflicting nature of these approaches, in addition to generating discussion, often results in a bargaining breakdown where neither side accepts an offer and both receive nothing. In that case, I don't have to pay out any cash, making this demonstration cheap to run.
2. Bergstrom and Miller (1999) have an excellent discussion of the experimental literature. For a more recent summary, see Camerer (2003).

APPENDIX: DEMONSTRATION INSTRUCTIONS

Bargaining

Today we are going to play a game in which the class will be divided into two teams, Team Lambda and Team Rho. The bargaining will be over how to split $8. At the end of the exercise I will randomly pick one member from each team and pay them their team's payoff.

Rules:

Team Lambda makes the first offer of how to split the $8. Team Lambda may make any offer between $0 and $8 to Team Rho, in multiples of $0.50. (Example: Team Lambda offers Team Rho $2.50, and would keep $5.50 for itself.)

Once Team Lambda has made their offer, Team Rho has the opportunity to accept or decline the offer. If Team Rho accepts, the game ends and both teams receive their agreed upon payoffs. If Team Rho declines, it then has the opportunity to make a take-it or leave-it offer to Team Lambda over how to split $6. Team Rho may make any offer between $0 and $6 to Team Lambda, in multiples of $0.50. (Example: Team Rho offers Team Lambda $1.50, and would keep $4.50 for itself.)

If Team Rho declines Team Lambda's initial offer and makes a counter-offer, Team Lambda may either accept or decline Team Rho's offer. If Team Lambda declines, both teams earn $0. If Team Lambda accepts, then both teams receive their agreed upon payoffs.

Both teams have 15 minutes to discuss their strategies.

Team Lambda	**Team Rho**
Initial Offer: $_____ Team Lambda $_____ Team Rho	Will accept any offer above: $_____ Team Lambda
If Initial Offer is Rejected, will accept any offer above: $_____ Team Rho	If Initial Offer is Rejected, Offer: $_____ Team Lambda $_____ Team Rho
Team Lambda earnings: $_____	Team Rho earnings: $_____

4. Bo knows property rights and futures markets: economics in *Trading Places*

Michael R. Hammock and Art Carden

4.1 INTRODUCTION

The early 1980s movie classic *Trading Places* illustrates several important points about basic economics, such as the fact that the value of labor is determined by the value of its marginal product (for example, when Randolph and Mortimer Duke are signing payroll checks and comment that they are paying Louis Winthorpe 'an awful lot of money'), the costs of discrimination, the role of property rights and the difference between accounting profit and economic profit. It also illustrates a serious blunder for people wishing to engage in illegal insider trading; those who wish to commit crimes may find it advisable not to leave paper trails. Our focus is on the basic economic lessons that can be learned by watching *Trading Places*.[1]

In this study, the position taken is that the most important economic lessons in the movie *Trading Places* involve futures markets. A futures contract is '[a] contractual agreement, generally made on the trading floor of a futures exchange, to buy or sell a particular commodity or financial instrument at a pre-determined price in the future' (investopedia.com). People buy and sell futures contracts based on their expectations about the prices of commodities or financial instruments in the future. On the one hand, someone who expects the price of oil to go up in the future may want to buy futures contracts at the current price (either because they want to take delivery of inexpensive oil at a time when oil is expensive or because they want to sell, in the future, the right to receive that oil and earn a profit). On the other hand, someone who expects the price of oil to go down in the future may want to sell futures contracts at the current price (because they will be able to realize a profit by buying inexpensive oil in the future to satisfy the promise they have made now).

The same logic applies to other markets. In the case of the movie, the Duke brothers (who own a commodities brokerage) attempt to illegally acquire the United States Department of Agriculture's (USDA) estimates of what the Florida orange crop will be. Fresh orange juice and frozen concentrated orange juice are substitutes. A bad orange harvest will mean a high price of oranges and, therefore, a high price of frozen concentrated orange juice. A good orange harvest will mean a low price of oranges and, therefore, a low price of frozen concentrated orange juice.

Louis Winthorpe III and Billy Ray Valentine (played by Dan Aykroyd and Eddie Murphy, respectively) trick the Dukes with a false crop report while hiding the real information for themselves. The Dukes are tricked into believing that the orange harvest will be relatively low when, in fact, the USDA has estimated that the crop has not been affected by recent severe weather.

The Dukes try to capitalize on this information by buying contracts for frozen concentrated orange juice; they continue buying even as the price increases dramatically on the anticipation that the final price will go still higher. This means that ultimately they will have paid a relatively low price for frozen concentrated orange juice (FCOJ), which they can then sell at a higher price later. Other traders, observing that the Dukes are attempting to corner the market, try to 'get in on it' and push the price still higher.

Winthorpe and Valentine, however, know the truth about what the orange crop will be. When the price reaches a certain level, they offer to sell FCOJ in the future. Note that they do not actually have any FCOJ; they are short-selling orange juice because they are selling orange juice that they do not yet possess. Quantity in this case is unclear, but they sell contracts for approximately $142 each.

When the real USDA crop report comes out, people panic because they acted on incorrect information. Winthorpe and Valentine then cover their position by buying contracts that will allow them to make good on their legal obligation to deliver orange juice at some future date. The closing price is $29 per unit, which means that Winthorpe and Valentine have effectively sold orange juice they did not actually have at a very high price, and then bought the orange juice they needed to fulfill their contractual obligations at a very low price.

What happens to the Duke brothers? Near the end of the movie, one of the directors of the exchange issues a margin call. Investment website Investopedia.com defines a margin call in the following way:

> A broker's demand on an investor using margin to deposit additional money or securities so that the margin account is brought up to the minimum maintenance margin. This is sometimes called a 'fed call' or 'maintenance call'.[2]

This is not made explicit but it is evident from the context that the Dukes were buying futures contracts on margin, that is, they were buying FCOJ futures contracts using borrowed money. Investors who buy on margin must satisfy a minimum margin requirement or minimum maintenance margin. This means that the value of the things they bought must meet some level at the close of the trading day, with the level depending on the amount borrowed. When a broker issues a 'margin call,' it requires the trader to deposit money into his account or sell some of his assets in order to bring the balance up to the minimum maintenance margin.[3] In the Dukes' case, they did not have the cash or the assets to cover their position and thus the assets of their company and their seats on the commodity exchange were confiscated and sold. The Dukes were ruined financially.[4]

4.2 THE MARKET FOR NATURAL RESOURCES

This discussion has implications for the future of any scarce resource as prices reflect our expectations about future supply and demand conditions. Consider again the case of oil. Many have argued that we are running out of petroleum, and indeed, there is likely only a fixed quantity of petroleum beneath the Earth's surface. There is indeed an entire body of theory built around the idea of 'peak oil,' which states that we will, at some point, reach a maximum practical ability to extract oil from the ground. This in itself is not a ridiculous idea; our abilities to extract some other resources have also peaked, and there is no reason that oil extraction could not, at some point, begin to fall. Hysterical manifestations of this theory, however, then usually posit that the world will devolve into a post-apocalyptic nightmare along the lines of the *Mad Max* movies.

If people truly believed that we are 'running out of oil,' and if they believed that the price of oil did not reflect this information, they would buy oil futures and drive up the price. A higher price of oil futures would send two important signals into the market place: conserve more and work harder to find substitutes. As economist Julian Simon has shown, societies have responded to these signals by conserving, by finding substitutes and by inventing new and better ways to use resources.[5]

What if people think we are 'running out of oil?' Someone who believes that we are 'running out of oil' in a meaningful sense must believe that as demand grows and supply grows more slowly, stops growing or actually begins shrinking, the price of crude oil will go up. If the investor believed that the current oil price did not fully reflect future scarcity, it would be in that person's best interest to buy crude oil futures. This would drive up the price, and it thereby conveys a benefit on society because our hypothetical investor-prophet's superior vision would provide the rest of us with a natural incentive to conserve.

4.3 TRADING PLACES AND DISCRIMINATION

In the movie, Billy Ray Valentine shows that he has a knack for commodity trading. The Dukes are revealed to be racists when it is discovered that they do not want Valentine running their company. They end up paying a very high price to indulge their 'taste for discrimination' (as well as their total lack of ethics). The people they try to destroy end up ruining them completely.

This scenario illustrates an important point about competitive labor markets. Those who wish to exercise a 'taste for discrimination' by allowing non-productivity characteristics (race, gender, sexual orientation, age and so forth) will tend to earn lower profits and possibly be competed out of the market. While the Dukes' racism is somewhat tangential to the story and, for the most part, used to establish the Dukes as truly unsympathetic villains, their unwillingness to look past their prejudices plays an important role in costing them absolutely everything.

4.4 ACCOUNTING PROFIT AND ECONOMIC PROFIT

Early in the movie, the Duke brothers are introducing Valentine to his new life, to his butler (Coleman) and to his new house (which formerly belonged to Winthorpe). The Dukes have to convince Valentine that he owns the house, that the things he is slipping into his pocket and trying to 'steal' are in fact being stolen from himself. Valentine is not convinced and begins playing with an oriental vase, passing it back and forth from hand to hand. He drops the vase. The vase shatters on the ground and Valentine apologizes. The Dukes assure him that it is OK, that he has broken his own vase and that everything will be OK.

Valentine asks if the vase was fake, and Randolph points out that they had paid $35,000 for it. Trying to lighten the mood, though, Randolph then says to Mortimer that they had reported the value of the vase at $50,000 for insurance purposes, and he laughs that even in a short time Valentine has already made them a profit of $15,000. The Dukes and Coleman begin laughing, and Valentine asks if they want him to break something else.

The Dukes and Coleman are unanimous: 'no,' apparently concerned that Valentine will break something else valuable. There are obvious possible implications of insurance fraud here, but more fundamentally, if the Dukes were upset that Valentine had broken the vase, can we then reasonably say that Valentine's actions have generated an economic profit? No. Breaking the vase may have generated an accounting profit in that the estimated value of the vase was $50,000 and they had paid only $35,000; however, we can reasonably infer that they earned an economic loss because the true value of the vase would be the discounted present value of whatever they expected the vase to be worth at some point in the future. Their dismay at the broken vase (and their reluctance to have Valentine break anything else) suggests that they in fact expected to sell the vase for more than $50,000 at some point in the future. Rather than a profit, Valentine's carelessness with the vase may have imposed an economic loss on the Dukes.[6]

4.5 PROPERTY RIGHTS AND CREDIT

The Dukes engage in a 'grand experiment' to simultaneously elevate Billy Ray Valentine (Eddie Murphy), a con man from the streets, while destroying the life of Louis Winthorpe (Dan Aykroyd), an Exeter- and Harvard-bred commodities broker who runs their firm (and in fact does so quite profitably). One of the ways the Dukes destroy Winthorpe is by setting him up as a thief and a drug dealer. Winthorpe's assets are frozen by the Internal Revenue Service, his credit cards are confiscated and he is left almost entirely without cash or credit.[7]

Winthorpe solves this problem by going to a pawn shop. Looking the part of a street person, Winthorpe ends up trying to pawn a sports watch worth thousands of dollars to a pawnbroker (played by musician Bo Diddley) who is only willing to pay $50. The broker accuses Winthorpe of trying to sell him a stolen watch (asking 'got a receipt?' when Winthorpe quotes the retail price) and says that at that point in time, the watch is only worth $50. Winthorpe reluctantly takes the deal. According to pawnbroker Diddley, 'in Philadelphia, it's worth fifty bucks.'

We may lament Winthorpe's plight, especially since we see him selling for $50 a watch worth many times that (though he uses the proceeds to buy a gun, which he employs in an attempted robbery). However, the fact that there exists a market for small loans – a pawn brokerage in this case – meant that Winthorpe had access to money when he clearly needed it most.

It is also important to note that Winthorpe's inability to prove that he has title to the watch sharply reduced its value. A watch that may have been worth thousands if it could be proved legitimate was worth instead only $50 in the absence of a clear property right. This reduction in value reflected the broker's risk of being prosecuted for receiving and trafficking stolen goods, as well as the fact that potential buyers may be unwilling to pay much for a watch that has a high probability of having been stolen. Had Winthorpe been able to prove his title to the watch, he likely would have been able to enjoy a higher price, and perhaps the pawnbroker would have been able to enjoy a higher profit from legally reselling a luxury wristwatch.[8]

4.6 PROPERTY RIGHTS AND STEWARDSHIP

Another role of property rights shows up in the film. After ruining Winthorpe, the Duke brothers tell Valentine that they are giving him a house, a butler, a car and a job – a new life. Valentine is initially, and perhaps quite reasonably, skeptical about the Duke brothers' generosity. He attempts to steal items from his own house and, as mentioned before, casually juggles a valuable vase, breaking it. This callous disregard for property makes some sense as he does not really believe that it is his property. People take care of the things they own; they take less care with things they do not own.

Valentine is soon convinced, however, that the car, the butler, the house and everything in the house are his. He invites an unruly crowd of bar patrons – acquaintances from his old life – over to his house, hoping to impress them with his newfound wealth. He is quickly frustrated by their slovenly habits. They spill drinks on his Persian rug, threaten to vomit on the stairs, put out cigarettes on his floor and fail to use coasters on his end tables. Valentine tries to restrain their behavior, but eventually becomes fed up with the damage to his property and throws everyone out of the house. He then tells the butler that his former guests were just 'freeloaders' treating his house like a 'zoo.' Valentine's new role – that of property owner – has completely changed his incentives and, therefore, his perspective.

4.7 CONCLUSION

Economists often need practical examples of the propositions that we discuss in the classroom. Many useful such examples are provided in *Trading Places*, which, in addition to being an entertaining movie, illustrates a number of important points about economics, including the role of property rights, the costs of discrimination, the importance (and definition) of profit and the role of expectations and information in determining resource allocation across space and time. The movie is rich in lessons about basic economics and would make a valuable addition to any economist's pedagogical toolkit.

NOTES

1. For more on using media in economics instruction, see Mateer and Li (2008), Mixon (2010), Crisp and Mixon (2012) and Mateer (2012, 2013).
2. http://www.investopedia.com/terms/m/margincall.asp (accessed 31 October 2006). See also lecture notes by John M. Abowd, 'How the market works', available at http://instruct1.cit.cornell.edu/Courses/econ101-dl/lecture-auction-explained.html (accessed 30 October 2006).
3. Ibid.
4. Don't feel too bad for them. They make a return in a cameo in Eddie Murphy's 1988 film, *Coming to America*.
5. See, for example, Simon's classic 'The ultimate resource II: people, materials, and environment', available at http://www.juliansimon.com/writings/Ultimate_Resource/ (accessed 6 November 2006).
6. There is another possibility, albeit one that is perhaps unlikely: the Dukes over-insured the vase, but not anything else in the house.
7. One of the comedic themes is that people keep forgetting which drugs Winthorpe was accused of dealing. He was accused of dealing PCP (phencyclidine), but people keep erroneously saying that he was accused of dealing heroin or other drugs. Winthorpe has to correct them.
8. Economist Hernando de Soto has done a great deal of meticulous research on the role of informal property rights in developing countries. He argues specifically that a lack of formal property rights limits individuals' access to capital. See in particular his *The Mystery of Capital: Why Capitalism Triumphs in the West and Fails Everywhere Else* (de Soto, 2003).

5. Crony capitalism in *The Gilded Age* by Twain and Warner and its relevance for today

Michelle A. Vachris

5.1 INTRODUCTION

The Gilded Age, A Tale of Today, written by Mark Twain and Charles Dudley Warner (1873) tells the story of crony capitalism in the United States after the Civil War. The novel is Twain's only co-authored novel and was inspired by a challenge from Twain's and Warner's wives to write a better novel than the ones they had been reading. The plot is a thinly veiled account of actual 'backroom deals, sexual intrigue, and high-powered deception' from that era, and it is the book that gave 'The Gilded Age' its name.

This chapter describes how *The Gilded Age* can be used in undergraduate courses to teach about crony capitalism. The public choice framework is used to analyse themes in the novel, and excerpts and assignments are provided that could be incorporated into an undergraduate upper-level field course in Public Choice, Public Sector Economics or United States Economic History.

5.2 USING LITERATURE TO TEACH ECONOMICS

There is a growing body of work that describes and encourages the use of literature to teach economics (Watts, 2003), and more economics conferences are including sessions on economics and literature. Bohanon and Vachris (2012) survey over 40 articles in economics journals that either use the tools of economics to analyse specific works of literature or describe how to incorporate literature into the teaching of economics. They also provide an overview of literature written by economists and students for the purpose of teaching and learning economics.

Why use literature to teach economics? Research into learning behavior, such as Bransford et al. (2000), demonstrates that students, especially students in introductory courses, learn best from memorable storytelling. Such stories abound in literature and can increase a student's ability to understand the formal models presented in class. In addition to the potential for increasing student learning, the use of literature in the economics curriculum can support the interdisciplinary and integrative goals of a liberal education.

Cowen (2008b) argues that novels and social science models have similar structures and uses, and, therefore, that they complement one another. When we economists use models, we begin by describing our initial assumptions and setting out propositions regarding how exogenous variables influence certain endogenous variables, for example, by outlining utility or production functions. After establishing the initial equilibrium for the model, we then introduce a shock to the system by changing one of the exogenous variables (for example, increasing the price of a substitute commodity). We then perform comparative statics analysis to trace the effects of this shock as the model adjusts to a new equilibrium. Models are judged not by how realistic they are but rather whether they are internally consistent and have empirically predictive power.

Some novels, according to Cowen (2008b), follow this comparative static pattern. Authors begin by describing the initial state of the characters' lives and their environments. This initial equilibrium is then disturbed by some event that changes the lives of the characters. For example, in *The Gilded Age,* Laura goes to Washington, DC to become a lobbyist. The rest of the novel describes the results of this shock to the system. Novels, then, can be seen as informal models that 'use a stylized setting to show how one set of causes lead to particular effects, working through a mechanism of some generality' (Cowen, 2008a, p. 11). These informal models are similar to the models used by economists 'before the mathematization of the economics profession' (Cowen, 2008a, p. 11).

Despite the potential gains from trade between literature and economics, only a very small proportion of instruction time in economics classes is reportedly spent on examples from literature. Watts and Schaur (2011) provide results from surveys of economic instruction that include a question on how much class time is spent on references to literature/drama/music. The survey results are reported for principles courses, intermediate theory courses, statistics and econometrics courses and upper-level field courses. Not surprisingly, the median response for statistics and econometrics courses in each of the surveys was no class time (0 percent) devoted to literature/drama/music. At the principles level, the median time reported was stable at 6 percent for the 2000, 2005 and 2010 surveys. Both the intermediate theory courses and upper-level field courses have seen slight increases in the use of such references. For the intermediate theory courses, the median increased from 0 percent in 2000 and 2005 to 6 percent in 2010, and for the upper-level field courses, the median increased from 0 percent in 2000 to 6 percent in 2005 and 2010. Analysis of the mean data reported by Watts and Schaur (2011) also reveals increases in the use of literature/drama/music, especially in the principles and upper-level field courses. Most of the recent gains are in upper-level field courses, and the rest of this chapter describes how parts of the novel, *The Gilded Age*, can illustrate economic concepts in these types of courses.

5.3 PUBLIC CHOICE THEMES FOUND IN *THE GILDED AGE*

The novel *The Gilded Age, A Tale of Today* provides three storylines that offer illustrations of public choice theory in action. The first storyline, attributed to Mark Twain, involves the poverty-stricken Hawkins family's attempts to become rich from the sale of a plot of undeveloped land in Tennessee. The second storyline, attributed to Warner, describes the quest for riches by two upper-class men, Philip Sterling and Henry Brierly. A subplot interwoven into these two main storylines involves Senator Dilworthy, who manages the backroom deals behind both efforts. Public choice topics such as rent seeking and incentives of politicians are well illustrated.

The various pieces of legislation introduced by Senator Dilworthy can be analysed using the format that Caplan (2007) describes in his piece about how the events in the novel *Atlas Shrugged* by Ayn Rand parallel public choice theory. Caplan explains that each of the pieces of legislation in *Atlas Shrugged* has the following components: (1) a public interest rationale; (2) supportive interest groups with a hidden financial agenda; and (3) negative consequences for the general public. These components are also found in the bills introduced in *The Gilded Age*.

Silas 'Si' Hawkins, the patriarch of the Hawkins family, holds title to 75,000 acres of land in East Tennessee, and he imagines that this purchase is an investment for his and his family's future. He foresees many possible fortunes arising from this land. The land is about 20 miles from a river where he expects steamboats to come and stimulate the local economy, and he holds a similar expectation about the as-yet-to-be-built railroad. These high hopes lead him to reject offer after offer to take the land off his hands, much to the dismay of his long-suffering wife. The lessons in public choice begin once the Hawkins's adopted daughter, Laura, goes to Washington to pursue the latest scheme – petitioning the federal government to fund the development of Knobs Industrial University on the land.[1]

Laura is invited to Washington by the Senate sponsor of the bill, Senator Dilworthy, who employs her brother (coincidentally named Washington). She is accompanied on her journey by Colonel Sellers, a long-time family friend, a 'flamboyant backwoods speculator and loud-mouth opportunist' (Twain and Warner, introduction, p. xxvi), who has enticed Si Hawkins over the years with many get-rich-quick schemes.[2] Signs of crony capitalism appear at the very start of the journey, as Laura and Colonel Sellers travel using tickets provided to Senator Dilworthy for free by the railroad companies.

Once in Washington, Laura, with her beauty and charm, quickly becomes the 'reigning belle' of the town (Twain and Warner, 1873 [2006], p. 235) and a powerful lobbying force under the Senator's tutelage. In true public choice colors, Senator Dilworthy instructs Laura on the importance of cloaking private interests in public interest terms:

> Don't misunderstand me, Laura. I don't deny that it is for the interest of us all that this bill should go through, and it will. I have no concealments from you. But I have one principle in my public life, which I should like you to keep in mind; it has always been my guide. I never push a private interest if it is not justified and ennobled by some larger public good. (Twain and Warner, 1873 [2006], p. 259)

The proposed bill would fund the purchase of the Hawkins's land and the founding and building of Knobs Industrial University, which would then provide much needed education to transform the unskilled labor of the South into the more skilled labor needed for industrialization. The student population targeted by this new university would be the newly freed Negroes. The Representative reporting the bill from committee predicts, 'In five years the increase in local wealth would not only reimburse the government for the outlay in this appropriation, but pour untold wealth into the treasury' (Twain and Warner, 1873 [2006], p. 329). The land itself was described as being rich in natural resources, including coal and metals for mining extraction (though no evidence is actually provided for the existence of such resources).

A moral foundation is also woven into the arguments for the bill as follows: 'God had given us the care of these colored millions. What account should we render to Him of our stewardship? We had made them free. Should we leave them ignorant?' (Twain and Warner, 1873 [2006],

p. 329). That this richly endowed land had never been developed before is interpreted as 'providence' that it was 'consecrated for some great use' (Twain and Warner, 1873 [2006], p. 329), as opposed to evidence that the land was worthless.

The combination of private interest with moral arguments is reminiscent of Yandle's (1983) account of the strange political bedfellows of 'bootleggers and Baptists.'[3] Yandle explains how the prohibition against selling alcohol on Sundays would be supported by both Baptists (who are against drinking on moral grounds) and bootleggers (who would profit from the lack of competition on Sundays). When such disparate groups support a regulation, it is difficult for that regulation to be dismantled by the political process. Bootleggers and Baptists actually come together (that is, become de facto allies) in *The Gilded Age* to promote the development of the Hawkins's land.

The public choice theory of the brokering function that politicians play in the provision of government regulation and policy is prevalent in the novel. The excerpt that most captures the corruption in voting from the Knobs Industrial University storyline is chapter 42, in which Laura meets with Representative Trollop, who opposes the House bill. Once she convinces Trollop that she has information about his past improper behavior, he agrees to promote her bill. Laura then explains the quid pro quo.

> [T]hese gentlemen are to vote and work for the bill, simply out of love for the negro – and out of pure generosity I have put in a relative of each as a member of the University incorporation. They will handle a million or so of money, officially, but will receive no salaries. A larger number of statesmen are to vote and work for the bill – also out of love for the negro – gentlemen of but moderate influence, these – and out of pure generosity I am to see that relatives of theirs have positions in the University, *with* salaries, and good ones, too. You will vote and work for the bill, from mere affection for the negro, and I desire to testify my gratitude becomingly. Make free choice. Have you any friend whom you would like to present with a salaried or unsalaried position in our institution? (Twain and Warner, 1873 [2006], p. 309)

Ironically, despite Laura's lobbying abilities, the bill ultimately loses all support once Dilworthy is accused of paying a bribe to keep his Senate appointment. The Hawkins family never realizes a fortune from their land.

The secondary plot line involving the speculative pursuits of Henry Brierly also contains lessons about crony capitalism. In this storyline, Colonel Sellers plays a larger role. He works with Henry to try to get Congress to appropriate funds for a project that would make the river running through his land in Missouri navigable enough for steamship traffic. Senator Dilworthy introduces the petition from the citizenry 'with the remark that he knew, personally, the signers of it, that they were men interested, it was true, in the improvement of the country, but he believed without any selfish motive' (Twain and Warner, 1873 [2006], pp. 166–7). The 'race card' is played, yet again, in that '[i]t pleased him to see upon the roll the names of many colored citizens, and it must rejoice every friend of humanity to know that this lately emancipated race were intelligently taking part in the development of the resources of their native land' (Twain and Warner, 1873 [2006], p. 167).

The appropriation of $200,000 is passed and work begins on the project. Workers are hired and supplies bought – on credit backed by the promise of the appropriated funds:

> Beautiful credit! The foundation of modern society. Who shall say that this is not the golden age of mutual trust, of unlimited reliance upon human promises? That is a peculiar condition of society which enables a whole nation to instantly recognize point and meaning in the familiar newspaper anecdote, which puts into the mouth of a distinguished speculator in lands and mines this remark: 'I wasn't worth a cent two years ago, and now I owe a million dollars.' (Twain and Warner, 1873 [2006], p. 192)

No appropriated funds ever reach the project and the workers eventually turn into a mob that runs Henry out of town. Henry meets with the president of the company financing the project to obtain the funds, only to realize that the whole project is nothing but a house of cards. Chapter 28 includes the following description of where the initial appropriation went.

> Why the – matter is simple enough. A Congressional appropriation costs money. Just reflect, for instance – a majority of the House Committee, say $10,000 apiece – $40,000; a majority of the Senate Committee, the same each – say $40,000; a little extra to one or two chairmen of one or two such committees, say $10,000 each – $20,000; and there's $100,000 of the money gone, to begin with. Then, seven male lobbyists, at $3,000 each – $21,000; one female lobbyist, $10,000; a high moral Congressman or Senator here and there – the high moral ones cost more, because they give tone to a measure – say ten of these at $3,000 each, is $30,000; then a lot of small-fry country members who won't vote for anything whatever without pay – say twenty at $500 apiece, is $10,000; a lot of dinners to members – say $10,000 altogether; lot of jimcracks for Congressmen's wives and children – those go a long way – you can't spend too much money in that line – well, those things cost in a lump, say $10,000 – along there somewhere; and then comes your printed documents – your maps, your tinted engravings, your pamphlets, your illuminated show cards, your advertisements in a hundred and fifty papers at

> ever so much a line – because you've got to keep the papers all light or you are gone up, you know. Oh, my dear sir, printing bills are destruction itself. Ours so far amount to – let me see – 10; 52; 22; 13; – and then there's 11; 14; 33 – well, never mind the details, the total in clean numbers foots up $118,254.42 thus far! (Twain and Warner, 1873 [2006], pp. 204–5)

In other words, the initial appropriation was merely seed money to buy off enough votes for future appropriations.

The subplot of Senator Dilworthy and the bribe includes a scathing description of influence peddling in politics. Indeed, Dilworthy's character is based on real-life Senator Samuel Pomeroy, who was removed from office in 1873 after offering a bribe to a state legislator to support his bid for re-election.[4] (Remember that prior to the passage of the 17th amendment to the US Constitution, state legislatures elected US Senators.) In the novel, Dilworthy offers $7000 (the same sum as Pomeroy) to state legislator, Mr Noble, to guarantee support for re-election. During the investigative hearings about the incident, described in chapter 59, Dilworthy is somehow able to turn the tables on Mr Noble. Dilworthy learns of the accusation and immediately demands an investigation into Mr Noble for attacking the reputation of a US Senator. Noble testifies that he received the bribe from Dilworthy, to which an investigative committee member exclaims:

> *At last*, Mr. Chairman, this shameless person has arrived at the point. This is sufficient and conclusive. By his own confession he has received a bribe, and did it deliberately. This is a grave offense, and cannot be passed over in silence, sir. By the terms of our instructions we can now proceed to mete out to him such punishment as is meet for one who has maliciously brought disrespect upon a Senator of the United States. (Twain and Warner, 1873 [2006], p. 433)

In Dilworthy's account of the incident, he describes how he merely gave the cash to Noble to deliver to a friend of his, who was borrowing the money from Dilworthy to start a bank. No receipts or borrowing agreement were necessary. The Committee ends up setting Mr Noble free and letting the whole matter drop.

The inability of the legislature to police itself is covered more generally in chapter 51, where Colonel Sellers explains to Washington Hawkins that the vote on their land bill will be delayed because Congress begins each session by making a show of cleansing itself. No one is ever actually expelled from the legislature, of course. The voting public's short-term memory is illustrated by the fact that no one gets upset at the lack of expulsions because 'the proceedings drag on so long that the country is sick and tired of it' (Twain and Warner, 1873 [2006], p. 377).

In contrast to these examples of rent seeking and corruption, the novel also contains a counter-example of honest-to-goodness capitalism in action in the case of Philip Sterling's eventual success at finding coal. For most of the novel, however, Philip, like his partner Henry, is described as follows:

> There are many young men like him in American society, of his age, opportunities, education and abilities, who have really been educated for nothing and have let themselves drift, in the hope that they will find somehow, and by some sudden turn of good luck, the golden road to fortune … He saw people, all around him, poor yesterday, rich to-day, who had come into sudden opulence by some means which they could not have classified among any of the regular occupations of life. (Twain and Warner, 1873 [2006], p. 369)

Eventually, however, Philip develops surveying skills and work habits that lead him away from wealth redistribution and towards the production of wealth. While Henry fakes learning enough surveying skills to participate in the various land deals, Philip actually learns the trade. He dedicates himself to finding ore in the land owned by the family of the woman he loves, and ultimately '[t]he mine turned out even better than was at first hoped, and would, if judiciously managed, be a fortune to them all' (Twain and Warner, 1873 [2006], p. 462). That the novel ends with Philip's success, both in business and in love, is a moral statement against crony capitalism.

5.4 *THE GILDED AGE* BEING USED IN THE CLASSROOM

Any of the excerpts described above could be used in the teaching of public choice topics such as rent seeking, politicians as vote-maximizing brokers, voter rational ignorance and crony capitalism. One way to incorporate literature into the teaching of upper-level economics courses is to have the students read the novel over the semester and hold several discussion days as they progress through the novel. Students can use the public choice model to analyse the various bills proposed in the novel using questions such as those listed in Appendix A.

Rather than reading the entire novel, students can be assigned to read certain chapters that stand alone, such as chapters 28, 42, 51 and 59 described above. These excerpts and associated questions listed in Appendix A can be used as homework assignments or exam questions.

For shorter exams or assignments, the notable quotes presented in Appendix B might prove useful.

5.5 *THE GILDED AGE* AND ITS RELEVANCE FOR TODAY

The Gilded Age can be used to illustrate specific public choice topics as outlined above, but the novel can also be used to help students understand parallels between today's economy and the roots of the Progressive Era, perhaps in a course on United States Economic History.

Two opposite narratives exist that portend to explain the rise of Progressive legislation in the United States during the late 1800s and early 1900s. The first narrative explains that as the US economy became more industrialized, and as improvements in transportation, especially the railways, expanded the reach of markets, there were increased economies of scale, which led to the concentration of power in various industries. Large Trusts were created, which were headed by 'Robber Barons,' who used their economic power to exert influence in the political realm. The political influence of the Robber Barons led to policies that favored big business over the working man. The concentration of economic power also led to vast income inequalities. Legislation of the Progressive Era, as early as the Interstate Commerce Act of 1887 and the Sherman Antitrust Act of 1890, was the result of widespread popular outcry against the crony capitalism of the day. Increased regulation was in the public interest to control the excesses of laissez-faire capitalism.

Another narrative holds that much of the Progressive Era legislation was determined by private as opposed to public interests. Specifically, regulation of big business was supported by small, inefficient businesses that could not compete with the larger companies. Increased regulation led to a cozy relationship between government and business as 'capture theory' would predict. Once the government had favors to hand out, crony capitalism resulted.

Which came first, the chicken (political power) or the egg (economic power)? A similar discussion is taking place today with regard to the causes of the financial crisis. One narrative, favored by the Occupy Wall Street movement, argues that big business, especially banks, used their economic power to lobby for deregulation, and once they became 'too big to fail,' used that power to obtain bailouts. The obvious solution is to increase regulation to prevent another crisis, and to use income redistribution to 'level the playing field.' Another narrative, favored by the Tea Party movement, maintains that the potential existence of political favors invites rent seeking, as those who cannot successfully compete in the economic marketplace instead resort to obtaining market share through the political sphere. Those who can compete do so, whereas those who cannot engage in rent seeking instead. The solution here is to restrict the power of government so that there are no rents available to seek.

While novels set in historical times are usually not unbiased accounts of actual events, it so happens that *The Gilded Age* includes characters based on real persons and includes some pretty accurate descriptions of the scandals of the day. More importantly, reading and discussing a novel such as *The Gilded Age* in a course covering United States Economic History is a way to introduce students to the cultural context of the events of the era. As McCloskey (2010) suggests, cultural context and rhetoric of the day are essential for understanding and explaining underlying economic trends.

To which narrative about the rise of the Progressive movement in the United States would Twain and Warner likely have subscribed? Well, they may not have been Tea Partiers, but Twain and Warner certainly seemed skeptical of the political process in general, so they would probably not see re-regulation as the preferred path. As the character Colonel Sellers states, 'in a free country like ours, where any man can run for Congress and anybody can vote for him, you can't expect immortal purity all the time – it ain't in nature … Even in these days, when people growl so much and the newspapers are so out of patience, there is still a very respectable minority of honest men in Congress' (Twain and Warner, 1873 [2006], pp. 375–6).

NOTES

1. Laura's character is based on 'the ranking femme fatale of the time, Laura D. Fair' (Twain and Warner, 1873 [2006], introduction, p. xxi).
2. Colonel Sellers's character is patterned after Twain's mother's cousin and the land speculations have roots in Twain's actual life (Twain and Warner, 1873 [2006], introduction, p. xxiii).
3. Indeed, the quote 'Politics makes strange bedfellows' is attributed to Charles Dudley Warner.
4. US Senate Reference (2001).

APPENDIX A: SAMPLE DISCUSSION/EXAM QUESTIONS

From the full novel:

1. Explain the public interest rationale for the Knobs Industrial University bill. Which interest groups with a hidden financial agenda would benefit by the passage of the bill? What might be some of the negative consequences for the general public and unintended consequences of the bill?
2. Explain the public interest rationale for the Appropriation for Improving the Navigation of the Columbus River. Which interest groups with a hidden financial agenda would benefit by the passage of the bill? What might be some of the negative consequences for the general public and unintended consequences of the bill?
3. Describe examples of rent seeking in the various get-rich-quick schemes undertaken by Colonel Sellers.
4. Describe examples of the brokering function that politicians play in the market for votes.

From specific excerpts:

5. Chapter 28: Use Henry's meeting with the president of the Navigation Company to explain the brokering function that politicians play in the market for votes.
6. Chapter 42: Use Laura's meeting with Mr Trollop to explain the brokering function that politicians play in the market for votes.
7. Chapter 51: Find examples of principal agent problems between politicians and voters in Colonel Sellers's explanation of how Congress pretends to police itself.
8. Chapter 59: Use the theory of voter rational ignorance to explain how Senator Dilworthy gets away with making a bribe.

APPENDIX B: OTHER NOTABLE QUOTES ON POLITICAL CORRUPTION

Relate the following quotes to public choice theory:

Colonel Sellers (Twain and Warner, 1873 [2006], p. 264): 'when you come to look at it you cannot deny that we would have to go without the services of some of our ablest men, sir, if the country were opposed to – to – bribery.'

Philip Sterling (Twain and Warner, 1873 [2006], p. 370): 'chances are that a man cannot get into Congress now without resorting to arts and means that should render him unfit to go there.'

Senator Dilworthy (Twain and Warner, 1873 [2006], p. 260) on the abuse of franking privileges to ship personal belongings home: 'Yes, yes, but child, all Congressmen do that. It may not be strictly honest, indeed it is not unless he had some public documents mixed in with the clothes.'

More on franking privileges (Twain and Warner, 1873 [2006], p. 174): 'postage stamps were not needed – the Senator's frank could convey a horse through the mails if necessary.'

6. Including short stories in economics courses

Philip J. Ruder

6.1 INTRODUCTION

Teaching economics effectively to a diverse undergraduate audience to some extent requires finding ways to engage the students who view the math of the subject as difficult and the concepts as abstract and irrelevant. Adding short stories to the reading list of traditional economics courses can increase student engagement while providing rich case studies that illuminate the subject matter in ways that textbook readings and news articles do not. Short story readings in the syllabus can surprise students, connect economic concepts to personal and intense situations and highlight important subtleties that traditional treatments of the topics miss. Student feedback on short story readings often suggests that most students find them enjoyable and useful elements of the course.

The use of literature in economics courses has been well documented in the literature on pedagogy in economics and in other fields. Watts and Smith (1989) and Watts (1998, 2003) describe how poems and excerpts from novels and plays can enhance otherwise traditional economics courses. Kish-Goodling (1998) discusses the use of a specific play and Scahill (1998) discusses the use of a particular novel in economics courses. Hartley (2001) uses classic texts to teach an introductory course for non-majors. Recent articles in this vein offer literary possibilities for economics courses that include historical novels (Cotti and Johnson, 2012) and Dr. Seuss (Miller and Watts, 2011) at the principles level, and excerpts from American novels (Vachris and Bohanon, 2012) in labor economics courses.

Adding literary selections to course readings and activities improves economics courses by surprising students with different and entertaining material laden with economic content. Many students see economic concepts as useful for understanding the business world – a domain that remains largely outside the experience of typical undergraduates. Examples from literature demonstrate the usefulness of economic insight for understanding many more phenomena than students expect.

Most students respond favorably to the literary readings and assignments. As a result, students seem more likely to do the reading before class and to participate thoughtfully in class activities based on those readings. Moreover, the unusual content in the course can increase the favorable 'buzz' on campus about it, and increase student enrollments in economics courses as well.

Literary examples in general, and short story cases in particular (Ruder, 2010), can provide a facsimile for experiences that students do not yet have. Students in the traditional 18–22-year-old demographic group seldom have managed a business, purchased a home or even supported themselves financially. As a consequence, the relevance of many economic concepts is not easily fully appreciated by students. The emotional power of literature can personalize economic phenomena and demonstrate the importance of economic analysis for understanding the situations under study.

In the experience of the author of this chapter, short stories serve the purposes of the economic instructor exceptionally well. Reading excerpts of novels and plays inevitably results in a loss of the context in which the excerpted scenes take place. Short stories, on the other hand, can tell a complete tale in a brief reading. Short stories generally work better than poems as well due to the relative ease of reading and interpreting the short stories versus the poems. Despite their brevity, short stories can be dense with economic content. Joyce Carol Oates describes the form as 'a prose piece that is not a mere concatenation of events, as in a news account or an anecdote, but an intensification of meaning by way of events' (Oates, 1992, p. 7). Short stories can deliver a 'big bang' for a brief reading assignment.

Short stories have constituted part of the principles courses taught by the present author for many years. The reading assignments of the course generally include 10 to 15 chapters of an introductory textbook, nine news articles and two short stories. Each week, students are required to read the assigned news article or short story in advance, and to submit via a course management website short written responses to several questions. Questions are intended to lead students to make the connection between the material in the textbook and course and the assigned reading, and to conduct some form of analysis using the tools under study in the course.

Table 6.1 Short stories with economic content

Author	Story	Source	Concepts	Synopsis
Akpan, Uwem	An Ex-Mas Feast	*The New Yorker*, 13 June 2005	development, informal economy, education	A poor family in one of Nairobi's shanty towns struggles and tries to send one child to school
Alarcón, Daniel	City of Clowns	*The New Yorker*, 16 June 2003	development, corruption, markets	A young man in Lima, Peru, contrasts making a living through thievery with participating honestly in the market economy
Crace, Jim	Talking Skull	*Continent* (New York: Harper & Row) 2005	demand, gains from exchange	The city-educated heir of a wealthy villager inherits the family business
Davis, Lydia	Break it Down	*Break it Down* (New York: Farrar, Straus and Giroux) 1986	benefit-cost analysis	A man estimates in dollar terms the benefits and costs of a romantic weekend away with his lover
Eugenides, Jeffrey	Early Music	*The New Yorker*, 10 October 2005	opportunity costs, labor markets, credit	A man struggles to support his family, pay the loan on his clavichord and nurture his musical skill
Gautreaux, Tim	Welding with Children	*The Atlantic Monthly*, March 1997	income inequality, social mobility	A grandfather tries to break the cycle of poverty for his grandchildren
Gautreaux, Tim	Same Place, Same Things	*The Atlantic Monthly*, June 1991	supply and demand, Great Depression	Pump repairman Harry Lintel follows droughts in Depression Era South to ply his trade
Hamid, Mohsin	The Third-born	*The New Yorker*, 24 September 2012	development, rural to urban migration, education	The third-born in a developing country family is the only child allowed to stay in school

Author	Story	Source	Concepts	Synopsis
Jen, Gish	Birthmates	*Ploughshares*, Winter 1994	creative destruction, signaling	Microcomputer software salesman finds himself stuck in a job at a firm in a declining industry
Jensen, Geeta Sharma	A Good Country	*The Atlantic Monthly*, May 2003	negative externalities, property rights, negotiation costs, public goods	Immigrants from Myanmar get caught in the middle of a dispute over zoning rules and enforcement that pits farmers and city people against each other in a Wisconsin exurb
Jones, Edward P.	Bad Neighbors	*The New Yorker*, 7 August 2006	income inequality, social mobility, race	Upwardly mobile African-American families interact with poor neighbors
Mueenuddin, Daniyal	Nawabdin Electrician	*The New Yorker*, 27 August 2007	development, entrepreneurship, corruption	An entrepreneurial and pilfering electrician strives to finance dowries for 12 daughters in Pakistan
Parker, Dorothy	The Standard of Living	*The New Yorker*, 20 September 1941	demand, relative poverty	Two young women in a steno pool in Manhattan fantasize about being wealthy

Author	Story	Source	Concepts	Synopsis
Proulx, Annie	What Kind of Furniture Would Jesus Pick?	*The New Yorker*, 18 August 2003	supply and demand, negative externalities, non-monetary benefits and costs	Gilbert Wolfscale is a rancher in the failing Wyoming open-range beef market. The decline of this industry, regulatory efforts to prevent stream erosion and the disruption of pronghorn migration and property rights and pollution issues related to coal bed methane make this story rich in economic content
Upike, John	My Father on the Verge of Disgrace	*The New Yorker*, 10 March 1997	precariousness of economic life	A child's observations of small-town economic life in Depression and World War II years
Vapnyar, Lara	Broccoli	*The New Yorker*, 5 January 2004	demand, utility	A Russian immigrant to the United States stocks up on broccoli and other vegetables but never gets around to cooking anything
Vapnyar, Lara	Cinderella School	*The New Yorker*, 22 May 2006	immigration, labor markets	A Russian immigrant to the United States teaches English to other immigrants at an office run by a charlatan
Wolff, Tobias	The Benefit of the Doubt	*The New Yorker*, 14 July 2003	Foreign aid	A foreign aid agency official allows himself to be robbed by gypsies in Rome

The short stories are of greatest use when some aspect of human behavior is central to the economic issue. As described in Ruder (2010), Annie Proulx's (2003) 'What Kind of Furniture Would Jesus Pick?' has been used to illustrate, among other concepts, the importance of implicit costs and benefits to explain the protagonist's perseverance at ranching when it seems to be such a losing venture. Jensen's (2003) 'A Good Country' has provided an excellent supplement to textbook treatments of the Coase Theorem.[1] The story illustrates how a violation of social norms regarding fairness can result in transactions costs that can make solutions to externality issues difficult to achieve. Table 6.1 presents 18 short stories and some of the economic concepts illustrated by each story.[2] The following section describes in greater detail how a short story can illustrate important concepts in an economics class.

6.2 TEACHING DEVELOPMENT ECONOMICS WITH 'NAWABDIN ELECTRICIAN'

A more detailed example demonstrates how adding short stories to the mix of readings and assignments can enrich an economics course. Students who have grown up in wealthy nations such as the United States can have a difficult time grasping many aspects of the development economics course because so many issues studied in that course lie so far outside of students' experience. Supplementing readings from textbooks, journals and the popular press with short stories emphasizes the human costs of underdevelopment, while also giving students a sense of the impediments to development that result from the nature of the incentives faced by citizens in developing nations.

One of the central issues in a development course is the effect on growth of the institutions present in a particular developing country. The level of corruption present in a nation can determine its prospects for economic growth. Easterly (2002) offers a very clear scholarly treatment of the impediment to growth posed by corruption. A news article such as Bajaj and Yardley (2012) can offer a very current example. Having students read Daniyal Mueenuddin's (2007) 'Nawabdin Electrician' provides students with a sense of the incentives facing an individual in a developing country, and it illustrates how difficult it might be to combat the problem of corruption.

'Nawabdin Electrician' tells the tale of Nawab, a skilled mechanic and electrician striving to earn enough to pay the dowries necessary to marry off his 12 daughters. Nawab is a skilled and likable protagonist, but also the perpetrator of numerous small crimes. Nawab's livelihood depends on his skill at these small thefts. 'He flourished on a signature ability: a technique for cheating the electric company by slowing down the revolutions of its meters, so cunningly performed that his customers could specify to the hundred-rupee note the desired monthly savings' (Mueenuddin, 2007, p. 73).

Nawab works maintaining the pumps at a farm of a wealthy and largely absent owner. On the side, Nawab is a clever but not completely honest entrepreneur. 'He set up a one-room flour mill, run off a condemned electric motor – condemned by him. He tried his hand at fish-farming in a pond at the edge of one of his master's fields' (Mueenuddin, 2007, p. 73). Even when Nawab engages in legal endeavors, he undertakes them by sneaking away from his job on the farm.

One evening, Nawab is ambushed and wounded by a desperately poor itinerant laborer. Several villagers come to Nawab's aid and shoot the thief. Nawab and the thief end up in adjacent beds in the local clinic, with Nawab receiving aid and the thief left to die. The thief apologizes and begs forgiveness from Nawab with his dying breath, but Nawab curses him for his crimes. 'Never. I won't forgive you. You had your life, I had mine. At every step of the road I went the right way and you the wrong. Look at you now, with bubbles of blood stuck in the corner of your lips. Do you think this isn't a judgment?' (Mueenuddin, 2007, p. 77).

Table 6.2 Possible discussion questions

Daniyal Mueenuddin's 'Nawabdin Electrician'
1. Make a list of Nawab's various jobs and business ventures mentioned by the narrator. Which are honest, which are not?
2. How do Nawab's actions affect the rate of return to the resources invested in K.K. Harouni's farm?
3. In an economy where most workers were only as honest as Nawab, how would the rate of growth compare with that of an economy where most workers were honest?
4. Despite the fact that Nawab makes a large portion of his income through petty thievery, he shows no understanding or mercy to the thief who tries to rob him. Why?

Nawab's sense of himself as an upright citizen and the deference shown him by other characters in the story illustrate the normalcy of corruption in this village economy. Table 6.2 presents several discussion questions related to this short story reading that evoke short written responses from students submitted electronically the night before the class discussion. In class, students work in groups of two or three to develop a group response to the questions on the required readings. After that exercise, the topic of the effect of corruption on growth is presented to and then discussed by the whole class.

6.3 STUDENT FEEDBACK

An economics instructor includes short stories or other literary readings in an economics course in order to offer readings that students might enjoy more than either textbook or news article readings, and to develop case studies that increase student understanding. The reading for the Spring 2012 section of the Principles of Microeconomics course at Pacific University consisted of one short story, nine news articles and 16 textbook chapters. The short story read by the class was Annie Proulx's (2003) 'What Kind of Furniture Would Jesus Pick?' – a story that touches on numerous economic issues that span the entire Principles of Microeconomic course. The news articles were selected from *The New York Times* and *The Wall Street Journal*; each article illustrated a single economic concept. The students read Mankiw's (2011) *Principles of Microeconomics* (6th edition). At the conclusion of the course, the instructor administered a survey that consisted of four questions that asked the 54 students in the course to assign numerical ratings to assess the enjoyment and instructional value of the single short story reading relative to the textbook chapters and news articles read by students during the semester. Table 6.3 presents the distribution of student responses to the questions. The survey gave students the option of providing written comments and 47 of the 54 students did write a sentence or two to supplement their numerical ratings.

The student survey was administered on an exam day in order to achieve maximum participation. Students received extra credit points for completing the survey, which was not anonymous. At the end of a semester that included weekly short-response exercises for which students received full credit for participation, not content, the lack of anonymity is not expected to result in limited student candor. Nevertheless, it is possible that the lack of anonymity may have compromised the usefulness of the student feedback.

In any case, the ratings that students assigned to questions one and two regarding student enjoyment of the short story reading relative to the textbook and news article readings indicate that a large majority of students found the short story reading at least as enjoyable as the other readings in the course. Exactly half the class found the short story reading more enjoyable than the textbook readings, and 22 of the 54 students found the short story more enjoyable than the news articles;

Table 6.3 Student feedback on short story readings

Question 1: Please rate your enjoyment of the short story you read in this class relative to the readings in the textbook.						
Less enjoyable	1	2	3	4	5	More enjoyable
Count	2	7	18	22	5	
Question 2: Please rate your enjoyment of the short story you read in this class relative to the readings in the other economic reasoning exercises.						
Less enjoyable	1	2	3	4	5	More enjoyable
Count	5	9	18	16	6	
Question 3: Please rate the usefulness of the short story for conveying economic concepts relative to the readings in the textbook.						
Less useful	1	2	3	4	5	More useful
Count	3	8	10	23	10	
Question 4: Please rate the usefulness of the short story for conveying economic concepts relative to the readings in the other economic reasoning exercises.						
Less useful	1	2	3	4	5	More useful
Count	2	12	20	13	7	

most students rated the short story reading as equally or more effective at conveying economic ideas relative to textbook and news article readings; 33 of 54 students rated the short story superior to the textbook for conveying economic concepts; and 20 out of 24 students indicated that the short story surpassed the news articles in ability to illuminate economic ideas.

Student comments help one to interpret the numerical ratings. Among the positive comments, the most common responses cited the story's effectiveness at providing real-world examples. One student wrote, 'the short story put the economics we were learning through graphs and such into perspective, or put it into a real world situation. This helped make the economics more understandable and realistic (especially because I was more interested in how these concepts played out in life/society/government).' Some students made positive comments about the change of pace and the humor offered by the short story reading.[3]

As Table 6.3 suggests, the negative comments were not nearly as numerous as the positive ones. The most frequent criticism of the short story reading focused on the length of that reading assignment. Although only 12 pages long, the story far exceeded the 2–4 page length of the news articles. Several students found it difficult to discern the connection between the short story and the economics. A few students simply did not enjoy the story. One student captured the sense of all the negative comments submitted when she wrote, 'The reading was too long and too slow and the questions asked were not anywhere near a focal point in the reading, making it a little confusing. Especially paired with the timing (we hadn't really talked about externalities in class yet) it was hard to figure out what the question was looking for. I sympathize with the apparent death of the family farm, which I like as a concept for illustrating externalities and subsidies, but this particular story was exceptionally depressing and pretty boring. I didn't sympathize with the character, or enjoy reading after the first page or two. I would recommend shortening it or choosing a relatively faster-paced story.'

In the experience of the instructor, the students who least appreciated the quantitative rigor of the course and struggled more with the textbook readings were more likely to enjoy and report learning from the short story reading. The students who found the quantitative work to be straightforward and for whom the textbook reading was clear seemed less likely to enjoy the short story reading or to find it useful. The several non-native English speakers in the class had a hard time reading the short story.

The success of the short story reading in engaging students who are alienated by the traditional economics course offers a compelling reason to include such material in one's syllabus. Very short stories focused tightly on one or two economic issues are likely to be more effective at pulling in students who are struggling with the technical elements of the course. The shorter, better targeted stories also seem less likely to put off students for whom the stories are not a fun element of the course.

6.4 CONCLUSION

The short story gives economics teachers and their students a great way to convey economic concepts and increase the variety of class readings and activities. As supplements to traditional economics courses or as readings in unconventional economics or interdisciplinary courses, short stories deliver a great deal of content from brief, enjoyable and relatively easy reading assignments. Sometimes the connection between the economic concepts and the world experienced by students is made clearer via a short story than by means of the textbook or a news article. Class discussions centered on short stories can also draw out the student who has only a weak grasp of the technical framework of the course but who has a comparative advantage in analysing literature. Positive student feedback on the short story reading in an introductory economics course at Pacific University provides evidence of the potential usefulness of short stories for increasing student enjoyment and understanding of economics courses (and the contents of such courses). More careful measurement of the effect on outcomes of short story and other literary readings remains to be done.

NOTES

1. See Chapter 11 by Beaulier, Mixon and Cebula in this volume for more on textbook and other treatments of the Coase Theorem.
2. See Ruder (2013) for more resources related to the use of short stories in economics instruction.
3. These types of benefits are also discussed in Bauman's Chapter 10 in this volume.

7. Some brief syllabus advice for the young economist

Emily Chamlee-Wright and Joshua C. Hall

7.1 INTRODUCTION

In the field of economic education, there are numerous articles on how to teach economics more effectively. For example, edited volumes by Becker and Watts (2000), Becker et al. (2006), Mixon (2005) and Mixon and Cebula (2009) brim with advice on how economists might improve what they are doing in the classroom. These volumes and the various economic education journals are filled with articles on how to teach specific courses differently or more effectively (for example, Chamlee-Wright, 2011; Coyne and Leeson, 2011; Hartley, 2001), how to incorporate popular culture (Hall, 2005), film clips (Crisp and Mixon, 2012; Mateer and Stephenson, 2011; Mixon, 2010) and even how to use taste tests to teach about protectionism (Powell, 2007). To our knowledge, however, there are no articles specifically geared toward economists about syllabus design outside of specific discussion of readings.

This is puzzling given the vast literature aimed at helping the young economist succeed in the Academy. For example, Thomson (2001) is widely read by graduate students in order to become acculturated to the profession. Similarly, Hamermesh (1992) provides advice to the young economist on professional etiquette that can be generally viewed as good career advice. There also exists advice for specific sub-groups within economics, from women (Hamermesh, 2005), individuals looking for teaching positions (Owens, 2008) and even Austrian economists interested in liberal arts college jobs (Horwitz, 2011). While this advice benefits young economists by getting them to be thoughtful about their teaching, research and interactions with fellow economists, it is a bit surprising that none of this literature touches at all on the classroom syllabus and the policies laid out therein.

In our opinion, this gap represents an important oversight. Many young economists become bogged down in the first few years of teaching because they have had neither the time nor the experience nor the mentoring to think through and develop how best to structure their syllabus. By 'syllabus structure' we do not mean which readings are assigned and when, or what textbook will be used, or whether to emphasize lecture or discussion. Instead, we are concerned about how exactly a faculty member's *expectations* for the class get expressed to students through the syllabus. In our experience, young faculty members often encounter trouble because of differences between their expectations and those of the students. Perhaps the most obvious case of this is with respect to grading, but teaching is filled with other examples such as availability for consultation outside of class, participation criteria and so on. Confusing or incomplete expectations in the syllabus inhibits the development of student agency and responsibility in the classroom itself.

What follows is a discussion of syllabus language that touches on three different areas of expectation management: managing out-of-class time; leading effective classroom discussion; and setting and maintaining grading expectations. While we are largely in agreement about these three points, the language and discussion in the first two come primarily from Emily Chamlee-Wright's experiences, and the latter from Joshua Hall's experiences. As we point out later in the chapter, much of what we discuss here has come to us from a variety of different sources and influences. Thus, we do not claim that these practices are unique or originated with us. At the same time, we hope that by discussing them in this format, more economists, particularly young economists setting out on their careers, will be exposed to and benefit from these elements of syllabus design that foster better expectation alignment.

7.2 MANAGING TIME OUTSIDE OF CLASS

One of the perennial problems professors face is how to manage time with students outside of class time. This issue is particularly pressing for faculty in small liberal arts colleges, where the expectation often is that faculty will remain very accessible to and develop close mentoring relationships with their students. Regular and posted office hours have become a sacred cow at such institutions. The assumption is that by maintaining regular office hours, students will know when they can find their professors and their professors will be accessible and eager to receive students during these appointed times. Experience suggests, however, that the exact opposite is true.

First, most faculty choose office hours that are spaced apart in such a manner that they complement their teaching schedule. So if the faculty member has no classes on Monday, Wednesday or Friday from 10:00 to 11:00, this may look like an ideal time to hold office hours. But this time is likely to overlap with courses that students are taking, making it impossible for them to come during this particular time slot. They thus default to the 'or by appointment' option, to which I turn in a moment. Non-course time slots in the weekly schedule – at Beloit College, where Emily Chamlee-Wright taught for 19 years, there are no courses offered between 4:00 and 7:00 p.m. – are no more helpful, as such times are typically cordoned off for co-curricular activities. In short, students are busy. No particular time slot, even if the number of hours is generous, is likely to work for the majority of advisees and students in one's classes.

Second, when office hours do not get used, faculty tend to rely on that time as preparation time, grading time or finishing that article to meet the deadline time. The unfortunate student who actually avails him or herself of the option to utilize the designated office hours is likely to encounter a professor who is now stressed out by the fact that she no longer has the time she had grown accustomed to using for other purposes. In short, the notion that faculty are eagerly awaiting students' arrival during their office hours is a myth. Smart, busy people find productive ways to fill that time when it is not used regularly. Smart, busy people come to rely on that space in their day, and they are not likely to be focused on the student before them if their work plan has been interrupted.

Thinking this through has led me to adopt a 'meetings by appointment only' policy. I (Emily Chamlee-Wright) have the one-line version of this policy posted on my door, but in my economics courses I use the following parable to explain my policy. Although it takes up an inordinate amount of real estate on my syllabus, I figure that the 'real estate' is cheap and the economic lesson it conveys is valuable.

> **Office Hours (a story of social coordination through the ages):** Once upon a time, office hours were the low cost way of solving a coordination problem: Student needs to talk to Professor; Student stops by Professor's Office. Alas, Professor has gone to think Deep Thoughts somewhere other than The Office. Student leaves frustrated. Then, someone invents the 'Office Hour,' a stretch of time in which Professor commits to thinking Deep Thoughts *in* The Office, ready to receive the company of any Student who comes by. Coordination problem solved! But, Professor notices a consistent and abhorrent waste of our most precious resource: Time. Professor observes that frequently Students do not use the appointed Office Hours, thus unnecessarily confining Deep Thinking to The Office when Professor is sure that much Deeper Thinking could be done over a latte (vente, non-fat please) in the café. At other times, say, just before a midterm exam, Professor notices a multitude of Students lined up (wasting *their* Time) outside Professor's door, all competing for what

> is now an all too scarce slice of Office Hour. The ubiquity of the telephone was an improvement ('Professor, may I schedule an appointment at 2:00 on Tuesday?') but still required Professor to be in the office to receive Student's telephone call. The dawn of the answering machine helped, but Student frequently failed to leave a number or, when call was returned, Roommate never gave Student the message from Professor that, 'no, 2:00 will not work, but how about 7:00 am? Bring coffee please.' Just when Professor was ready to give in to the barbaric waste of Time, some wise and gentle soul invented Email. With Email, Student could send Note: 'Would love to meet with you this week. I am free on Thursday between 2:00 and 4:00,' to which Professor responds, 'That would be lovely. If you like, we can meet over lattes at 2:00.' How civilized! No wasted hours trapped amongst the dusty old books, when a walk to fetch a caffeinated beverage would surely dredge up those Deep Thoughts from the dark recesses of the mind. No wasted time waiting in lines outside Professor's door. Ah, the emancipating power of Email and the phrase, 'Meetings can be arranged by appointment.'
>
> By the way, Tuesdays and Thursdays are the best days to arrange an appointment with me. When requesting an appointment, please suggest several times that can work with your schedule.

As I suggest above, one of the critical benefits this policy conveys, at least in my experience, is that I feel prepared to receive the student who has made an appointment to see me at 2:00 on Thursday afternoon. At ten minutes before the hour my Google Calendar reminder pops up with '2:00 Meeting with Amanda RE: Senior thesis.' I search for my last email exchange with Amanda, quickly remind myself of the thesis she is attempting to pursue and the issues she was facing in the last draft. This takes, at most, five minutes. When Amanda arrives, I am mentally prepared and collegially receptive. With this system, no student ever feels like they have interrupted me or thrown me off my plans for the day.

The 'meetings by appointment only' policy offers one further benefit in that it sets appropriate expectations for professional life. Once students graduate, when and where will they ever again face the 'regular office hours regime'? I dare say, never. I doubt seriously that on his first day of work Young Graduate will hear his new boss say, 'Young Graduate, I will set aside 2:00–4:00 every Tuesday and Thursday for you to come see me, or not, as you see fit. Don't bother making an appointment. You can rest assured that I will be there waiting for you.' Preparing students to meet expectations beyond the college environment is one of the most important things we do as educators, and the office hour regime runs counter to this purpose. In professional life, we make (and keep) appointments. There is no good reason not to establish this practice in the college years.

I should offer this note of caution. I instituted this policy as a tenured full professor at Beloit College, knowingly violating Beloit's Administrative Policy Manual. Silly rules are easy to make fun of and ignore as a senior member of the faculty, but my junior colleagues would often say, 'your approach sounds like such a smart way to manage time with students, but I don't want this to come back and haunt me in my tenure review.' I like to think that at Beloit, faculty and administrative colleagues would never hold a niggling policy violation against someone in their review so long as they were living up to the intended spirit of the rule. Yet I understand my junior colleagues' concerns. And at another institution, one that does not value common sense as much as my Beloit colleagues, there may be very good reasons to be concerned. Thus, before instituting such a practice, junior faculty would be wise to seek official sanction from a department chair or appropriate administrative supervisor. One might propose this as an experiment that can inform future debate on the subject. Any innovative chair or dean ought to welcome fresh ideas and faculty experimentation that can improve faculty–student interaction.

7.3 DEVELOPING INTELLECTUAL AGENCY THROUGH FORMAL CLASS DISCUSSION

I love to lecture. And I particularly prize the pedagogical value of a well-crafted lecture. That said, even the best lectures – even those that are appropriately interactive and engaging – can leave many students with the sense that their primary job is simply to absorb what the professor has said. In order to reinforce the point that students are expected to be active contributors in the production of new knowledge, I have always integrated discussions of primary texts into my courses. I do this at the introductory level and increase the emphasis on discussion in courses taught later in the curriculum, culminating in a senior seminar course that is almost entirely focused on discussion and development of original research.

Anyone who practices class discussion on a regular basis is familiar with the common frustrations: passive students who never say anything; students who dominate the discussion and crowd out more reluctant students; discussions that go off track; the difficulties of knowing how to grade student contribution in discussions; and so on. The framework for formal discussions I offer below is not a panacea, but it goes a long way toward addressing some of these common frustrations. Most importantly, the rules of formal discussion I deploy foster the expectation that students will contribute to (not merely absorb) the body of knowledge that informs the field of inquiry we are studying.

Let me begin with a disclaimer that I have not come up with these rules on my own. Shamelessly, I have adapted them from Liberty Fund seminar rules. They are described below, as I describe them to my students.

Formal Discussion Rules:

Discussions will begin promptly at the start of class and run (without break) for 90 minutes. Please come on time and be prepared to sit for that length of time. If you do need to step out, try to do so quietly.

Chairs and tables will be arranged in a rectangle in advance. (If you arrive early and the chairs are not arranged this way, please help by making the appropriate adjustments.) Students will be assigned specific seats with the placement of nameplates. Nameplates are used to encourage mutual reference between discussion participants, e.g., 'I want to respond to something John said earlier …'

The discussion will begin with the Discussion Leader (that's me) highlighting some points within the reading and posing questions to which discussion participants might wish to respond. These questions will be posted on the course website in advance. My introductory remarks should take no more than 10–15 minutes, leaving the balance of the discussion time for discussion participants to respond to my queries, present your own questions, and respond to other discussion participants. This means that you are duty-bound to come prepared, with the text read very carefully, with notes and/or questions written down so that you can contribute to a lively and engaged discussion.

After I finish my introductory remarks, the 'queue' is then opened for participants to respond and/or pose their own questions. You may indicate your interest in making a comment by raising your hand upward. If, while another discussion participant is speaking you decide that you would like to make your own points, you should 'catch my eye' by raising your hand quietly, and wait for a silent nod indicating that you have been placed on the queue.

If discussion participants wish to make a *very brief* comment that pertains to something that was *just* said, you can be put on the 'brief comment' queue which allows you to get your short point in right away before the conversation moves too far beyond the specific issue being raised. Participants wishing to be put on the short comment queue indicate this by putting their finger and thumb together (as if to say, 'this will be short, I promise'). A position within the brief comment queue does not eliminate a position in the main queue. This helps to assure that brief comments remain brief and that participants will have time to articulate their longer points when their turn in the long comment queue comes around.

The Discussion Leader may participate in both queues, but she will have to abide by the same rules as everyone else (i.e., I have to wait my turn just like everyone else). The Discussion Leader does however reserve the right to change the order of the queue toward the end of the discussion time to make sure that everyone who wants to speak gets the chance. The Discussion Leader also reserves the right to cut short comments that go on too long and to take other appropriate measures necessary to maintaining order and decorum.

Mutual respect is an absolute in these discussions. That said, one can be respectful while still engaging in lively argument. Striking this balance is the key to a successful discussion and is the responsibility of everyone at the table.

Each discussion day, students will earn 0 to 10 points. A score of '0' is attributed to those who do not attend on the designated discussion day and time. A score of '2' is attributed to those who attend but appear inattentive or disengaged from the discussion. A score of '5' is attributed to those who attend, do not say anything, but who appear to be engaged and are focused on the conversation. (Now, I know what you are thinking. 'How does she know whether I am engaged or disengaged? She cannot read my thoughts!' True enough. But I can tell whether you *appear* to be engaged – or not – and this makes a difference. A student who appears to be disengaged creates a negative externality that causes the slow death of what might otherwise have been a lively discussion. Students who appear to be engaged, even if they are silent, encourage others to continue their active participation, hence the 5 points.) The student who speaks up a few times during the course of the discussion earns 7 points. The student who offers frequent thoughtful commentary, connects their comments to the comments of others, sparks debate, and so forth, earns 10 points. While it is perfectly acceptable to not speak on any given discussion day, consecutive discussion days with no active participation earn successively lower scores.

Weekly grades will be posted, using a system of anonymous codes, on the course website.

I have used this formal discussion methodology for the past six years or so. There are some costs. At first, students can greet the formal rules with reluctance. 'In my other classes, I get to chime in whenever I want,' say some students. Yet the corresponding benefit is that for these students, the queue acts as a governor, giving them space, but not at the expense of other more reluctant students.

The rules do not completely solve the problem that some students will not contribute much to the discussion. The formal grading process, however, does provide an incentive to at least try, and if a reluctant student weighs in with even two brief comments in a given discussion, the posted grades for the week give them immediate feedback that such contributions make a difference. Most importantly, the rules make it perfectly clear that it is the student's responsibility to enter into the discussion. The professor does not pick and choose a single student out of a sea of raised hands. If a student raises her hand, she gets a spot on the queue. That is all that is required. Their discussion grade is entirely in their control.

One of the things students do not like when they first encounter these rules is that the discussion often ebbs and flows between and across different discussion topics raised within a given reading. The queue dictates what is said next. This means that one topic may get abandoned (temporarily) as the next person on the queue raises a different point, only to be brought back up again by a student further down in the queue. A few weeks with the rules, however, give students an opportunity to experience what I call the 'Liberty Fund Rules (LFR) Magic'. The LFR Magic is the phenomenon whereby a discussion that at first appears to be scattered across and jumping between disparate themes, at some point, begins to cohere. Forced to listen to their fellow discussion participants while they wait for their spot on the queue, students often discover and describe connections between readings or ideas or topics that they didn't see on their own. As the course proceeds through the semester, this thematic looping can happen between topics addressed across the entire term, lending coherence to the course as a whole.

While I am an enthusiastic advocate of these formal rules, I wish to offer the following words of advice:

- In order for the rules to work, the discussion leader must keep a strict discipline in managing the queue. The instructor should not be tempted to bypass one student for another (except to favor a quiet student toward the very end of the session). Students will notice and the instructor will lose legitimacy as a discussion leader if she breaks with the discipline of the queue.
- The formal discussion rules will only work if they are practiced regularly (so students can gain confidence operating within the rules) and consistently. Introducing two or more different rule structures in the same course will be confusing and the more formal process will meet with greater resistance.
- The discussion leader should never violate the rules to get his or her point in first. I will often put myself on the queue only to hear another discussion participant make my point before I have the opportunity to do so. In such cases, I quietly count this as a 'win' on my mental scorecard and cross my name off the list.

- A neat circular or rectangular table arrangement and the nameplates are essential components in building a learning community. If students do not face one another and do not know one another's names, they will direct their commentary to the professor rather than to each other. The discussion leader should make sure that the nameplates are printed on a high-quality cardstock; that everyone's name is spelled correctly; the nameplates are replaced if they get damaged; and that they bring the nameplates to and collect them after each discussion. This may sound a bit obsessive. But I believe that the precise table placement and the nameplates have a kind of ritual effect, transforming a regular classroom into a wonderfully special place in which students become the co-creators of their own intellectual emancipation.

7.4 SUCCESSFULLY FRAMING GRADING STANDARDS

Often students are upset about grading because they feel they have earned an A. Grade inflation is a real problem in higher education. In small departments (like at most liberal arts colleges), grade inflation can be especially problematic as students are advanced onto future classes for which they are unprepared. Thus, grade inflation in earlier classes produces negative spillovers onto faculty downstream in the form of unprepared students or students unwilling to accept appropriate grading standards. Over time, concern over grades can often result in even the hardest grader easing up.

At my former institution (Beloit College), we had written grading standards in our Academic Policy Manual (APM). In order to mentally prepare students for my relatively 'tough' grading, I (Joshua Hall) copied these standards directly from our APM into my syllabus. I also included a little joke that highlights the fact that while I was not curving to meet that standard, students should not expect to come out of the class with everybody earning As and Bs.

Here is the language in the section titled 'Grading Philosophy' as it recently appeared in my syllabi:

Grading Philosophy

I have no pre-set grade distribution in mind. Note, however, that Section IX of the Beloit College Academic Policy Manual (APM) clearly discusses the definitions of specific grades (see http://www.beloit.edu/apm/). According to the APM, grades of A are for 'credit earned in a manner that demonstrates unusual ability and distinctive achievement.' B grades are for 'credit earned in

> a manner that demonstrates articulate, above-average performance' and C grades are for 'credit earned in a manner that demonstrates satisfactory performance.'
>
> I note this language for two reasons. First, I want to highlight that a C is not a failing grade. It is, by definition, satisfactory performance. Unless your class is Lake Wobegon ('where everyone is above average'), several of you might find yourselves in and around that range. This grade merely reflects that while your work is satisfactory, you need further work on certain concepts, skills, or capabilities. Second, it is important to note that As are rewarded for *exceptional* performance. Any questions regarding a particular grade must be made with reference to why your performance was mischaracterized.

This can be thought of as the beginning of properly framing grading standards in a classroom. The above is insufficient in that many students have little idea what 'above-average' or 'exceptional' performance might entail. Unlike a 100-yard dash where students can easily know how much slower they are than Usain Bolt, students often do not have a good idea of other students' performance in written assignments or non-multiple choice exams. Thus, it is hard to demonstrate to students how their efforts fail to meet a classroom standard.

In order to provide students with a standard that helps to frame the professor's grade expectations, I often use anonymous student answers as the answer key. That way a student can directly see how their work stacks up to their peers. While this requires a little more work than other approaches, it has at least two benefits. First, I do not have to come up with an answer key directly. Second, students can see first-hand the anonymous answers of their peers. For many college students, this is the first time they are directly confronted with strong evidence that they are not working as hard or not doing as high-quality work as their classmates. In my experience, this approach (and the conversations that the approach creates the space for) engenders the proper response in many students. For some students, the proper response might be accepting their C grade, while for others it means stepping up their effort in order to obtain a higher grade. The key advantage is that the focus is off the faculty member for giving unfair grades and back on the student for failure to meet classroom standards.

Here is an example of the language I have used in my syllabi to describe my grading approach for a take-home final exam in an upper-level elective course in economics:

Exams

The final exam will be delivered to you by Sunday, April 29th and will be due by noon on Saturday, May 5. As with the midterm, **I ask that it be emailed to me as well as delivered to me via hard copy to my office**.

I ask for them in both forms so I can provide an answer key and in order to employ my grading approach (see below). For each exam you will be given a list of *n* questions, from which you will have to answer n–1 questions. You will typically have a week to work on these exams. The recipe for success on the exams therefore is to pay good attention in class and take good notes, so that you will be able to come up with appropriate answers fairly quickly. Class lectures are generally not sufficient background for doing well on the questions, however, thus you need to revisit and employ the underlying readings in your answers.

My grading standard for these questions is **not** the answer *I* would give. You do not want to be held to that standard. Instead, the standard is a relative one. In my opinion, being 'correct' is only sufficient to get you to 80 percent. Some correct answers are better than others because they are: 1) better written, 2) more nuanced, 3) incorporate relevant outside material, 4) clearly synthesize the relationship among readings, 5) and so forth.

Thus in grading, I read all of the answers to one question, checking to see if they are correct and looking for the 'best' answer. The 'best' answer receives 100 percent of the value for that question and becomes the standard by which the other answers are judged. It is possible to have other answers be so close that they also receive perfect grades, but this only happens occasionally. All other correct answers will then be placed somewhere on the 100 to 80 percent continuum, depending on the quality of the answer. This process is then repeated for each question on the exam. Each exam is worth 25 percentage points of your final grade.

In my experience, this approach has led to a separating equilibrium. The competitive students (not always the best students) work really hard to try to get the 'best' grade on a particular question. In order to do so, they have to go back to the original readings and engage with those texts as well as the secondary literature. The 'best' answers will often draw on numerous relevant papers that we did not have time to cover in class. From my perspective, this is a great outcome because I can tell it stimulated a tremendous amount of out-of-class effort and learning.

The second group can be thought of as satisficers. These students do the bare minimum necessary to make their answers correct in order to get the B– they want. The only time I have difficulty is when a person thinks they are being competitive but is actually a satisficer, but that situation is quickly resolved when they are confronted with the 'best' answers and I ask them how their answers are comparable.

7.5 CONCLUDING REMARKS

In this chapter, we have touched on three major pieces of syllabus language that we think can help young economists in thinking through how they want to manage their economics classes. As with the writing of a constitution, it is not enough to just copy the words on the page in order for them to be effective. Instead they must fit the 'facts on the ground' and the day-to-day experiences of students. If the syllabus talks about valuing everyone's time and yet the classroom experience does not reflect that, the syllabus language is useless. As with constitutions (Wenzel, 2010), however, syllabi are useful as a starting point for nurturing a mental model of the rigorous economics inquiry and discourse.

8. Using literature to teach the economics of the Soviet-type and centrally planned economies

Zenon X. Zygmont*

8.1 INTRODUCTION

The recent anthology by Watts (2003) shows the wealth of examples available for instructors who choose to integrate literature in their economics courses. However, as Watts (2003) acknowledges, the examples consist mainly of the contributions by American and British writers (Watts, 2003, p. xvi). This chapter extends the range of literary examples by concentrating on the writings (in translation) of selected Russian, Soviet and East Central European authors. The purpose of the present chapter of this book is to describe a writing assignment that will assist students in understanding the classic Soviet-type economy/centrally planned economy (hereafter STE/CPE).

While the STE/CPE still lingers in only a handful of nations (for example, North Korea and Cuba), understanding the failures of centrally planned economies remains important for a variety of reasons. At the time the Berlin Wall fell, respected members of the economics profession were still professing that 'the Soviet economy is proof that contrary to what many skeptics had earlier believed, a socialist command economy can function and even thrive' (Samuelson and Nordhaus, 1989, p. 837).[1] This kind of statement suggests that many areas of research remain to be explored to fully understand the structural problems of the old system, the post-communist transition and even specific policy initiatives in the West that are imbued with a degree of central planning (for example, agriculture and health care). For an undergraduate student, studying the STE/CPE offers the opportunity to explore a variety of economic concepts including, among others, pervasive shortages, principal-agent issues, entrepreneurship, black and gray markets, de facto vesus *de jure* property rights, disguised unemployment, income distribution, health care and environmental degradation.

Relatively few instructors who use literature in the classroom have applied it to a Soviet socialist or central planning perspective.[2] This chapter will begin to fill the gap. The scope of the chapter is modest; the list of authors and economic concepts in the Appendix is designed to provide a starting point, a representative sample of books to stimulate interest in this literature. The Appendix does not provide a complete list of the relevant authors and texts. While I have tried to provide the widest geographic coverage possible, the list of authors is dominated by those from the Soviet Union and further research would benefit by focusing on writers from smaller STE/CPE nations, such as Bulgaria, Hungary or the Baltic states. Also, to provide the greatest possible variety, I have listed no more than one book per author. The Appendix follows the same format as Watts and Smith (1989).

8.2 THE EXERCISE

In my course on the STE/CPE, I require the students to read a work of fiction and then write an essay. The rich literature from the Soviet bloc nations offers students myriad opportunities to understand the theory and practice of the system and, in particular, its impact on the everyday life of the average citizen. A classic example of this literature, albeit in the form of a short story, is Gorenstein's 'Bag in Hand.' The intent of the assignment is to complement class lectures and the primary textbook(s) (for example, Gregory and Stuart, 2001; Kornai, 1992). The assignment is described in the syllabus as follows:

> The book essay is an exercise designed to allow you to illustrate your understanding of the STE/CPE through the analysis of a work of fiction. Your essay must address two questions. First, how does understanding the STE/CPE help you understand the book? Second, how does the book help you understand the STE/CPE? As you answer these questions, make sure that you are integrating economic concepts – especially those you are learning in class – in your paper. This assignment is an essay and not a book report; you should only provide a summarization of the plot to the extent it will help me understand what is going on. The date of publication and/or plot setting should be between 1930 and the late 1980s (but avoid books about World War II). The paper must be typewritten, double-spaced, and approximately 7 pages in length).

The two questions are open-ended enough that any student exhibiting even a modicum of effort should find enough examples in the book to complete the essay. They also let the student focus on those examples of greatest interest to them. The primary hurdle is choosing an appropriate book. This decision sometimes proves frustrating to the student, especially those with little prior experience of literature. To help students identify a book, I discuss the range of writing they are likely to encounter as they search for a book, and I provide the following guidelines (these can be easily incorporated into the syllabus).

First, it is necessary that they differentiate between fiction and non-fiction. This problem is compounded by the fact that many excellent non-fiction books exist, often written by journalists with extensive experience in STE/CPE nations.[3] These books offer an excellent alternative for instructors who prefer works of non-fiction without changing the nature of the writing assignment.[4]

Second, my preference is that students avoid the well-trodden path of classic dystopia literature, such as Orwell's *Animal Farm* or *1984*, Huxley's *Brave New World*, Rand's *Anthem* or Zamiatin's *We*. Students may have read at least one of these in high school, in other college courses or may be familiar with the main themes from film (for example, *Animal Farm* or *1984*). Part of the purpose of the exercise is to have them read something 'out of the ordinary.'

Third, there are a variety of ways for students to identify a suitable book. An obvious first step is to consult with a reference librarian and establish a research strategy. This will likely yield reference resources such as literature bibliographies and compendiums (examples include Brown's *The Last Years of Soviet Russian Literature* and *Soviet Russian Literature since Stalin*).[5] There are also online resources like Sovlit.com and literature lists from reputable book sellers, such as Powell's Books.[6] One point of caution is that many novels have yet to be translated into English. If a student identifies a candidate author but is unsure if the author's work has been translated, I recommend using World Cat (an online database resource that should be accessible through most college and university libraries). Another useful web-based approach is to browse Amazon's editorial reviews, customer reviews and links to related books (using the 'customers who bought this item also bought …' feature).

Fourth, novels vary greatly in length, from 100–150 pages to well beyond 400 pages. Instructors might consider offering extra credit or some sort of bonus to those students who choose a lengthier book. An alternative is to assign a short story (like Gorenstein or Soloukhin).

Finally, to minimize 'selection anxiety' among her students, the instructor may provide students with a list of books from which they may choose. In any event, to ensure they have a suitable text, I ask students to get my permission before they undertake the assignment. This also ensures a minimum of duplication among the students.

NOTES

* This chapter is dedicated to the memory of Chuck Isenberg.

1. For a concise discussion of how economists and other observers got it wrong about the Soviet economy, see Boettke (1993).
2. See Roback (1985), Bogart (1995), Scahill (1998) and Hamlen (2000).
3. Some examples are Anne Applebaum's *Between East and West*, Mark Brzezinski's *Casino Moscow*; Michael Dobbs'*s Down With Big Brother*, *Moscow Days* by Galina Dutkina, *Vodka,Tears and Lenin's Angel* by Jennifer Gould, Eva Hoffman's *Exit into History*, *Comrade Criminal* by Stephen Handelman, Timothy Harper's *Moscow Madness*, *Imperium* by Ryszard Kapuczynski, Mark Kramer's *Travels with a Hungry Bear*, *Reeling in Russia* by Fen Montaigne, *Lenin's Tomb* and *Resurrection,* both by David Remnick and Tina Rosenberg's *The Haunted Land*.
4. An additional variation could focus on the extensive body of prison memoirs by victims of communism such as *Beyond all Hope* by Armando Valladares, Wu Ming Shih's *Red in Tooth and Claw*, *The Long Walk* by Slawomir Rawicz, Victor Herman's *Coming Out of the Ice*, Irina Ratushinskaya's *Grey is the Color of Hope*, *Diary of a Survivor* by Ana Rodriguez or even Solzhenitsyn's *One Day in the Life of Ivan Denisovich*, a novelization of his own experience as a captive in the Soviet Gulag.
5. Other examples are Miloscz's *The History of Polish Literature* or Ekmanis's *Latvian Literature Under the Soviets 1940–1975*.
6. The Powell's URL is http://www.powells.com/section/literature/eastern-europe/. Another example is the University of Pittsburgh's The World Wide Web Virtual Library for Russian & East European Studies, available at http://www.ucis.pitt.edu/reesweb/ (accessed 21 March 2013).

APPENDIX

Table 8A.1 *Representative list of Soviet and East European literature containing economic content*

Author	Title	Publisher	Date	Pages	Economic Concepts
Abramov, Fyodor	*The New Life: A Day on a Collective Farm*	Grove Press, New York	1963	19–21, 99–100, 130–5	Defects of planning
				25–6, 29, 33–4, 46, 50–2, 55–6, 89–90, 94–7, 127–8	Incentives
				36, 38–9, 42–4, 67–70, 72–3, 77,85–9, 94–5,105–7, 122–3	Collective farms
Chukovskaya, Lydia	*Sofia Petrovna*	Northwestern University Press, Evanston, IL	1967	14, 26, 40	Consumer life

				28	Aspects of planning
Dovlatov, Sergei	*The Suitcase*	Grove Weidenfeld, New York	1986	16, 44	Black/gray markets
				18–19, 103	Consumer life
				21	'lifting'
				69, 113	Nomenklatura privileges
				121–2	Queuing
Dudintsev, Vladimir	*Not by Bread Alone*	E.P. Dutton & Co., New York	1957	53–5	Housing
				60, 92, 100, 116, 173, 212, 300, 323, 412	Planning bureaucracy
				71, 76	Health care
				78, 86, 104	Nomenklatura privileges
				127, 146	Shortages/rationing
				250	Monetary policy
				478	Labor policy
Ehrenburg, Ilya	*The Thaw*	Henry Regnery Company, Chicago, IL	1955	13, 32, 176	Shortages
				20, 186	Opportunity cost
				20	Quotas
				25	Incentives

Author	Title	Publisher	Date	Pages	Economic Concepts
				25, 81	Central planning
				62–3, 169–70	Collective farms
				122, 139	Housing
				123	Consumer life
Gladkov, Feodor	*Cement*	International Publishers, New York	1929	5, 21	Rationing
				22	Theft
				67, 95, 136	Labor requisitioning
				94, 118, 133	Food requisitioning
				93	Threat of plan failure
				97, 208–9,	Planning
				241	bureaucracy
				185, 188–9, 200	New Economic Policy
				99, 100	Central planning
				171	Expropriation of personal property
Glowacki, Janusz	*Give Us This Day*	St Martin's, New York	1981	3, 10, 14	Consumer life/shortages
				12, 35	Labor conditions
				22, 31	Aspects of planning

				26, 32	Black/gray markets
				28, 38	Housing
				14, 33, 63, 91	Nomenklatura privileges
Gorenstein, Friedrich	'Bag in Hand' *Glas: New Russian Writing*		1993, vol. 4	all (116–34)	Consumer life
Ovechkin, Valentin	'Visitors at Stukachi' *Collective Farm Sidelights*	Foreign Languages Publishing House, Moscow	n.d.	all (5–84)	Collective farming, incentive structure
Preda, Marin	*In a Village*	The Book Publishing House, Bucharest, Romania	1955	52, 54, 88, 134, 172, 184	Collective farming
Soloukhin, Vladimir	'Stepanida Ivanova's Funeral'	Abbeville Press, New York	1989	all (279–95)	Shortages
	Zalygin, *The New Soviet Fiction*			283	Queues
				290, 293–5	Bureaucracy
Sorokin, Vladimir	*The Queue*	Readers International, New York	1988	7–11, 14, 17	Queuing
				20, 23–5, 43–50, 64–8, 86, 90–1, 131–2, 150, 184, 196	Shortages

Author	Title	Publisher	Date	Pages	Economic Concepts
Tarsis, Valeriy	*The Bluebottle*	Alfred A. Knopf, New York	1963	30	Collective farms
				30	Private property
				31	Black markets
				32	NEP
				32, 106-7, 120	Shortages
				33, 118-9	Bureaucracy
Zagrebelny, Pavlo	*From the Point of View of Eternity*	Progress Publishers, USSR	1978	24, 54, 59–64, 76, 98, 127	Aspects of planning and working conditions
				141	Nepman

9. Not so *Bleak House*: business and entrepreneurship in Dickens

Sarah E. Skwire

9.1 INTRODUCTION AND BACKGROUND

All of us who love literature and who love private enterprise are familiar with the problem. In literature, as John Blundell reminds us, we are presented again and again with 'prodigiously wasteful, yet Scrooge-like businessmen who are abnormal and antagonistic; corrupt, cunning and cynical; dishonest, disorderly, doltish, dumb and duplicitous; inhumane, insensitive and irresponsible, ruthless, unethical and unprincipled; and villainous to boot' (Blundell, 2000, p. viii). Literature, we are told, hates business – or at least holds it in contempt – and hates – or at least holds in contempt – those who engage in it.

And the most contemptuous, the most opposed of all authors to the power and the capabilities and the promising potential of private enterprise is, of course, Charles Dickens. We know this because, when we – even we – need a term of repugnance for a businessman of a certain type we instinctively think of Ebenezer Scrooge from *A Christmas Carol*. How instinctive is that thinking? Since the 1950s *The Oxford English Dictionary* has recorded multiple uses of Scrooge's name as a common noun used as a synonym for miser in a wide range of contexts that have no explicit bearing on Dickens's work or any explicit or implicit reference to Christmas. For example, in October of 1976 *The Monitor*, a newspaper out of McAllen, Texas, noted that, 'Jim "Catfish" Hunter, baseball's foremost "money" pitcher, turned in a Scrooge-like performance Saturday.' Disney's Scrooge McDuck is a familiar character to most Disney and comic fans.

And this common vision of Scrooge is no surprise. We are supposed to hate him. Dickens built him that way. And because Dickens is a writer of undeniable power and influence, we can't resist. How could we, with descriptions like this?

> Oh! But he was a tight-fisted hand at the grindstone, Scrooge! a squeezing, wrenching, grasping, scraping, clutching, covetous, old sinner! Hard and sharp as flint, from which no steel had ever struck out generous fire; secret, and self-contained, and solitary as an oyster. The cold within him froze his old features, nipped his pointed nose, shrivelled his cheek, stiffened his gait; made his eyes red, his thin lips blue; and spoke out shrewdly in his grating voice. A frosty rime was on his head, and on his eyebrows, and his wiry chin. He carried his own low temperature always about with him; he iced his office in the dog-days; and didn't thaw it one degree at Christmas. (Dickens, 1843 [1997], p. 8)

Scrooge is a villain, and we take our pleasure from his story as we see him get punished, and we undergo our catharsis as we see him reform. At least, most of us do.

Apparently tired of the endless drubbing that Scrooge takes as an exemplar of every form of financial evil, and possibly even more tired of sugar-coated financial advice books that use Scrooge's fictional transformation as their model for how rational people should handle their money (witness *The Financial Wisdom of Ebenezer Scrooge*, which comes with a foreword by that esteemed financial wizard, Naomi Judd), the economists Bruce Bueno de Mesquita and Steven Landsburg have both published defenses of Scrooge's 'miserly' behavior before his reformation.

Landsburg's 2004 article in *Slate*, 'What I like about Scrooge: in praise of misers' is a ringing defense of the social – not just individual – virtues of saving money. He writes:

> Put a dollar in the bank and you'll bid down the interest rate by just enough so someone somewhere can afford an extra dollar's worth of vacation or home improvement. Put a dollar in your mattress and (by effectively reducing the money supply) you'll drive down prices by just enough so someone somewhere can have an extra dollar's worth of coffee with his dinner. Scrooge, no doubt a canny investor, lent his money at interest. His less conventional namesake Scrooge McDuck filled a vault with dollar bills to roll around in. No matter. Ebenezer Scrooge lowered interest rates. Scrooge McDuck lowered prices. Each Scrooge enriched his neighbors as much as any Lord Mayor who invited the town in for a Christmas meal.

With his tongue firmly in cheek, but his economic principles firmly intact, Landsburg (2004) concludes his article by noting that 'Great artists are sometimes unaware of the deepest meanings in their own creations. Though Dickens might not have recognized it, the primary moral of *A Christmas Carol* is that there should be no limit on IRA contributions.'

While Landsburg's article uses Dickens's novel and its representation of Scrooge as an example of one kind of thinking about miserliness and then challenges the reader to re-examine that kind of thinking in ways that are productive of intelligent economic thought, Bruce Bueno de Mesquita (2001) actually rewrites the novel. In his *The Trial of Ebenezer Scrooge,* he engineers a new history for Scrooge – one of consistent and consistently hidden charitableness, of grinding personal poverty that is only increased by the many sacrifices Scrooge makes to help others, of a man who is misunderstood, misjudged and wrongly punished. While he asserts that he does this by 'relying on evidence found within the body of Dickens's great work,' he finds himself driven to borrow characters from other novels by Dickens and other Victorians, to accuse Charles Dickens of non-specific but damning 'unhallowedness' and to blacken the reputation of Tiny Tim in order to defend Scrooge.

I understand the impulse. For those who are exhausted by yet another negative representation of the businessman in literature, it must sometimes seem as if the whole problem could be solved if Scrooge can just be turned into a hero. If he's the root of the problem, we should just be able to reinterpret Scrooge and 're-vision' Dickens until the problem goes away.

The problem with this approach, though, as contrasted to Landsburg's (2004) use of the Scrooge story as a springboard for one of those always intriguing economic counter-intuitive phenomena, is that it is all but guaranteed to enrage people who love literature. Now, that may be your goal. In that case, go ahead. But if the goal is, instead, to open up a conversation between lovers of literature and lovers of private enterprise, there may be a more productive technique to use. And interestingly, the work of Charles Dickens is perfectly suited to it.

It is my contention that in order to rescue the representation of business in literature – more specifically, in literature written by Charles Dickens, that great enemy of private enterprise – all we need to do is … do the reading.

With novels that frequently weigh in at over 800 pages, with thousands of characters (*Little Dorrit* has around 45 named characters, and countless unnamed shopkeepers, maidservants, beggars, tavern keepers and so on), and with scores of characters and scenes that are so memorable and so engrained in our popular culture that we think we remember them before we have even read them, the danger when reading Dickens is that we assume that we actually know what it's 'about.' This danger is only increased when we approach the novels wanting to prove a point, particularly a point about something we care about as much as private enterprise. We know, in other words, that Dickens created Scrooge. We know that he wrote *Hard Times*, where Coketown, his analogue of nineteenth-century Manchester,

> lay shrouded in a haze of its own, which appeared impervious to the sun's rays. You only knew the town was there, because you knew there could have been no such sulky blotch upon the prospect without a town. A blur of soot and smoke, now confusedly tending this way, now that way, now aspiring to the vault of Heaven, now murkily creeping along the earth, as the wind rose and fell, or changed its quarter: a dense formless jumble, with sheets of cross light in it, that showed nothing but masses of darkness: Coketown in the distance was suggestive of itself, though not a brick of it could be seen.
>
> The wonder was, it was there at all. It had been ruined so often, that it was amazing how it had borne so many shocks. Surely there never was such fragile china-ware as that of which the millers of Coketown were made. Handle them never so lightly, and they fell to pieces with such ease that you might suspect them of having been flawed before. They were ruined, when they were required to send labouring children to school; they were ruined when inspectors were appointed to look into their works; they were ruined, when such inspectors considered it doubtful whether they were quite justified in chopping people up with their machinery; they were utterly undone, when it was hinted that perhaps they need not always make quite so much smoke. (Dickens, 1854 [1997], p. 110)

We know that we won't find anything in the writing of the man who produced this jeremiad against commerce and industry that supports business, private enterprise, free markets or the kind of financial responsibility that is so important to a free society. The problem is we're wrong.

The works of Charles Dickens – and I'm thinking of the major novels here, not obscure short stories or forgotten magazine articles – provide a range of counter-arguments to the anti-private enterprise arguments made in other places in his own works. Indeed, it is not at all unusual for those arguments in support of private enterprise to occur in the same books as arguments that criticize it. Whether it is support for the importance of innovation, or the respectability of work, or the moral challenge of irresponsible management of one's personal finances, it is available in Dickens. It only remains for those of us who care about these issues – and not merely heart-wrenching accounts of families ruined by malevolent, dishonest schemers – to draw attention to these moments and create a fuller and more sophisticated picture of Dickens's work and thought.

9.2 DICKENS AND INNOVATION

When we think of *Little Dorrit*, we think of its portrayal of the Marshalsea – London's notorious debtors' prison, about which more later on – and its account of the financial chicanery of Mr. Merdle, upon whose demise (by his own hand, out of shame at being exposed), it is discovered that:

> Numbers of men in every profession and trade would be blighted by his insolvency; old people who had been in easy circumstances all their lives would have no place of repentance for their trust in him but the workhouse; legions of women and children would have their whole future desolated by the hand of this mighty scoundrel. Every partaker of his magnificent feasts would be seen to have been a sharer in the plunder of innumerable homes; every servile worshipper of riches who had helped to set him on his pedestal, would have done better to worship the Devil point-blank … [He] was simply the greatest forger and thief that had every cheated the gallows. (Dickens, 1857 [1997], p. 710)

Certainly, I am not going to make the claim that Dickens's portrait of Mr. Merdle – the Bernie Madoff of nineteenth-century London – is in any way intended to encourage private enterprise, or the sort of risk acceptance that is needed for investment. But Mr. Merdle is not the only character and not the only businessman in *Little Dorrit*.

An important foil to Merdle and his criminal misuse of funds is Dan Doyce. We are introduced to Dan Doyce by Mr. Meagles, a kindly retired banker (and please note that despite some character flaws, he is kindly. Dickens even describes him as such in the list of characters). As Meagles tells us, Doyce:

> is a smith and engineer. He is not in a large way, but he is well known as a very ingenious man. A dozen years ago, he perfects an invention (involving a very curious secret process) of great importance to his country and his fellow-creatures. I won't say how much money it cost him, or how many years of his life he had been about it, but he brought it to perfection a dozen years ago. (Dickens, 1857 [1997], p. 119)

Doyce is, in other words, an independent businessman, an inventor and an entrepreneur. Notice that Dickens is very careful to specify both the enormous utility of Doyce's invention and the cost of the time, intelligence, money and energy he has invested in it. Doyce's invention, we are told repeatedly throughout the novel, will be of great benefit to England, if he can only get a patent and put it into production. However, in order to do this, Doyce must get past Parliament and the infamous Circumlocution Office:

> [T]he trials were made in the presence of a board of six, of whom two ancient members were too blind to see it, two other ancient members were too deaf to hear it, one other ancient member was too lame to get near it, and the final ancient member was too pig-headed to look at it … How the Circumlocution Office, in course of time, took up the business as if it were a brand new thing of yesterday, which had never been heard of before; muddled the business, addled the business, tossed the business in a wet blanket. How the impertinences, ignorances, and insults went through the multiplication table. How there was a reference of the invention to three Barnacles and a Stiltstalking, who knew nothing about it; into whose heads nothing could be hammered about it; who got bored about it, and reported physical impossibilities about it. How the Circumlocution Office, in a Minute, number eight thousand seven hundred and forty, 'saw no reason to reverse the decision at which my lords had arrived.' How the Circumlocution Office, being reminded that my lords had arrived at no decision, shelved the business. (Dickens, 1857 [1997], p. 120)

Dickens makes it very clear to his readers, as he takes us through Doyce's rough but accurate accounting methods and business practices, that the problems Doyce faces in achieving his patent and in being allowed to produce his invention and profit from his own innovation are not due to any failing on Doyce's part. He does everything right. He is hampered only as a result of an ossified government structure, a crew of bureaucrats who are too stupid to recognize a good thing when they see it and an endlessly circumlocutory process.

Entrepreneur and innovator that he is, Doyce takes the only possible action. He tries another market. He packs up his invention and the considerable personal capital contained in his innovative brain, and heads for 'other countries.' The result of this move (a fine example of the need for international capital/labor mobility) is that at the end of the novel Meagles is able to tell us:

> Don't talk about happiness until you see Dan. I assure you, Dan is directing works and executing labours over yonder, that it would make your hair stand on end to look at. He's no public offender, bless you, now! He's medalled and ribboned, and starred and crossed, and I don't-know-what all'd like a born nobleman. But we mustn't talk about that over here … Britannia is a Britannia in the manger – won't give her children such distinctions herself, and won't allow them to be seen when they are given by other countries. (Dickens, 1857 [1997], pp. 822–3)

As a result of this outstanding success, Doyce is able to return at the end of the novel, to pay off the debts of his business partner, Arthur Clennam, the novel's romantic hero who lost the firm's money by investing it with Merdle, and to enable the marriage of Arthur to Little Dorrit.

All of this good is achieved through Doyce's innovation and entrepreneurship. Wealth and happiness are assured through Doyce's good auspices, and Dickens's readers are assured, through some final comments by the narrator, that the firm of Doyce and Clennam will continue long into a fictional 'afterward.'

Perhaps business, as represented in Dickens's novels is not so bad after all. And perhaps the businessman is not intrinsically malevolent and untrustworthy. Certainly his innovation, entrepreneurship, creative thinking and ability to create wealth can bring happiness and solvency not only to himself but others whom we care about.

9.3 DICKENS AND WORK

It is a truth universally acknowledged that the Victorians considered work ungentlemanly. It has been endlessly pointed out that the only occupations available to Jane Austen's heroes are either landowning gentry, officer in the military or member of the clergy. Trollope manages a bit better, with some lawyers, engineers and others added into the mix. Wilkie Collins gives us the occasional drawing master and a police detective or two. In Dickens, however, almost everyone works. Donald Hawes notes that 'In his *Everyone in Dickens*, George Newlin lists 1,024 occupations and vocations for males and 137 for females' and that 'Drawing from a more restricted range of Dickens's work … Gilbert A. Pierce and William A. Wheeler in their *Dickens Dictionary* … compiled a "Classed List of characters, Etc". In that, about 150 professions, trades, and occupations can be distinguished' (Hawes, 2000, p. 3). Ergo, at a minimum, in the novels of Dickens we have a fuller picture of the world of work than one might anticipate in Victorian fiction.

But a fuller picture of the world of work does not make much difference if the work is described by a writer who, like Austen's 'Netherfield ladies (who) would have had difficulty in believing that a man who lived by trade, and within view of his own warehouses, could have been so well bred and agreeable' (Austen, 1813, p. 137). Happily, this is not the case with Dickens.

For the young heroes of Dickens's novels, there are generally two central questions. First, whom should they marry? And second, what ought they to become? For both David Copperfield and Richard Jarndyce of *Bleak House* that second question becomes an enormous driving factor for the plot of their respective stories.

David Copperfield is initially established as an articled clerk, apprenticed to Mr. Spenlow, who is a proctor at nautical and ecclesiastical courts of Doctors' Commons. Purchasing his articles costs his Aunt Betsy Trotwood 1000 pounds and commits David to years as an unpaid apprentice, but the expectation is that entering David into the profession will assure him of a comfortable income for the rest of his life.

All of this changes when Betsy Trotwood's money is lost though the machinations of the vile Uriah Heep. Suddenly, she has no income out of which to support herself, let alone David and her friend, the mentally challenged Mr. Dick. Someone needs to earn some money. After a fruitless attempt to get his articles cancelled and have the 1000 pound investment returned to him, David sets out to earn his living. David's determination to do this leads him to work for his old tutor as a secretary and ghost writer, to try to learn short-hand in order to be able to report Parliamentary debates for the newspapers and eventually to establish himself as a respected writer of novels and non-fiction. What is notable is that after one night of complete despair where David tells us, 'thought and thought about my being poor … about my not being what I thought I was, when I proposed to Dora … about how I should contrive to live, during the long term of my articles, when I was earning nothing; about doing something to assist my aunt, and seeing no way of doing anything…'(Dickens, 1850 [1997], p. 505), his focus shifts to hope and to practical consideration. Knowing that he must support himself, that he hopes to be able to support his future wife, Dora, and that he must help support his aunt as well, he resolves:

> What I had to do, was, to show my aunt that her past goodness to me had not been thrown away on an insensible, ungrateful object. What I had to do, was, to turn the painful discipline of my younger days to account, by going to work with a resolute and steady heart. What I had to do, was, to take my woodman's axe in my hand, and clear my own way through the forest of difficulty. (Dickens, 1850 1997], p. 520)

David Copperfield is a model – perhaps a particularly useful model for these times – of the way in which those of us who believe in free enterprise and personal initiative should respond to reversals in fortune. He may grieve over lost opportunities and destroyed wealth, and he is well justified in doing so. But he never lets that grief stand in the way of his determination to find work and to do it well. Rather, it is the work and the determination to do well and to improve and to support himself and his family that carries David through the maddening years of his marriage to his utterly charming and utterly irresponsible 'child-wife' Dora. His work is what pulls him out of depression after Dora's death. Indeed, by the close of the novel, David has become a successful novelist:

> I worked early and late, patiently and hard. I wrote a Story, with a purpose growing, not remotely, out of my experience, and sent it to Traddles, and he arranged for its publication very advantageously for me … After some rest and change, I fell to work, in my own ardent way, on a few fancy, which took strong possession of me … (Dickens, 1850 [1997], p. 816)

His work – specifically the self-examination and contemplation required by working as a novelist – turns David Copperfield into an adult who is able to realize that his love for Dora was a true, but childish passion, and that his love for Agnes is a full, lasting and adult love. It is work, learning to do it and finding the right kind that helps David Copperfield to his happy ending.

Less happy is the ending that awaits Richard Carstone of *Bleak House*, another Dickens hero in search of a profession. As one of the 'heirs in Jarndyce,' Richard is waiting, and will spend his life waiting, for the resolution of Jarndyce and Jarndyce, the longest running suit in the history of the Courts of Chancery. In one of the novel's several lengthy discussions about 'what Richard was to do' (Dickens, 1853 [1997], p. 167), Richard's guardian John Jarndyce suggests that this interminable waiting has left Richard incapable of making such decisions.

> How much of this indecision of character … is chargeable on that incomprehensible heap of uncertainty and procrastination on which he has been thrown from his birth, I don't pretend to say; but that Chancery, among its other sins, is responsible for some if it, I can plainly see. It has engendered or confirmed in him a habit of putting off – and trusting to this, that, and the other chance, without knowing what chance – and dismissing everything as unsettled, uncertain, and confused. (Dickens, 1853 [1997], p. 167)

With such a character driving his decision-making process, Richard tries medicine, law and the military, and fails at all three. Unable to make a commitment to working diligently, Richard alienates his affectionate guardian, falls into debt, begins compulsive and expensive pursuit of the hopeless Jarndyce and Jarndyce case and eventually dies destitute, leaving a wife and infant son behind him.

Much of the blame for Richard's death is squarely laid at the feet of the lawsuit, which is a great evil hulking over the entire novel. But nearly equal responsibility lies with his failure to find a profession that would carry him through the vicissitudes of a life darkened by the madness of Jarndyce and Jarndyce. On his deathbed, Richard himself seems to realize this, saying, 'I have to begin the world … I will not begin in it in the old way now … I have learned a lesson now'(Dickens, 1853 [1997], p. 869). This resolution to 'begin the world' echoes, tragically, the hope and determination of the job-seeker setting out to the market or the young apprentice beginning his profession. The suggestion is clear. With a real profession to steady him and help him grow up – as David Copperfield's profession does – Richard might have made it out of Jarndyce and Jarndyce alive. Without it, there was never any hope.

9.4 DICKENS AND DEBT

That Richard Carstone slides into debt while waiting for some sort of resolution to the case of Jarndyce and Jarndyce is not in any way unusual for Dickens's characters. Dickens is justly famed for his grim representations of the dire conditions and the Alice-in-Wonderland logic that drove the creation and existence of England's debtors' prisons. *Little Dorrit* is the novel that most focuses on debtors' prison in particular, but it is the secondary characters in *David Copperfield* and in *Bleak House* that best serve to illustrate the complex relationship that Dickens had with debt and debtors.

Without giving into the fraught temptations of a psycho-analytic reading of Dickens's novels, it is important to remember that his father was imprisoned in the Marshalsea for debt, and that as a result of this, the twelve-year-old Charles was sent to work in a blacking factory to support himself, his family and attempt to pay his father's debts. It was only the death of his grandmother and a 450 pound legacy that released Dickens's father from prison, and that eventually allowed Charles to stop work and return to school. Knowing that, it is no surprise that Dickens's portraits of the financially improvident, personally irresponsible debtors Wilkins Micawber and Harold Skimpole are drawn with a mixture of both affection and disgust.

Mr. Micawber is famously based on Dickens's father, and since his appearance in *David Copperfield*, he has been one of Dickens's most beloved characters. Portrayed in film by stars like W.C. Fields, Micawber's comic language, his irrepressible good cheer in the face of self-created adversity, and his unending faith that 'something will turn up' has made it seem to some as if his portrait is an example of a moment when Dickens is being overly kind to a dangerously flawed character.

Certainly, it would be ridiculous to argue that Micawber's portrayal isn't affectionate. Described in the list of characters as 'a jaunty, grandiloquent, recklessly good-natured, improvident man,' Micawber is funny and charming and inspires unceasing devotion in his wife and friends. He also gives one of the best pieces of financial advice ever given in a work of fiction: 'Annual income twenty pounds, annual expenditure nineteen pounds nineteen and six, result happiness. Annual income twenty pounds, annual expenditure twenty pounds ought and six, result misery'(Dickens, 1850 [1997], p. 175). Micawber's inability to abide by his own advice is the source of much of the comedy of his story – and much of its tragedy.

For despite every scene where Micawber makes us laugh – one thinks of his plans to put bow-windows into his house the minute 'something turns up,' although he has just sold all the family's cutlery – there is a distinct air of sadness and even potential menace surrounding him. He and his family are forever traveling from one place to another in search of promising opportunities that – even when found – Mr. Micawber is incapable of pursuing to the point of achieving success. In the course of these travels, they are often separated, often destitute and often imprisoned. Their exigencies, in the end, drive Micawber to what initially appears to be an unholy alliance with Uriah Heep, surely one of the most revolting characters in Dickens's long catalogue of memorable villains. Heep is exploiting the growing alcoholism and irresponsible behavior of David's friend and mentor Mr. Wickfield in order to pillage and ruin his business. Heep's plan is that, by so doing, he will render Wickfield's daughter (David's future wife) into such a state of submission that she will agree to marry him purely in order to save her father's reputation. We know that this is Uriah Heep's plan. We have, with David, loathed Uriah Heep since his first appearance in the novel. To hear Micawber tell David, 'I have entered into arrangements, by virtue of which I stand pledged and contracted to our friend Heep, to assist and serve him in the capacity of – and to be – his confidential clerk' (Dickens, 1850 [1997], p. 531) makes us shudder. And when Micawber further specifies, 'My friend Heep has not fixed the positive remuneration at too high a figure, but he has made a great deal, in the way of extrication from the pressure of pecuniary difficulties, contingent on the value of my services; and on the value of those services I pin my faith' (Dickens, 1850 [1997], p. 532), we are sickened. It is instantly evident to us that Uriah Heep has purchased Mr. Micawber and will do with him as he likes.

For the next 200 pages we believe, entirely, that Mr. Micawber is in league with Uriah Heep and all his plans. It is no more of a relief to him than it is to us when he finally breaks forth to tell David, 'I'll know nobody and – a – say nothing – and – a – live nowhere – until I have crushed – to – a – undiscoverable atoms – the – transcendent and immortal hypocrite and perjurer – HEEP!'(Dickens, 1850 [1997], p. 711). And crush him he does. After serving as his confidential clerk, Micawber knows every detail of Heep's plots and plans. He is able to expose Uriah Heep, to save Agnes Wickfield from marrying him, to protect Mr. Wickfield's reputation and to help return Betsy Trotwood's lost fortune to her. He is, in the end, heroic. But he is also, in the end, impossible. And like others of Dickens's impossible characters – the Artful Dodger, for one – Micawber cannot possibly remain in England to fall back into debt and trouble his friends. He must emigrate to Australia. Here, we are told, he finally finds a country that can appreciate his capacities, and he becomes a magistrate.

Micawber's happy ending may still trouble those who want to argue for the importance of personal financial responsibility. Such critics may find themselves more satisfied with the story of Harold Skimpole in *Bleak House*. One of John Jarndyce's innumerable friends/charitable cases, Skimpole introduces himself to us as 'a mere child' who has 'two of the oldest infirmities in the world: one was, that he had no idea of time; the other that he had no idea of money. In consequence of which he never kept an appointment, never could transact any business, and never knew the value of anything!' (Dickens, 1853 [1997], p. 69). Upon their initial meeting with Skimpole, our young hero and heroines confess themselves 'enchanted' and 'dazzled.' Later that same evening, however, Skimpole is arrested for a debt of more than 24 pounds. Utterly charmed by him, and sympathetic to his plight, Richard and Esther give him all the money they possess to clear him of his debt. The mercurial John Jarndyce is at first horrified that Skimpole has squeezed Richard and Esther 'like a couple of tender young Saint Michael's oranges' (Dickens, 1853 [1997], p. 78) but calms himself by remembering what a 'child' Skimpole is.

This initial encounter leaves the reader feeling nervous about Skimpole, however. And as the novel continues and he blithely fails to pay his butcher's bill, blaming the butcher for wanting to be paid when he could have paid himself by not wasting his time trying to collect money from Skimpole, and has all his furniture (unpaid for) confiscated until he pays his rent, the expense of which he cheerfully refers to John Jarndyce. To ensure that we are further troubled by this sort of behavior, Dickens is careful to have Esther remind us that 'I always wondered on these occasions whether he ever thought of Mrs. Skimpole and the children, and in what point of view they presented themselves to his cosmopolitan mind. So far as I could understand, they rarely presented themselves at all' (Dickens, 1853 [1997], p. 253). It is possible, even with this discomfiting reminder that Skimpole has a family he is utterly neglecting, to still find him comical, particularly if one is familiar with Mr. Micawber.

But once the pathetic character of Jo, the sweeper, crosses paths with Skimpole, such comic sympathies are no longer possible. Jo first wins our sympathies as the loyal friend of the mysterious law writer, Nemo. An utterly uneducated, all but totally solitary orphan who sweeps the streets of London in hopes of getting tips, Jo is one of the lost and the least of Victorian society. He is one of Dickens's most pathetic orphaned children, made all the more pathetic by the death of his only friend, Nemo, early in the book. That death, for a variety of plot reasons too intricate to detail here, leads to Jo being hounded through the city by the police. Skimpole enters his life when Jo appears, sick and harried, near to Jarndyce's home. Esther brings him inside, 'like some wounded animal that had been found in a ditch' and Skimpole argues that the child should be turned out into the street instantly.

> He's not safe, you know. There's a very bad sort of fever about him … I *am* a child, and I never pretend to be anything else. If you put him out in the road, you only put him where he was before. He will be no worse off than he was, you know. Even make him better off, if you like. Give him sixpence, or five shillings, or five pound ten … I recommend your turning him out before he gets still worse. (Dickens, 1853 [1997], pp. 433–5)

This child's utter lack of sympathy and human compassion for an actual child – and remember that Skimpole is a doctor, as well as a father – is chilling.

It would be chilling enough if Skimpole's effect on Jo were to end there, but it does not. Jo is put into a comfortable bed in the hayloft, where he will be warm and safe and not risk infecting the occupants of the house. The plan is to take him to the hospital in the morning. But in the morning Jo is gone. No one in the house knows what to make of his disappearance, and they all worry that he has wandered off in a moment of delirium, 'all of us, that is to say, but Mr. Skimpole, who repeatedly suggested, in his usual easy light style, that it had occurred to our young friend that he was not a safe inmate, having a bad kind of fever upon him; and that he had, with great natural politeness, taken himself off' (Dickens, 1853 [1997], p. 437). We find out though, at the end of the novel, that Skimpole knows precisely what has happened to Jo, because it was Skimpole who, in return for five pounds, turned him in to the police, who harry Jo so relentlessly from place to place that he dies from exhaustion, from fear and from the illness that Skimpole can be partially blamed for.

As Mr. Bucket, the policeman who paid Skimpole, notes:

> Whenever a person says to you that they are as innocent as can be in all concerning money, look well after your own money, for they are dead certain to collar it, if they can. Whenever a person proclaims to you 'In worldly matters I'm a child' you consider that that person is only a-crying off from being held accountable, and that you have got that person's number, and it's Number One. (Dickens, 1853 [1997], p. 775)

Skimpole is reprehensible, and any whimsical charms that he possessed at the beginning of the novel turn our stomachs by the end.

We should note, too, that Skimpole's final treachery – telling the police where to find Jo – is driven by his financial irresponsibility. Incapable, as he claims, of understanding the value of money, he does nothing but waste it, chase it and spend other people's. When he is presented with the chance of a five pound note, it would be madness in us to expect Skimpole to do anything other than what he does. It is in this moral turning point that the difference between Micawber and Skimpole comes to light. Micawber turns against the villain who has bought him and emerges heroically (though still in debt) from the moral challenges he faces. Skimpole simply continues as he always has.

9.5 CONCLUDING COMMENTS

There are other aspects of Dickens's novels that while perhaps of somewhat less specific interest to fans of private enterprise and free markets, address other pertinent economic concerns. Dickens often uses his novels for extensive discussions about charity. While his vision of private charity is complex – with the competent and helpful Cheeryble brothers and John Jarndyce contrasting with figures like Mrs. Jellyby, who is so devoted to helping the poor and neglected children in Africa that she utterly ignores her own children, his vision of public charity is much less nuanced. He hates it. The workhouse. The orphanage. The charity school. All of these are places of horror for Dickens. Surely, those of us who believe in private charity can make something of this acknowledgment that while private charity has its problems (issues), public charity has even more.

It would also be an interesting – although enormous – project to track the stories of young lovers in Dickens's novels. How many of them who claim – as many of them do – that they do not need money find that their happy endings are resolved through money they have earned, inherited or been 'put in the way of'? *Bleak House* is a fine example of this. Esther Summerson's happy ending is ensured by her receipt of a house from her guardian, her husband's receipt of an excellent position made possible through her guardian's influence, and (presumably) their expectations of inheriting her guardian's wealth when he dies. Of all this, Esther notes, 'We are not rich in the bank, but we have always prospered, and we have quite enough'(Dickens, 1853 [1997], p. 879). I find it difficult to decipher what Esther could mean here by the apparently oxymoronic 'not rich in the bank' but 'prospering,' although I suspect it has more to do with the Victorian difficulty of attaining ready money than with any sort of claim of actual poverty. Regardless, in each of the three books that I have discussed most extensively here – *Little Dorrit*, *Bleak House* and *David Copperfield* – the happy endings enjoyed by more than one pair of lovers are enabled by prosperity.

It would be madness and folly to try to turn Dickens into a thoroughgoing fan of private enterprise, free markets and business. There is far too much evidence in his work that goes against that, and to ignore it would be an injustice to the work and to the man. But it is equally an injustice to allow Dickens to be thought of as some sort of mealy-headed overly-emotional romantic who thinks that all rich people are evil, all work is oppression, all business is corruption and all financially irresponsible people are charming butterflies. We have the tools to argue against this within Dickens's own work. And within Dickens's work, we may find the tools to support some of our own most important arguments.

10. Beyond the can opener: a top ten list of economics humor

Yoram Bauman

10.1 INTRODUCTION

In his 'Introduction' to the inaugural issue of *The Teaching Economist*, McEachern (1990) implores economics instructors to make good use of humor when exposing students to economics. According to McEachern (1990, p. 5), '[i]f you have a sense of humor, don't be afraid to use it … [t]he use of humor does not mean telling jokes or trying to go for big laughs, but seeing the humor in simple things and putting a humorous twist on the material.' More recently, Welker (2007) adds, '[a]ll the talk about economics being the "dismal science" is totally wrong. In fact, this subject is [funnier] than people know! … [s]o, add humor to your list of tools in your attempt to make economics stick with your students.'

This chapter builds on the advice of both McEachern (1990) and Welker (2007) by providing examples of economics humor that come directly from published economic literature, and that could perhaps be integrated into upper-level undergraduate course discussions, or included, as an occasional break from traditional texts and articles, on reading lists in graduate courses. These examples, which come from some of the top economics humor contributions to the literature, are accompanied by background information that in some cases arose from communications with the authors, and so has not previously appeared in print. Lastly, note that three of the economics humorists highlighted below are among the past winners of the Nobel Prize in Economic Sciences, while two are also among the past winners of the prestigious John Bates Clark Medal. These credentials help dispel many of the myths about economists, economics and humor.

10.2 THE TOP ECONOMICS HUMOR FROM THE ACADEMIC LITERATURE

Below, I provide a chronological list of what I consider to be the top economics humor journal articles. This is naturally a subjective endeavor, so readers are welcome to fault me for selecting one of my own articles for inclusion in the list. Most of these articles are from the 'Miscellany' section in the *Journal of Political Economy*, dating back to the days when George Stigler was the editor, and/or from a similar section (that I am fortunate enough to presently oversee) in *Economic Inquiry*. A previous editor-in-chief of that journal, Robert Clower, went on to become editor-in-chief of the *American Economic Review*, and he deserves special mention for helping two of these papers (Leijonhufvud, 1973; McAfee, 1983) see the light of day in the pages of those journals. Lastly, some of these humorous contributions can be found in Clotfelter (1997) or in the compendium of economics humor that I maintain (see Bauman, 2013). Clotfelter is one of the few women engaged in the field of economics humor, and I have high hopes that women will be more prominently featured in future top ten lists of economics humor.

10.2.1 Leijonhufvud on the Econ Tribe

Axel Leijonhufvud is a Swedish-born economist who is currently a professor emeritus at both University of California Los Angeles (UCLA) and the University of Trento. Educated at Northwestern University (PhD, 1967), Leijonhufvud has become, over the course of his academic career, a very well-known macroeconomist (Snowden, 2004). At the time of Leijonhufvud (1973), *Economic Inquiry* was called *Western Economic Journal*. I intend to ask *Economic Inquiry* to republish this article on or before the 50th anniversary of its original publication. Excerpts from Leijonhufvud (1973) appear below.

> The Econ tribe occupies a vast territory in the far North. Their land appears bleak and dismal to the outsider, and travelling through it makes for rough sledding; but the Econ, through a long period of adaptation, have learned to wrestle a living of sorts from it. They are not without some genuine and sometimes even fierce attachment to their ancestral grounds, and their young are brought up to feel contempt for the softer living in the warmer lands of their neighbors, such as the Polscis and the Sociogs.
>
> Almost all of the travellers' reports that we have comment on the Econ as a 'quarrelsome race' who 'talk ill of their fellow behind his back,' and so forth.

> The Econ word for caste is 'field.' Caste is extremely important to the self-image and sense of identity of the Econ, and the adult male meeting a stranger will always introduce himself with the phrase 'Such-and-such is my field.' The English root of this term is interesting because of the aversion that the Econ normally have to the use of plain English.
>
> [S]tatus is tied to the manufacture of certain types of implements called 'modls.' The status of the adult male is determined by his skill at making the 'modl' of his 'field.' The facts (a) that the Econ are highly status-motivated, (b) that status is only to be achieved by making 'modls,' and (c) that most of these 'modls' seem to be of little or no practical use, probably accounts for the backwardness and abject cultural poverty of the tribe.
>
> The dominant role of 'modl' is perhaps best illustrated by the (unfortunately very incomplete) accounts we have of relationships between the two largest of the Econ castes, the 'Micro' and the 'Macro' … If a Micro-Econ is asked why the Micro do not intermarry with the Macro, he will answer 'They make a different modl,' or 'They do not know the Micro modl.'
>
> It would be to fail in one's responsibility to the Econ people to end this brief sketch of life in their society without a few words about their future. The prospect for the Econ is bleak. Their social structure and culture should be studied now before it is gone forever.

Thanks to Leijonhufvud (1973), we have some indication as to how the Macro and the Micro appeared. These are depicted in Figure 10.1.

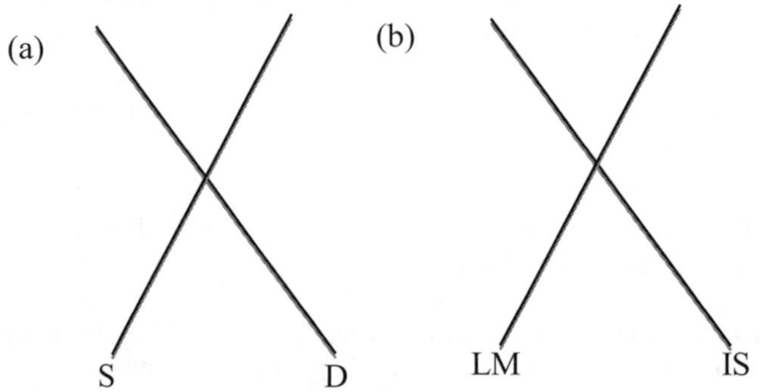

Source: Leijonhufvud (1973).

Figure 10.1 Totems of (a) the Micro and (b) the Macro

Readers interested in more about the Econ should track future issues of *Economic Inquiry* for a republication of Leijonhufvud (1973).

10.2.2 Krugman on Interstellar Trade

Paul Krugman, economics professor at Princeton University, won the Nobel Prize in Economic Sciences in 2008. An international economics scholar, Krugman also won the John Bates Clark Medal 17 years earlier, in 1991 (Mixon and Upadhyaya, 2014). Students of economics are introduced in principles courses to the benefits of trade between nations. Krugman (2010) introduces us to interstellar trade. Excerpts from Krugman (2010), including the paper's abstract, are provided below.

> Abstract: This article extends interplanetary trade theory to an interstellar setting. It is chiefly concerned with the following question: how should interest charges on goods in transit be computed when the goods travel at close to the speed of light? This is a problem because the time taken in transit will appear less to an observer traveling with the goods than to a stationary observer. A solution is derived from economic theory, and two useless but true theorems are proved.
>
> Many critics of conventional economics have argued, with considerable justification, that the assumptions underlying neoclassical theory bear little resemblance to the world we know. These critics have, however, been too quick to assert that this shows that mainstream economics can never be of any use. Recent progress in the technology of space travel … make this assertion doubtful; for they raise the distinct possibility that we may eventually discover or construct a world to which orthodox economic theory applies.
>
> It should be noted that, while the subject of this article is silly, the analysis actually does make sense. This article, then, is a serious analysis of a ridiculous subject, which is of course the opposite of what is usual in economics.

The original version of this paper is from 1978, but was never published, and the background story here might be of interest to readers. Krugman told me (personal correspondence, 25 April 2008) that 'many years ago I actually did submit it to the *JPE* [*Journal of Political Economy*] for the back-of-the-journal funny stuff … [but *JPE* editor George] Stigler sent it back demanding revisions – what's Trantor, he asked – and I said stuff it.'[1]

The paper might have disappeared had it not been for Joshua Gans, who told me (personal correspondence, 7 March 2013) that he was Krugman's teaching assistant in 1993 and ended up with a paper copy of the article, which came up 'in 2008, [when] a discussion arose on the Internet about interstellar trade.' Gans sent Krugman a scanned version of the article, which Krugman posted online (Krugman, 2008), noting that

'Thirty years ago I was an oppressed assistant professor, caught up in the academic rat race. To cheer myself up I wrote – well, see for yourself.'

Krugman's post (Krugman, 2008) appeared shortly after Editor-in-Chief Preston McAfee asked me to be the Specialized Co-Editor for Miscellany for *Economic Inquiry*. McAfee and I emailed Krugman to ask him if we could publish it, and he wrote back that 'if I can do it without revisions, that would be great.' Krugman also presented this paper at the 4th Annual American Economic Association Humor Session at the Allied Social Science Associations (ASSA) meeting on 7 January 2012.

10.2.3 Heckman's Empirical Work on Prayer and God

In some ways, James Heckman, the Henry Schultz Distinguished Service Professor of Economics at the University of Chicago, has a career path similar to that of the previous author, Paul Krugman. Heckman won the Nobel Prize in Economic Sciences in 2000, 17 years after winning the John Bates Clark Medal in 1983 (Mixon and Upadhyaya, 2014). As with Krugman (2010), Heckman (2010) is a paper from decades ago that was finally published in 2010.[2] Excerpts from Heckman (2010) are presented below.

> This article uses data available from the National Opinion Research Center's survey on religious attitudes and powerful statistical methods to evaluate the effect of prayer on the attitude of God toward human beings.
>
> The technique – due to Singh (1977) – is briefly described here. Let Y be God's attitude arrayed on a scale ranging from 0 to 1. This is an unobserved variable. Let X be the intensity of prayer in the population. It too is scaled between 0 and 1. The population density of prayer is summarized by a univariate density f(X), which has been estimated by Father Greeley (1972).
>
> Accept on faith that the conditional density of X given Y is of the form: $g(X|Y) = a(Y)\exp(XY)$ … [From this, Singh's technique can be used to calculate $E(Y|X)$.] Thus, from the population distribution of prayer, we can estimate the population regression function of God's attitude as a function of prayer.
>
> The empirical conclusion from this analysis is important. A little prayer does no good and may make things worse. Much prayer helps a lot.
>
> We conjecture that this powerful method can be extended to the more general case when X is not observed either.

Incidentally, the 'Father Greeley' referenced in the paper – in fact, the paper includes some correspondence from Greeley – was Anthony Greeley, who passed away in May of 2013. His obituary in *The New York*

Times ('Priest, Author, Scholar, Scold', 30 May 2013) notes that he 'wrote more than 120 books [including many scholarly works plus at least ten best-selling novels] many of them rife with Vatican intrigue, straying priests and explicit sex.' According to the obituary, Father Greeley once wrote that 'Sometimes I suspect that my obituary in *The New York Times* will read, "Andrew Greeley, Priest; Wrote Steamy Novels."'

10.2.4 Stigler on Economics Conferences

The late George Stigler earned his PhD in economics (in 1938) from the University of Chicago, where he spent much of his academic career in the economics faculty. Like Krugman and Heckman, Stigler won the Nobel Prize in Economic Sciences. Excerpts from Stigler (1977, from the same year he won the Nobel Prize) are presented below.

> There is an ancient joke about the two traveling salesmen in the age of the train. The younger drummer was being initiated into the social life of the traveler by the older. They proceeded to the smoking parlor on the train, where a group of drummers were congregated. One said, '87,' and a wave of laughter went through the group. The older drummer explained to the younger that they traveled together so often that they had numbered their jokes. The younger drummer wished to participate in the event and diffidently ventured to say, '36.' He was greeted by cool silence. The older drummer took him aside and explained that they had already heard that joke. (In another version, the younger drummer was told that he had told the joke badly.)
>
> This parable has often recurred to me as I attend conferences of economists. Economists travel together a great deal, and there is no reason why the discussions which follow the presentation of papers should not utilize a handbook of commentary. The following is a preliminary list of numbered comments, which itself will cover a large share of the comments elicited in most conferences. If the proposal meets approval, the list can be extended, and a second list of the standard replies to these comments can be provided.

Some examples follow.

> I can be very sympathetic with the author; until 2 years ago I was thinking along similar lines.
>
> This paper contains much that is new and much that is good.
>
> Theorizing is not fruitful at this stage: we need a series of case studies.
>
> Case studies are a clue, but no real progress can be made until a model of the process is constructed.

> The conclusions change if you introduce uncertainty.
>
> The central argument is not only a tautology, it is false.

As noted above, Stigler was also the editor responsible for the Miscellany section in the *Journal of Political Economy*, which published many funny articles (not including Krugman, 2010).

10.2.5 Snower on Vampire Economics

The Vampire Diaries (CW Network) and *True Blood* (HBO) are two popular television drama series among older teens and young adults. Both involve vampires, as does the humorous economics publication by Dennis Snower (1982), a Princeton University graduate (PhD) and an economics professor at the University of Kiel. Given the subject matter of Snower's article, it would likely be of interest to upper-level undergraduate and/or PhD students of economics. Excerpts from Snower (1982) are presented below.

> Although human beings have endured the recurring ravages of vampires for centuries, scarcely any attempts have been made to analyze the macroeconomic implications of this problem and to devise socially optimal policy responses.
>
> Over the past few centuries, a number of prominent investigators … have suggested that all vampires should be destroyed … [I show that] such a policy would not be socially optimal.

In doing so, Snower (1982) develops a formal/graphical model of the optimal production of stakes and the optimal destruction of vampires. Figure 10.2 depicts what Snower (1982) refers to as the Vampire Neutrality Theorem.

In addition to the Vampire Neutrality Theorem, Snower (1982) also derives a Vampire Impossibility Theorem. His article inspired at least one additional article, that by Hartl and Mehlmann (1982). Interest in the economics of vampires and the undead continues to this day, as evidenced by the call for abstracts for a forthcoming book to be titled *Economics of the Undead* (Whitman and Dow, 2013).

10.2.6 McAfee on the Voyage of Columbus

The spotlight now turns to Preston McAfee, who penned a humorous economics study on Christopher Columbus's voyage in the 1400s. Below are excerpts from McAfee (1983).

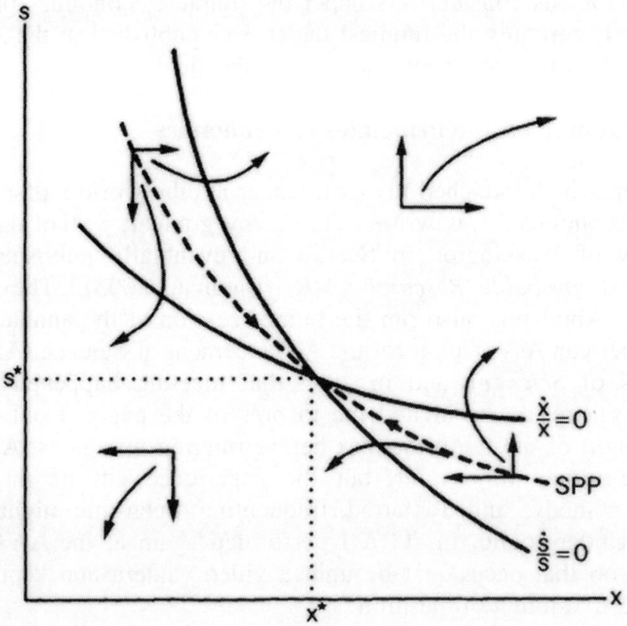

Source: Snower (1982).

Figure 10.2 The Vampire Neutrality Theorem

Since the imaginative, pathbreaking, inventive analysis of Robert Fogel (1962), the counterfactual analysis has intrigued and scintillated a generation of economists. Fogel considered the state of the American economy in 1890, had the railroads never been invented. He found that less than 10 percent of the American output could be attributed to the single innovation of railroads, thus demonstrating irrevocably that the loss of trains would not derail the American economic juggernaut.

In order to perform a valid test of the invincibility of the American economic cornucopia, the counterfactual must predate the development of the celebrated entrepreneur and the waves of immigrants whose sweat was an important input into the production process. Consequently, it is hypothesized that, rather than stumble upon the two American continents, Columbus fell off the edge of the earth. Certainly this is a valid test, for if America were to be virtually unchanged, despite not being discovered, certainly the 'American century' was inevitable. I choose the year 2000 as a target date, and compare America as it will be in the year 2000 to the way it would have been then, had Columbus fallen off the edge.

Many economists consider this paper the funniest economics paper ever written. It is certainly the funniest paper ever published in the *American Economic Review*, the premier journal in the field.

10.2.7 Bauman on the Principles of Economics

This paper, which launched my own career as 'the world's first and only stand-up economist,' was written during my graduate school days at the University of Washington in Seattle and eventually published in the *Annals of Improbable Research* (*AIR*) (Bauman, 2003).[3] The editor of *AIR*, Marc Abrahams, also ran the humor session at the annual meeting of the American Association for the Advancement of Science (AAAS, the publishers of *Science*), and in 2004 that meeting happened to be in Seattle. As a result, he invited me to present the paper. I only made it through eight of the ten principles before running up against Abraham's strict five-minute time limit, but the experience got me hooked on stand-up comedy, and I started frequenting open-mic nights at the Comedy Underground. In 2007, I performed again at the AAAS meetings, and on that occasion I brought a video camera and kept my talk within the five-minute time limit.[4]

Here are some excerpts from the paper.

> The cornerstone of Harvard professor N. Gregory Mankiw's introductory economics textbook, *Principles of Economics*, is a synthesis of economic thought into Ten Principles of Economics (listed in … Table 10.1 …). A quick perusal of these will likely affirm the reader's suspicions that synthesizing economic thought into Ten Principles is no easy task, and may even lead the reader to suspect that the subtlety and concision required are not to be found in the pen of N. Gregory Mankiw.
>
> I have taken it upon myself to remedy this unfortunate situation… [Table 10.1] … summarizes my attempt to translate Mankiw's Ten Principles into plain English, and in doing so to provide the uninitiated with an invaluable glimpse of the economic mind at work. Explanations and details can be found in the pages that follow, but the average reader is advised to simply cut out the table … and carry it around for assistance in the (hereafter unlikely) event of confusion about the basic Principles of Economics.

Many of my other economics humor videos (and a compendium of humorous economics writing) can be found at http://www.standupeconomist.com. I am also currently working (with Kurt R. Verkest) to publish some research we have done on 'Hyperinflation in Hell.'

Table 10.1 Mankiw's Principles translated

Mankiw's Principles	Yoram's Translations
#1. People face tradeoffs.	#1. Choices are bad.
#2. The cost of something is what you give up to get it.	#2. Choices are really bad.
#3. Rational people think at the margin.	#3. People are stupid.
#4. People respond to incentives.	#4. People aren't that stupid.
#5. Trade can make everyone better off.	#5. Trade can make everyone worse off.
#6. Markets are usually a good way to organize economic activity.	#6. Governments are stupid.
#7. Governments can sometimes improve market outcomes.	#7. Governments aren't that stupid.
#8. A country's standard of living depends on its ability to produce goods and services.	#8. Blah blah blah.
#9. Prices rise when the government prints too much money.	#9. Blah blah blah.
#10. Society faces a short-run tradeoff between inflation and unemployment.	#10. Blah blah blah.

Source: Bauman (2003).

10.2.8 Dynan, Elmendorf and Fichel on Financial Innovation

Getting back to the top ten, the next article ('Can Financial Innovation Help Explain the Reduced Volatility of Economic Activity?', published in 2006) comes from a trio of economists: Karen Dynan of the Brookings Institution, Douglas Elmendorf of the Congressional Budget Offce and Daniel Sichell, a professor of economics at Wellesley College. The abstract from the paper by Dynan et al. (2006) is provided below.

> Abstract: The stabilization of economic activity in the mid 1980s has received considerable attention. Research has focused primarily on the role played by milder economic shocks, improved inventory management, and better monetary policy. This paper explores another potential explanation: financial innovation. Examples of such innovation include developments in lending practices and loan markets that have enhanced the ability of households and firms to borrow and changes in government policy such as the demise of Regulation Q. We employ a variety of simple empirical techniques to identify links between the observed moderation in economic activity and the influence of financial innovation on consumer spending, housing investment, and business fixed investment. Our results suggest that financial innovation should be added to the list of likely contributors to the mid-1980s stabilization.

This paper was not written as a humor paper. However, given the role of financial innovation in producing the greatest increase in the volatility of economic activity since the Great Depression, the paper arguably deserves a place in the economics humor pantheon as a modern-day equivalent of Irving Fischer's proclamation three days before the 1929 stock market crash that '[s]tock prices have reached what looks like a permanently high plateau.' Lastly, given that this is not a real humor paper, I have added an additional article. So this top ten list 'goes to eleven.'

10.2.9 Smith on Japan's Phillips Curve

In 2008, Gregor Smith, the Douglas D. Purvis Professor of Economics at Queen's University in Canada, published a neat article 'looking at' Japan's Phillips Curve. Excerpts from Smith (2008) are provided below.

> Japan's Phillips Curve is shown in the right-hand panel of [Figure 10.3]. The data are monthly from January 1980 to August 2005.
>
> For ease of viewing, the left-hand panel of [Figure 10.3] rotates the Phillips Curve around the vertical axis so that minus the unemployment rate now is on the horizontal axis. Clearly visible are the islands of Hokkaido and Honshu, though it is somewhat difficult to separately distinguish the southern islands of Kyushu and Shikoku. The Noto-Hanto Penninsula is evident to the north of the southern end of the main island of Honshu. Tokyo Bay is also visible. The data point to the far left in [Figure 10.3] is the island of Fukue-Jima.

Smith's web page once provided a link to a version of the paper along with a note indicating that 'the title is also the abstract and, frankly, most of the text.'

10.2.10 Oxoby on AC/DC

The use of music as an instruction tool in economics is growing in popularity (for example, see Hall and Lawson, 2008; Hall et al., 2008, 2013; Lawson et al., 2008; Mateer and Rice, 2007). Robert Oxoby, a professor of economics at the University of Calgary, reverses the usual scope of this literature with his humorous article using game-theoretic concepts from industrial economics to evaluate music. The abstract and acknowledgments from Oxoby (2009) are presented below.

> Abstract: We use tools from experimental economics to address the age-old debate regarding who was a better singer in the band AC/DC. Our results suggest that (using wealth maximization as a measure of 'better') listening to Brian Johnson (relative to listening to Bon Scott) resulted in 'better' outcomes in an ultimatum game. These results may have important implications for

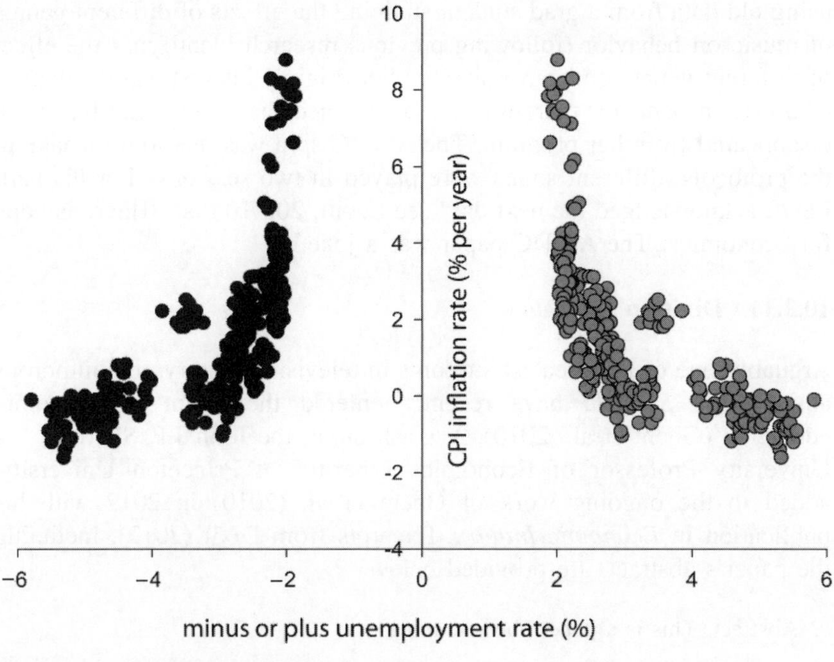

Note: CPI is consumer price index.

Source: Smith (2008).

Figure 10.3 Japan's Phillips Curve

> settling drunken music debates and environmental design issues in organizations.
>
> Acknowledgments: We thank Steven Levitt for his support and popularization of this research (see, for example, Levitt 2007). We thank Nathan Berg, Gary Charness, Bill Harbaugh, and Kendra McLeish for valuable suggestions and comments. We also thank a delayed Air Canada flight and a bar in the Vancouver airport for providing the time, space, and resources necessary to pursue this research. All errors are attributable to Air Canada.

Oxoby also deserves much credit for having a second (non-humorous) publication in the same issue of the journal (Spraggon and Oxoby, 2009). Unfortunately, Steven Levitt failed to get the joke in the AC/DC paper, prompting him to post on the Freakonomics blog (see Levitt, 2007a) that '[t]his is what happens to people who listen to too much AC/DC … I hope for this guy's sake he has tenure.' Oxoby commented that 'I have tenure,' and added some details on the paper: 'The paper was written using old data from a grad student studying the effects of different genres of music on behavior (following previous research identifying the effect of different genres on heart rate, etc.; her original interest was on the use of music in behavior therapy). She abandoned the project and has since disappeared from her program. The AC/DC spin was due to a mistake in the protocols: different songs were played in two sessions.' For his part, Levitt acknowledged the next day (see Levitt, 2007b) that '[t]here is hope for economics: The AC/DC paper was a joke.'

10.2.11 Dixit on *Seinfeld*

Arguably one of the greatest sit-coms in television history, the humorous antics from *Seinfeld* have recently entered the realm of economic education (Ghent et al., 2010). Avinash Dixit, the John J.F. Sherrerd '52 University Professor of Economics Emeritus at Princeton University, added to the ongoing work of Ghent et al. (2010) in 2012 with his publication in *Economic Inquiry*. Excerpts from Dixit (2012), including the paper's abstract, are provided below.

> Abstract: This is a paper about nothing.
>
> In an episode of the sitcom *Seinfeld* (Season 7, Episode 9, original air date December 7, 1995), Elaine Benes uses a contraceptive sponge that gets taken off the market. She scours pharmacies in the neighborhood to stock a large supply, but it is finite. So she must 're-evaluate her whole screening process.' Every time she dates a new man, which happens very frequently, she has to consider a new issue: Is he spongeworthy? The purpose of this article is to quantify this concept of spongeworthiness.
>
> When Elaine uses up a sponge, she is giving up the option to have it available when an even better man comes along. Therefore using the sponge amounts to exercising a real option to wait and spongeworthiness is an option value. It can be calculated using standard option-pricing techniques. However, unlike the standard theory of financial or many real options, there are no complete markets and no replicating portfolios. Stochastic dynamic programming methods must be used.

Dixit, an economist trained at the Massachusetts Institute of Technology, served as the President of the Econometric Society in 2001 and as the President of the American Economic Association in 2008. As such, he is not unlike several of the aforementioned luminaries who has added his name to the roster of humorists in the field of economics.

10.3 CONCLUDING COMMENTS

Economics humor is clearly a field of endeavor with a fine history and a promising future. A frequent challenge, however, is finding a suitable venue for publishing economics humor. A Miscellany section currently exists in *Economic Inquiry*, and in the past a similar section existed in the *Journal of Political Economy*, but they exist at the whim of editors and could easily cease to exist. And even when Miscellany sections exist, papers are subject to the imperfect judgment of editors: consider that a rejection by Stigler almost meant the loss of Krugman (2010) and that a rejection by yours truly has denied the light of day to McAfee's 'The cookie caper,' considered by some economists to be the second-funniest economics paper ever written. In light of all this, and given that this chapter is not being peer-reviewed, it seems fitting to include, as an honorable mention and conclusion, the following poem from Pannell (2002).

> You've posted in your paper
> To a journal of repute
> And you're hoping that the referees
> Won't send you down the chute
>
> You'd better not build up a sense of
> False security
> I've just received your manuscript and
> I'm the referee
>
> This power's a revelation
> I'm so glad it's come to me
> I can be a total bastard with
> Complete impunity
>
> I used to be a psychopath
> But never more will be
> I can deal with my frustrations now that
> I'm a referee

NOTES

1. For the record, Trantor is a planet in the science fiction writings of Isaac Asimov.
2. It is unknown if Heckman ever submitted it for publication in 1980.
3. These ten principles are also available on YouTube (see Bauman, 2013).
4. In the YouTube video (see Bauman, 2013), you can hear the timekeeper's dings every minute, and at the very end a shadow crosses the screen, preparing to end my talk if I was not going to end it myself.

11. Can't see the tacking for the trees? Try a Coasian solution

Scott A. Beaulier, Franklin G. Mixon, Jr and Richard J. Cebula

11.1 INTRODUCTION

The use of movies, television, music, literature and other aspects of (popular) culture has taken on a greater emphasis in recent years regarding the teaching of economics principles. Mateer (2004, 2009), Sexton (2006), Mateer and Li (2008), Mixon (2010) and Mateer and Stephenson (2011) offer resources for integrating films and movies into economics instruction. Use of television clips and shows, as explained in Mixon (2001), Sexton (2006), Ghent et al. (2010), Luccasen and Thomas (2010), Mateer et al. (2011) and Crisp and Mixon (2012), is the most expansive stem of this particular branch of economic education. In terms of music, Lawson et al. (2008) and Hall and Lawson (2008) represent seminal pieces instructing economics professors on how to incorporate music into the economics classroom. The use of literature, as exemplified by Watts (2003), is one of the oldest forms of imparting economics principles to business and economics students. Finally, Lawson (2006), Kjar (2009) and Mateer (2011) offer examples of how to use comic strips, video games and YouTube videos to, along with the other tools mentioned above, enhance the instruction of economics.

However, many instructors find it difficult to employ the tools and techniques highlighted above in their principles and other economics courses. A common perception is that the time costs required to do so are prohibitive, meaning that entertaining these instructional tools and techniques results in a loss of coverage of those economics principles that are not being illuminated by movies, television or other media. In this case, and given that these techniques arose in order to address media-savvy, yet perhaps attention-short, students of the twenty-first century, it is incumbent upon textbook authors and economic education scholars to provide more modern examples of the types of issues examined in principles of economics courses and beyond. This chapter offers such a modern pedagogical vignette dealing with economic approaches to negative externalities.

11.2 SOME BACKGROUND

The history of economic thought surrounding human beings' dealings with externalities is one of the more interesting dimensions of that particular field. Arguably, the most prominent branches of that thought that have emerged over the past century are Pigouvian taxes (Pigou, 1932) and Coasian bargains (Coase, 1960, 1988). In point of fact, it is these two approaches, particularly the latter one, that are most typically included in classroom and textbook discussions of solutions to negative externalities in principles of economics courses. Table 11.1 provides a brief account of the coverage in several leading economics principles texts of both the Pigouvian and Coasian approaches to negative externalities.[1] Although most of these texts cover the Pigouvian approach, almost half actually include his name (that is, A.C. Pigou) in the process. Almost all of these texts include both the Coasian approach and reference to Ronald Coase in their discussions of negative externalities.[2]

Table 11.2 provides a list of the types of vignettes used by popular principles texts in explaining how the Coase Theorem applies to negative externalities. Each text relies upon a hypothetical situation, with some using examples from the original writing on the subject. Specifically, the texts provide scenarios dealing with pollution generated by chemical and manufacturing firms, loss of farm crops due to neighboring cattle ranching, and economic and social activities that produce noise that disturbs people nearby these activities.

It seems reasonable to assume that the types of examples used by texts in examining Coasian bargains that address negative externalities are not the types of situations or stories that usually appeal to traditional college and university students. Thus, this chapter provides a more modern story for principles instructors to use as a supplement to traditional textbook accounts of the problems associated with externalities and the applicability of the Coase Theorem.

Table 11.1 Textbook coverage of Pigouvian and Coasian approaches to externalities

Book	Chapter	Chapter Title	Pigou	Coase
Arnold (2011)	31	Market failure: externalities, public goods, and asymmetric information	X	X
Bade and Parkin (2011)	11	Externalities and the environment		X
Boyes and Melvin (2011)	27	Market failures, government failures, and rent seeking	X	X
Case et al. (2012)	16	Externalities, public goods, and social choice		X
Colander (2010)	21	Market failure versus government failure	X	X
Frank and Bernanke (2011)	9	Externalities and property rights	X	X
Mankiw (2012)	10	Externalities and the environment		
McConnell et al. (2012)	17	Market failures: public goods and externalities		X
McEachern (2010)	5	Externalities		X
O'Sullivan et al. (2012)	17	External costs and environmental policy		X
Parkin (2012)	31	Economics and the environment	X	X

11.3 THE ORACLE CHIEF EXECUTIVE OFFICER AND THE REDWOOD TREES: A NEW COASIAN CASE

Our story begins in July of 1988, when Oracle Corporation Chief Executive Officer (CEO) Larry Ellison paid $3.9 million for a home in the Pacific Heights neighborhood of San Francisco – a property that provided Ellison with a prized view of San Francisco Bay below (Carleton, 2011).[3] However, later, in 2004, a $6.9 million home below Ellison's was purchased by Bernard and Jane von Bothmer. After taking ownership of the property below Ellison, the von Bothmers allowed three redwood trees and an acacia (located in their backyard) to grow by several feet (Carleton, 2011; Ferrato, 2011a). As depicted in Figure 11.1, the redwood and acacia growth came at the expense of Ellison's view: due to the taller trees, Ellison could no longer see San Francisco Bay from the third-story living room of his four-story home on the Bay (Carleton, 2011).

Table 11.2 Textbook vignettes of Coasian approach to negative externalities

Hypothetical case of a cattle rancher whose cattle stray onto adjacent farm and eat and/or damage the farmer's crops.
Hypothetical case of a chemical company that dumps waste into a river, harming the people who live near the river and use it for fishing and boating.
Hypothetical case where Ralph mows his lawn before 8 a.m. on Sunday mornings, disturbing his neighbor Louis.
Hypothetical case of Harry, whose dorm room is next to Jake's. Harry plays noisy video games, thus disturbing Jake. Also, hypothetical case of a power company in Pittsburgh that emits pollution, harming the 100,000 nearby residents.
Hypothetical case of a factory that dumps toxins into a river, harming the people who fish the river.
Hypothetical case of Dick, whose dog Spot barks, disturbing Dick's neighbor, Jane.
Hypothetical case of manufacturer of heavy machinery located next to research laboratory that tests delicate equipment – manufacturing process causes vibrations that disturb the lab's equipment.
Hypothetical case of a steel mill that dumps wastes into a lake, harming a nearby fishing firm.
Hypothetical case of a chemical company that dumps waste into a river, harming the people who live near the river.

As Carleton (2011) points out, San Francisco's hilly terrain and prized vistas often generate such tree disputes – so many, in fact, that the City of San Francisco passed a Tree Dispute Resolution Ordinance in 1988 that requires complainants to (1) attempt to reconcile the dispute with the other homeowner(s); (2) file a 'tree claim' in the event that (1) fails; and (3) submit the dispute to arbitration should both of the aforementioned remedies fail to resolve the issue.[4] If the resolution process fails altogether, the complainant can seek a formal remedy in the court. Ellison attempted to resolve the issue using steps (1) to (3) above during the years 2008 and 2009, but his attempts failed. At that point, Ellison sought a court-ordered remedy.

Ellison filed suit against the von Bothmers in June of 2010, and the courts agreed to hear his case on 6 June 2011, in San Francisco's California Superior Court (Carleton, 2011). Before the case went to trial, though, Ellison attempted to resolve the dispute privately by offering the von Bothmers $27 million for their hillside home (Dalton, 2011). Though Ellison's offer was nearly four times the 2004 purchase price of the home, the von Bothmers rejected the offer.[5] Ellison did not give up easily, and he wanted the issue resolved (ideally in his favor) in advance

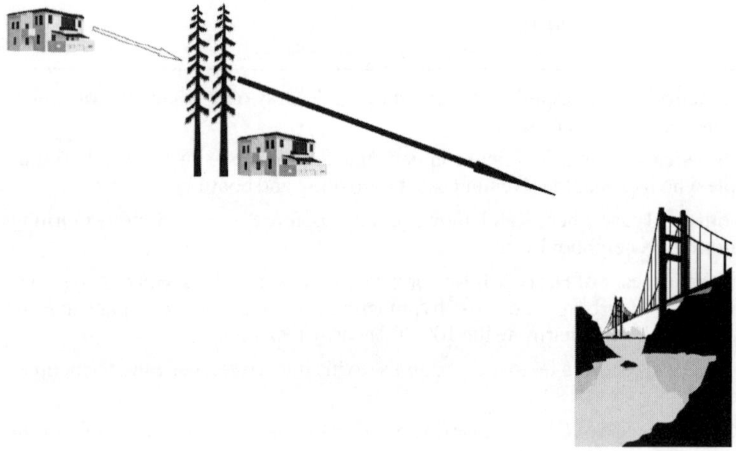

Figure 11.1 Bay view obscured

of the 2013 America's Cup race, which was ultimately won by Ellison's Oracle Team USA, representing the Golden Gate Yacht Club (Coté, 2010).[6] After more back and forth, he and the von Bothmers ultimately reached an out-of-court settlement before the 2011 trial whereby the von Bothmers agreed to keep the height of the trees within two feet of the elevation of the second floor level of Ellison's home (Ferrato, 2011b; Hickman, 2011; Staff, 2011).

11.4 PEDAGOGICAL 'TAKE-AWAYS'

The story of Larry Ellison's battle for a clear view of San Francisco Bay is a classic example of a property dispute that has the potential for settlement so long as rights are established. Law and economics scholars and teachers will recognize the similarities between the Ellison story and a number of legal cases, such as the conflict over competing uses in *Bryan v. Lefever,* 1879 and *Fontainebleau Hotel Corp. v. Forty-five Twenty-five, Inc.*, 1959.[7] All of the key features for a Coasian bargain to work itself out are present – the ownership rights are clearly defined, transaction costs and communication costs are fairly low and there are well-established markets in tree services and land. Many different outcomes could have emerged from this arrangement, but it is clear that the final outcome was the one where resources – particularly Ellison's uninhibited view of San Francisco Bay flowed to the person who valued the good most highly.

In addition to being a more contemporary example of the Coase Theorem, and in addition to being an example that involves a major personality in the business world, the Ellison story also gives scholars an opportunity to talk about the 'Invariance Hypothesis' and the role that endowments and wealth play when Coasian bargains are made. The Invariance Hypothesis states that if an unobstructed view is worth more to Ellison than the trees and land are worth to the von Bothmers, the rights to the view will be purchased – either by paying for trees to be cut or by buying up the property – so long as Ellison has enough funds to entice the von Bothmers into allowing the transaction. If the trees are more valuable to the von Bothmers than the view is to Ellison, the trees will not be chopped (or land will not be sold), so long as the von Bothmers have sufficient funds. The key condition for the Invariance Hypothesis to hold, therefore, involves the parties' relative willingness and ability to buy rights. A whole literature focuses on the issue of wealth effects, and it is clear that the initial assignment of rights does affect parties' relative wealth.[8] Given that the assignment of a right to one party has wealth effects, the final outcome may, *contra* the Invariance Hypothesis, be affected by the initial rights assignment.

In terms of the Ellison case, wealth and initial endowments certainly seemed to play some role in the final outcome. Ellison's tremendous net worth and wealth made him fairly insensitive to the von Bothmers's unwillingness to sell, and it is difficult to imagine the von Bothmers being able to offer Ellison a sum of money sufficient to leave him content having an obstructed view of San Francisco Bay.

NOTES

1. Table 11.1 contains the numbers of the textbook chapters to which discussion of externalities are assigned, as well as the titles of those chapters.
2. Examination of more advanced presentations might include Baumol and Oates (1988) and Cornes and Sandler (1996).
3. Oracle Corporation is a computer technology company located in Redwood Shores, California. It was founded in 1977 by Ellison and two others. Oracle's fiscal 2011 revenues exceeded $35 billion. At the same time, Ellison's personal wealth was estimated at just under $40 billion, ranking him fifth worldwide.
4. Interestingly, Ellison resolved a similar case involving redwoods that he planted at his Woodside, California home. There, a neighbor complained that Ellison's redwood trees blocked that neighbor's views, at which point Ellison removed the trees (Carleton, 2011).
5. Carleton (2011) reports an early offer of $15 million, a figure that is still more than twice the purchase price. Ferrato (2011a, 2011b) indicates that the von Bothmers

rejected 'two offers' from Ellison. Thus, it is possible that both figures, $15 million and $27 million, were offered by Ellison for the von Bothmers's home. In another interesting twist to the story, reports (Ferrato, 2011a, 2011b) in the spring of 2011 indicated that Ellison was attempting to purchase the house next door to his, which was owned by the late San Francisco socialite Dodie Rosekrans. Rosekrans's home had an unobstructed view of the Bay, and Ellison was rumored to have offered $40 million for the property. Interestingly, that sale never occurred.

6. As Coté (2010) indicates, San Francisco officials plan to raise $270 million to host the 2013 America's Cup race in San Francisco Bay. Ellison's own racing team, BMW Oracle Racing, is the current Cup holder, and is now creating an 'event authority' management group to administer much of the 2013 race.
7. See Barnes and Stout (1992) for a discussion of the case.
8. Calabresi (1970) is a good starting point for those interested in discussions of distributional effects.

12. Teaching the economics of income tax evasion

Richard J. Cebula and Maggie Foley

12.1 INTRODUCTION

The phenomenon of income tax evasion is a common component of both undergraduate- and graduate-level courses in public finance, public economics and public policy. In the United States, personal income tax evasion effectively consists of taxable income that is either unreported or underreported to the Internal Revenue Service (IRS) by individuals or couples. Income tax evasion can also take the form of spurious or inflated tax deductions, such as might be misrepresented on Form 1040, Schedule A[1] or on Form 1040 Schedule C[2] by individuals or couples. Income tax evasion, which is illegal, is distinguished from income tax avoidance, which is legal. Income tax avoidance, which can take many different forms, is simply a legal way to reduce one's federal personal income tax liability. An example of the latter is the interest paid on tax free municipal bonds, which is not subject to federal income taxation; to the extent that one owns tax free bonds, one receives a flow of interest income that is exempt from federal government income taxation.

The purpose of this pedagogical chapter is to provide a straightforward and easily understood framework that can be used to teach the economic behavior underlying income tax evasion. We begin with presenting a brief background that reflects the research that has been done, especially for the case of the United States, on income tax evasion. This brief section is meant to provide the student with some overall perspective on the issue. Once this literature overview is completed, the main section of this study provides a framework, based in cost-benefit analysis, to enable the student to easily understand factors underlying personal income tax evasion.

12.2 EXISTING STUDIES OF PERSONAL INCOME TAX EVASION

Studies of income tax evasion behavior essentially fall into three categories. First, there are the principally theoretical models of tax evasion behavior, such as Allingham and Sandmo (1972), Falkinger (1988), Klepper et al. (1991), Das-Gupta (1994), Pestieau et al. (1994), Caballe and Panades (1997) and Gahramanov (2009). These models tend to be very technical and mathematical in form. Their intent is to identify behavioral factors that would either, in theory, create incentives to engage in income tax evasion or disincentives to do so. Such studies are often mathematically elegant, although they typically are not subjected to formal empirical testing.

Second, there are a number of studies that either (a) use questionnaires or (b) undertake experiments, such as Baldry (1987), Alm et al. (1992), Thurman (1991) and Alm et al. (1999). These studies are effectively empirical in nature, deriving the data largely (if not entirely) from the experiments. Certain of these studies indicate an aversion to the prospect of being audited while others reveal a lack of such risk-averse behavior; still others imply that taxpayers may be averse to tax evasion on moral grounds. Additionally, the incentive to try to evade taxation by underreporting income in the face of higher marginal income tax rates is also revealed in most of these studies.

Third, there are those studies that largely or in some cases exclusively adopt what is referred to as 'official data,' that is, data obtained from the IRS (or its counterpart outside the Unites States) and/or some other 'official,' that is, government source, and/or from a publicly available source. Among the types of information thus obtained and analysed are data on the magnitude of income tax evasion in the economy, income tax rates and audit rates. Such studies endeavor typically either to estimate the aggregate degree of tax evasion or identify the determinants thereof (Ali et al., 2001; Alm and Yunus, 2009; Bawley, 1982; Carson, 1984; Cebula, 2001, 2004, 2008; Cebula and Coombs, 2009; Clotfelter, 1983; Connelly, 2004; Erard and Feinstein, 1994; Feige, 1994; Feinstein, 1991; Klepper et al., 1991; Ledbetter, 2004; Long and Gwartney, 1987; Musgrave, 1987; Pozo, 1996; Pyle, 1989; Tanzi, 1982, 1983).

In this literature, it is widely believed that the degree of federal personal income tax evasion in the economy as a whole is positively affected by income tax rates (Clotfelter, 1983; Feige, 1994; Tanzi, 1982). Interestingly, Yaniv (1994) characterizes Clotfelter (1983) as 'the most relevant study' with respect to the impact of income tax rates on tax evasion, whereas Cox (1984) questions his findings. In any event, this particular perspective is simple: the higher the income tax rate, the greater the benefit (in terms of a reduced tax liability) from not reporting taxable income, *ceteris paribus*. It is also widely accepted that the greater the risk associated with underreporting or not reporting taxable income, the less the degree to which economic agents will choose either to not report or underreport their taxable income (Erard and Feinstein, 1994; Spicer and Thomas, 1982).

12.3 EXPECTED BENEFITS FROM AND COSTS TO ENGAGING IN INCOME TAX EVASION

To help create an understanding of income tax evasion/compliance behavior, we start with a basic premise. In particular, it is assumed that the probability that an individual will not report all of his or her taxable income to the IRS and/or that an individual will overstate tax deductions or engage in other means to illegally evade income taxation (*PTE*) is treated as positively related to the expected gross benefits (*EGB*) to the individual of engaging in that income tax evasion and treated as negatively related to the expected gross costs and risks (*EGC*) to the individual of engaging in that income tax evasion. Thus, the probability that the individual will engage in income tax evasion can be expressed as:

$$PTE = f\,(EGB,\ EGC),\ f_{EGB} > 0,\ f_{EGC} < 0 \qquad (12.1)$$

12.3.1 Expected Benefits of Income Tax Evasion

The expected benefits of income tax evasion arguably can assume two different forms: expected primary or direct benefits and expected secondary benefits. Expected primary or direct benefits of income tax evasion can be regarded as obvious or transparent. Expected secondary benefits are less tangible but can nonetheless be very real.

The best example of direct benefits from income tax evasion would be the value of the taxes not paid to the IRS. To the extent that an individual engages in income tax evasion and underpays income taxes by, say, \$X, those \$X are a direct benefit to the individual, who can (in theory) spend and/or save the \$X. In this case, the higher the federal income tax rate (*FEDTXRATE*) that the individual is subject to, the greater the pecuniary benefit from underreporting his or her income and/or from exaggerating tax deductions by any given amount. For instance, if the income tax rate is 10 percent, tax evasion in the amount of \$5000 would be expected to yield the tax evader \$500; however, if the individual faced a 25 percent income tax rate, the expected benefit to this degree of tax evasion would be \$1250. Thus, it is logical to deduce that, *ceteris paribus*, the higher the income tax rate, the greater the incentive to engage in income tax evasion because the higher the income tax rate, the greater the expected benefits of the tax evasion behavior.

It is noteworthy that taxpayers living in a state that imposes an income tax (*STXRATE*) are provided an additional incentive to underreport taxable income and/or exaggerate tax deductions or exemptions, namely, they can evade state-level income taxes in addition to federal-level income taxes. This is especially likely since in many states one's state income tax liability is largely based on one's federal taxable income. Thus, the higher the state marginal income tax rate facing the taxpayer, the greater the incentive to evade federal income taxes. This is obviously because the higher the state marginal income tax rate in the individual's state of legal residence, the greater the total direct expected benefits to be derived for the individual from income tax evasion behavior in terms of lower taxes paid and hence higher levels of funds to spend and save.

Thus, it is argued that:

$$EGB = g\ (FEDTXRATE,\ STXRATE) \tag{12.2}$$

such that the expected gross benefits of federal income tax evasion are positively related to the individual's applicable federal income tax rate and to the individual's applicable state income tax rate.

Aside from the issue of tax rates, persons who have taxable income may be able in certain cases to derive secondary benefits from income tax evasion behavior. For example, if people disapprove of the way in which the federal government is spending their tax dollars, they may be angered or frustrated. To relieve this anger or frustration, they may consider income tax evasion as an outlet (Feige, 1994).

Consider the case of the federal government being engaged in an unpopular war (*UNPOPWAR*). For example, there is evidence (Cebula, 2001) that the unpopularity of the Vietnam War so angered the public that many chose to underreport their income and/or exaggerate their deductions. This form of income tax evasion behavior was undertaken because of the disapproval by much of the public of the federal government's involvement in and expenditures to finance the Vietnam War using their tax dollars. Whereas the Vietnam War raged on, at least some portion of the public received secondary benefits/gains from the experience that they were withholding financing of that military action.

Interestingly, other factors can work much the same way. For instance, the greater the public's dissatisfaction with government (*DIS*), the greater the degree to which the public is likely to experience a secondary gain from engaging tax evasion (Feige, 1994). Indeed, a low job approval rating for the sitting president can act in the same way, that is, to induce tax evasion based on secondary gains from tax evasion behavior (Cebula, 2008). Alternatively stated, the higher the president's job approval rating per se, the lower the degree of federal income tax evasion because if the president is regarded as doing a good job, there is less (if any) secondary gain from tax evasion.

Thus, Equation (12.2) can be expanded in various ways, as shown in Equation (12.3):

$$EGB = g\ (FEDTXRATE,\ STXRATE,\ UNPOPWAR,\ DIS) \quad (12.3)$$

such that the expected benefits from tax evasion are directly related not only to income tax rates (*FEDTXRATE*, *STXRATE*) but also directly related to the waging of an unpopular war (*UNPOPWAR*) or greater public dissatisfaction with government (*DIS*).

12.3.2 Expected Costs and Risks of Income Tax Evasion

Income tax evasion, because it is illegal, involves certain forms of costs and risks, which in turn lead the individual pondering income tax evasion to have expected probabilities of both detection by the IRS and penalties that would then be imposed by the IRS. These expected costs and risks act to discourage the would-be tax evader. In other words, the expected gross costs of tax evasion are hypothesized to be positively related to the expected risks/costs thereof (Alm et al., 1992; Caballe and Panades, 1997; Cebula and Coombs, 2009; Erard and Feinstein, 1994; Pestieau et al., 1994).

According to this perspective, to the representative individual taxpayer, the expected risks/costs from not reporting or from underreporting taxable income and/or of exaggerating tax deductions to the IRS are increased by an increase in *AUDIT*, the percentage of filed federal personal income tax returns that is formally audited by IRS examiners. Thus, the higher the proportion of income tax returns that is audited by IRS personnel, the greater the likelihood that the tax evasion activities of an individual will be detected. If an individual is selected for an audit, they are typically notified by mail that they must make an appointment for a face-to-face encounter with an IRS agent. The appointment usually occurs at the local IRS offices. The person(s) being audited must bring tax records such as receipts and other records.

Interestingly, if an individual has not intentionally engaged in tax evasion, the meeting might be just an inconvenience (the value of lost time), although the possibility that the 'innocent' taxpayer has illegally evaded taxes is not 0 because mistakes do happen. For example, a person with a consulting business or with numerous clients might have misplaced or failed to receive his or her Form 1099-MISC and therefore unintentionally evaded income taxation by understating gross income. Alternatively, an individual might have misunderstood IRS tax forms and made filing mistakes as a result. Thus, even the innocent taxpayer can incur costs from an audit in addition to the value of lost time.

For the taxpayer who is an actual or would-be tax evader, the experience of an IRS tax audit could imply non-pecuniary ('psychic') costs (such as anxiety) along with costs in terms of the value of lost time, as well as pecuniary costs. The latter could involve outlays for legal or other representation above and beyond any potential unpaid taxes, interest and penalties that are assessed by the IRS on detected unreported taxable income. Clearly, then, the higher the audit rate, the higher the expected costs of tax evasion and the greater the disincentive to evade taxes.

In addition to *AUDIT*, it is hypothesized that the expected risks/costs of tax evasion also include the magnitude of the IRS imposed penalties (*PENALTY*) should one's tax evasion activities be successfully detected by the IRS. This penalty has two components: (1) interest due on unpaid taxes[3] and (2) penalties per se. The latter form of penalty kicks in when the individual is found to owe more than \$5000 in unpaid federal taxes. In such a circumstance, the penalty is 20 percent of the total amount of the unpaid taxes. Thus, if a tax evader has engaged in substantial tax evasion, the tax liability consists of:

$$[(\text{unpaid taxes} + 20\% \times \text{unpaid taxes}) + \text{interest} \times (\text{unpaid taxes} + 20\% \times \text{unpaid taxes})$$

Clearly, the greater the value of *PENALTY*, *ceteris paribus*, the greater the expected costs of income tax evasion and hence the lower the degree of aggregate personal income taxation that is expected (Baldry, 1987; Cebula, 2001).

Accordingly, the expected gross costs of income tax evasion can be expressed as:

$$EGC = h\ (AUDIT,\ PENALTY) \qquad (12.4)$$

where the expected costs of tax evasion are positively related to the IRS audit rate and the IRS taxes and penalties imposed on detected tax evasion behavior. It should be noted that additional factors could be included among the expected costs of tax evasion. One notable example would be the possibility/probability of imprisonment for felony tax evasion.

12.4 THE DECISION TO ENGAGE IN INCOME TAX EVASION

Once an individual (or couple) evaluates the expected benefits from income tax evasion and the expected costs of income tax evasion, they are so situated as to make the decision as to whether or not to evade income taxes. This in reality requires information on a variety of factors, such as their anticipated tax rate and tax liability if they are in compliance with tax laws, their subjective secondary benefits (if any) from tax evasion, recent if not current IRS audit rates, recent if not current IRS penalty interest rates and their skills in 'hiding income' and/or exaggerating tax deductions.

In theory, if the individual/couple has the above information, a necessary condition for a rational decision maker to engage in income taxation is that

$$EGB > EGC \tag{12.5}$$

In other words, a necessary condition for the individual to be willing to engage in income tax evasion is that the value of the expected benefits from tax evasion outweigh the value of the expected costs of that tax evasion.

Naturally, the more risk averse a person is, the greater the weight assigned to the *EGC* factors. Hence, risk aversion behavior would tend to induce a lower probability of income tax evasion.

NOTES

1. Schedule A is used to report deductions, such as home interest, charitable contributions and the like.
2. Schedule C is used to report net profit from independent contractor income.
3. This interest is computed on a monthly basis.

13. The black market and the silver screen: economics in *The Third Man*

Michael R. Hammock and Art Carden

13.1 INTRODUCTION

Like many other parts of Europe, Vienna, Austria, following the Second World War was an unpleasant place. Postwar Vienna is the setting of *The Third Man*, one of the great noir films from the height of popularity of that classic style of film-making.[1] It tells the story of an American, Holly Martins (played by Joseph Cotten), who comes to Vienna to meet a friend, Harry Lime (played by Orson Welles). He arrives only to find his friend has died in a traffic accident. But two questions linger: 'Was it really an accident?' and 'Is Harry Lime really dead?' It turns out that the solution to the mystery revolves around the black markets that have sprung up as a result of rationing in postwar Vienna. Black markets are a natural consequence of rationing, price controls and other forms of interference with the market. Unfortunately, while the movie hints at the issues surrounding drug rationing, it does not explicitly make clear the economics of the problem. These hints are nonetheless useful for demonstrating some of the consequences of interfering with free-market mechanisms. *The Third Man* is, fundamentally, an exploration of the economic and social origins of villainy. Once we understand the economics, the motivation of an important character becomes clearer, and we are compelled to wonder if he is truly the real villain – is Harry Lime the real cause of the suffering of the sick?

In *The Third Man*, we learn that some form of penicillin rationing is in place in postwar Vienna. The main character, Holly Martins, arrives in Vienna intending to meet with Harry Lime, who has asked Martins to come to write for his medical charity. Martins arrives only to find that Lime has recently been hit by a truck and killed. The police force (which is jointly operated by the British, French, Russians and Americans) are interested in Martins, and Martins soon discovers that this is because they had been searching for Harry Lime. Police Major Calloway informs

Martins that Harry Lime was involved in black market activities, and he notes that the police had been looking for him for some time. Martins incorrectly guesses that Lime was involved in something petty – gasoline, or tires, perhaps. He eventually learns that it was more serious: Harry Lime was in business in the black market for penicillin.

What social forces produced the Harry Lime character? Lime's involvement in the black market for penicillin has several important implications, and it illustrates important economic principles. The first is straightforward: price controls and rationing produce black markets. Black markets are generally those in which commerce is conducted not by legitimate businessmen but by 'legitimate businessmen' – those with a comparative advantage in illegal and unethical activities.[2] Black markets in some commodities, such as gasoline or tires, may be regarded as relatively innocuous. In this case, Harry Lime was involved in a far more serious black market and one with even more dire consequences. The film also raises a more subtle point. People are often willing to concede that the market produces and allocates most goods with relative efficiency. 'Essentials,' like water, health care and other goods are somehow 'different.' They are regarded by some as simply 'too important' to be left to the market. *The Third Man* illustrates what happens when we decide that the provision of a certain good – penicillin, in this case – is deemed to be 'too important' to be left to the market.

13.2 THE BLACK MARKET FOR PENICILLIN

Why was there a black market for penicillin? Answering that question requires a brief look into the price controls and rationing policies of the period. Many governments during the Second World War used price ceilings to hold down the prices of goods, making operation of the military less expensive (as well as allowing politicians to achieve domestic political goals). A price ceiling set below the market price will increase the quantity that consumers want to purchase,[3] while at the same time decreasing the quantity that businesses are willing to produce. This gap between the quantity demanded and the quantity supplied is a shortage. Shortages have been the result of price ceilings throughout history. This artificially created shortage (by price controls) is illustrated in Figure 13.1.

The price control creates a shortage equal to the difference between quantity demanded under price control and quantity supplied under price control. The impact on social welfare is straightforward. In an unhampered market, consumers would enjoy a surplus equal to the area of

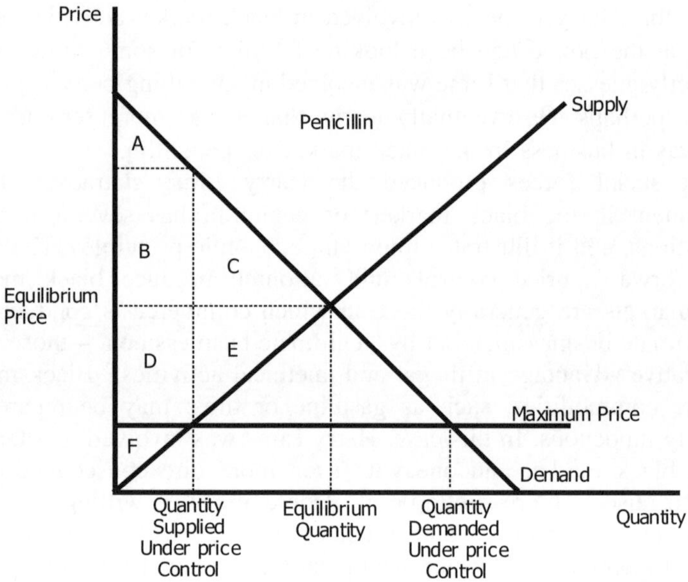

Figure 13.1 The penicillin price ceiling

polygons A, B and C. Producers would enjoy a surplus equal to the area of polygons D, E and F. Under the price control, rectangle D is transferred to consumers, but society at large loses C + E in the form of deadweight loss. Those aren't the only costs: the rectangle given by C + D also disappears as people 'pay' for the penicillin with their time rather than money. These shortages are the natural, albeit unintended, consequences of price control. It is true, of course, that in the unregulated market not everyone who wants penicillin (that is, not everyone who places a value greater than zero on penicillin) gets it, but under the price control, even fewer get penicillin!

Eliminating these pervasive shortages required a more elaborate solution. Governments have used consumption quotas to limit the amount that consumers could buy, while guaranteeing a certain quantity of the good could be purchased.[4] In the USA and Britain, cards, coupon books and stamps were issued, redeemable for a certain quantity of goods, such as meat, sugar, clothing and other goods. In Vienna, rationing cards were issued monthly on a per-person basis for meat, butter, beans, peas, cooking oil, sugar, milk and other goods.[5] The plot of *The Third Man* revolves in part around penicillin rationing.

Penicillin's medical uses were discovered between 1941 and 1943, and it began to be used by the US military to fight infections. Eventually, it was released for public consumption for Americans, but demand grew rapidly once its effectiveness became known. Penicillin initially was issued by a committee according to its efficacy in treating particular illnesses, which angered the public. Many were upset that the military received priority, since one of the primary uses of penicillin by the military was to treat gonorrhea, which was arguably the fault of the soldiers who contracted it.[6] In the movie, Austria is apparently pursuing (or is being forced by the Allies to pursue) a similar policy. Penicillin is scarce, and its price is set by the government. It is unclear exactly what rationing mechanism, if any, the government is using to deal with the shortage.

We still have not answered the question of why the police are so interested in Lime and his black market activities. When Martins presents Major Calloway with the possibility that Lime was murdered, Calloway says, 'I'm not interested in whether a racketeer like Lime was killed by his friends or by an accident. The only important thing is that he's dead.' The authorities are so interested in black market activities that they cannot be bothered to investigate a possible murder.

The problem confronting the police is that when governments impose restrictions on markets, markets try to find ways around them. The price controls and rationing of penicillin have created a 'black market' for illegally sold penicillin. Those who have the financial means and the contacts can buy this penicillin from people like Harry Lime, albeit at high prices. But here buyers run into one of the problems with black markets. Because competition in a black market cannot take place in the open, it is difficult for customers to get information about product quality and the trustworthiness of sellers. Harry Lime has been using a medical orderly named Harbin to steal penicillin from military hospitals. Lime dilutes it in order to increase the quantity, and then resells it to sick people at £70 per tube. The diluted penicillin is ineffective, however, which results in significant harm, and even death, to patients. Calloway takes Martins to a children's hospital in order to show him the suffering Lime has created.

None of this would come as a surprise to an economist. A similar phenomenon occurs with illegal narcotics and rent-controlled apartments today (Miron and Zwiebel, 1995). Black markets have also appeared in the USA when price controls were placed on meat, clothing and gasoline (Anderson, 1991). The gap between quantity supplied and quantity demanded means that there are people who would benefit from buying and people who would benefit from selling, but these people cannot legally conduct trade – so they trade illegally. But a black market operates without some of the normal mechanisms of a market. There is no court or arbitrator to judge and enforce contracts; deals can be enforced or broken with violence. It is difficult for reputation to work as a mechanism, because advertising and public knowledge are inherently harmful to a criminal enterprise. Even competition is constrained since the government is actively trying to drive producers out of the market. The producers who remain in the market are men like Harry Lime, who reveals his own perspective toward the end of the film. He delivers a chilling speech about his willingness to repeatedly swindle customers, dooming them to death for '£20,000 … free of income tax.' It is true that even in a black market sellers generally do not want to kill their customers, as it is unprofitable. In some circumstances, however, a man like Lime can make a quick profit from selling a dangerous and unreliable product. He is not in the market for the long term, and it is difficult to see how there could be such a market in the case of diluted penicillin – there are no repeat customers.

But are we taking away the correct lesson from this? Undoubtedly Lime is a villain, but is he the ultimate cause of the suffering of the ill? What we do not hear is what would happen if the rationing were perfectly enforced. The shortage would still exist. Some people would still go without penicillin. There would still be suffering and death, but more directly at the hands of the state. The price controls themselves are the cause of suffering. The black market is a response to the price controls – it is a symptom, not the disease itself. Harry Lime himself is a product of the price controls; it is inevitable that such people will appear given this social context. It would be unreasonable to expect a criminally inclined entrepreneur such as Lime to ignore an opportunity for profit.

If it had not been for the price controls on penicillin, Lime would surely have been in some other business – perhaps legal (probably not), but almost certainly less harmful to his customers. Perhaps he would have been in the business of forging papers (passports, visas and so forth), as he did for his girlfriend, Anna Schmidt. That would surely have been less harmful than selling diluted penicillin. It may have even been a beneficial act, helping people evade the efforts of governments (particularly Eastern European governments coming under the Soviet shadow) to restrict their movements. At the end of the movie, we are left with the unpleasant likelihood that Anna, whose false papers have been discovered, will be forced back to Czechoslovakia. Who ensured that the Russians would find out about Anna's forged papers? Harry Lime, who traded knowledge of the forged papers for his own safety, within the Russian-controlled zone of Vienna.

The Third Man carries implications for another aspect of the academic and popular debate about health care. It has often been maintained that basic health care is a 'fundamental right' that should be provided without regard to cost. Some might ask, 'what price life?' and indeed there are some who find the thought of placing a price tag on health care morally repugnant. Still, a lower price is more attractive than a higher price. It is possible to argue that the government has an interest in making penicillin more easily available to the public by reducing its price.

One might be concerned about the access to penicillin by the poor. A price ceiling below the equilibrium market price, however, puts one in the awkward moral position of advocating the death of more than one wealthy person (who can afford the penicillin at its unregulated price) in order to save one poor person. This further assumes that the poor will be the ones able to obtain the (very scarce) penicillin after the price control is implemented. It is likely that those most able to secure penicillin will still be those with the resources and connections to do so – the wealthy. In other words, even if one believes that the life of a wealthy person is worth less than the life of a poor person, the price control probably will not redistribute penicillin in the desired direction. Finally, by restricting the profit to be had from producing pencillin, the price control reduces the incentive to expand production with long-term investments in new capital for penicillin production, condemning future victims to death, rich and poor alike. The policymakers have these deaths on their hands.

The character of Harry Lime is instructive. Lime is a black market opportunist responding to the incentives laid out by society. Production and distribution of penicillin are sharply controlled by the allied government (as are the production and distribution of many goods, such as tires and gasoline). Price controls and government rationing are usually undertaken by those who wish (however naively) to see that everyone gets his or her 'fair share,' irrespective of willingness or ability to pay. However, underpriced resources will lead entrepreneurs to strive to fill demand through legal or illegal means as incentives dictate. When different forms of otherwise legitimate economic activity are deemed illegal, those with a comparative advantage in villainy (like Harry Lime) will move to fill the gap.

To the extent that price controls and rationing are used as part of health care reform, we will get a similar result: shortages will occur, and black market producers will try to fill these gaps, sometimes with dangerous results. In a free market, Lime perhaps would have been a small-time dealer of questionable used cars. In this case, however, the prospect of rents accruing to those who can distribute penicillin meant that Lime could enter a business that was considerably more lucrative and dangerous. It is still possible that he would have sold adulterated penicillin, even without price controls. There are, for example, scam artists on eBay who rip off buyers, and disappear, even though eBay's prices are completely market-determined. It is unlikely that Lime could do this persistently on a large scale, however, due to the legal recourse available to consumers and due to the open competition Lime would face.

So if not for the price controls, things might have turned out very differently. But how, then, can we distribute drugs to the sick? How can the government get the penicillin it needs for the military? The answer is simple: buy them. If the government needs drugs, let it buy them at market prices. If it drives the price up, the higher price will lure a greater quantity of penicillin onto the market. The price of penicillin conveys crucial information to producers. When it goes up, the price signals to producers that more penicillin is wanted. The fact that the production and distribution of penicillin is a life-and-death matter does not cause the principles of economics to be revoked. By refusing to pay this price – by legally mandating a lower price – the government is prohibiting an increase in the quantity of penicillin supplied, effectively sentencing sick people to death and creating villains like Harry Lime. In postwar Vienna, when communist central planning was in vogue and there were economists who believed that incentives do not matter, we might be able to understand how 'well-meaning' people could impose price controls. Fast forward 60 years and consider someone who imposes price controls after a natural disaster. This is the moral equivalent of selling tainted penicillin; it is a false solution that can change a problem from 'serious' to 'fatal'.

Certainly we can agree that the Harry Lime character is a ruthless black market con man. His actions resulted in the death and anguish of many sick people. An understanding of the incentives created by the system of price controls, however, lays the real blame where it belongs. The real villains are those responsible for the price controls that drive legitimate businesspeople out of the market and increase the relative returns to fraud and racketeering. Harry Lime is but a symptom; the price controls are the disease (cause).

If government intervention gets too extensive, the 'black market' may become the only viable market. If a particular line of business is legally proscribed – to the point that the government is willing to use violence to stop it – then the only viable market interactions may take place on the 'black market' (and they will invariably be characterized by a constant struggle between the state and those with a comparative advantage in racketeering).

13.3 CONCLUDING COMMENTS

The Third Man illustrates but does not explicitly elucidate a fundamental problem with government intervention. Price controls, on the one hand, create shortages; on the other hand, they provide incentives for people to engage in criminal activities. We see this in the fact that Harry Lime – later revealed to be a reprehensible human being – is running a penicillin racket in price-controlled Vienna. The movie stands as one of the great noir films of the 1940s, but its achievements go beyond classic film-making. *The Third Man* illustrates the human consequences of government intervention gone bad.

NOTES

1. The film is described by the Internet Movie Database, available at http://imdb.com/title/tt0041959/, as a political/economic film. It is reviewed by Stephen W. Carson of the Ludwig von Mises Institute at http://www.mises.org/content/film.asp#Third (accessed 12 March 2013).
2. We are grateful to Stephen W. Carson for this point.
3. It is likely, however, that the increase in quantity demanded is small, as demand for penicillin is likely to be inelastic.
4. In some cases, governments instituted coupon rationing without price controls in order to limit private consumption of certain goods, leaving the remaining quantity for military purchases, and redirecting production into other areas.
5. When this chapter was originally written, we were able to learn more about postwar rationing in Vienna from the city's website, http://wien.gv.at. Unfortunately, the specific page containing information on rationing and coupons no longer appears to be available. Based on this now-extinct page, the rules appear to have been somewhat complex, with exceptions and programs for special groups. For example, a couple celebrating a golden anniversary could receive extra flour, cooking oil, sugar, wine and one cake. The limits were raised as conditions improved. Some additional information about price controls and rationing in Vienna can be found in Lewis (2000) and Bischof et al. (2000). According to Lewis, price controls and rationing were a part of aid under the Marshall Plan.
6. For a brief history of penicillin rationing in the USA, see: McGough et al. (2005).

14. Assessing the economic and financial knowledge of adults

Kenneth C. Rebeck and William B. Walstad

14.1 INTRODUCTION

Interest in the financial literacy of adults has increased significantly over the past few decades. The reasons for the change have to do in part with the increased responsibility for personal financial decisions related to retirement contributions, student loans, home purchases, health insurance and other matters. At the same time, the financial world presents more complex financial choices for adults that can lead to serious consequences if there is poor financial decision making. In addition, greater uncertainty affects economic and financial prospects for individuals because of persistent unemployment or underemployment arising from the Great Recession and continuing debates over the fiscal and monetary course for the USA. The results of increased responsibility, greater complexity and a rise in uncertainty are that adults need to know more than ever before about how to manage their personal finances and understand the economic forces that are shaping their current living standard and their future prospects.

The turbulent events related to the economic and financial health of the USA in recent years led us to wonder about the link between adult knowledge of economics and personal finance. Specifically, do factors that influence adults' understanding of personal finance concepts, such as managing a budget or saving for the future, also influence their understanding of basic economics concepts such as cost-benefit decision making and the functioning of markets? Or, alternatively, is a better understanding of economics and effective decision making influenced by a separate set of factors than those that influence personal finance matters? Answers to these questions are important when considering the future approach to creating financial literacy programs and materials for adults. For example, making sound financial decisions about when and how to borrow requires not only knowledge of the available credit alternatives but also an understanding of the benefits and costs of borrowing and the factors that influence interest rates. If programs designed to increase financial knowledge do not at the same time generate an increase in the understanding of economics, this outcome raises questions about the effectiveness or efficiency of such programs because adults benefit from an increase in both types of knowledge.

A substantial amount of important research has been conducted on adult financial literacy and how it affects behaviors related to retirement planning, stock market participation and other financial matters (for example, Hilgert et al., 2003; Lusardi and Mitchell, 2007; Van Rooij et al., 2011). There is debate in this research about how to define and measure financial literacy (Huston, 2010). When financial literacy is assessed it is often measured with only three to five items (Hastings et al., 2012). We decided to use a more comprehensive measure for this chapter so that we could investigate the relationship between the understanding of personal finance (which could be labeled as financial literacy) and the understanding of economics.

In this chapter, we conduct a preliminary investigation of the complementary relationship between economic and personal financial knowledge with a sample of adults. We explore this relationship using a standardized test of personal finance and economic knowledge with 50 items that provides a comprehensive and reliable instrument to study the factors that influence both types of adult knowledge. We administered this test, along with a background questionnaire, to more than 240 adults. Test items were categorized as capturing: (1) personal finance concepts and relationships and (2) economics concepts and decisions. Separate scores were calculated for personal finance and economics. A seemingly unrelated regression system was estimated to measure the influence of background characteristics of adults, including their non-academic life experiences, education level, and prior high school and/or college coursework in personal finance and economics on adult knowledge of both personal finance and economics.

14.2 DATA AND INSTRUMENTS

The approach we used to sample adult knowledge of personal finance and economics followed closely the approach taken in a study of adult economic literacy (Gleason and Van Scyoc, 1995). To obtain the sample, we asked students enrolled in a course on the Principles of Microeconomics at a university in Minnesota to administer a survey to seven to ten semi-anonymous adults. These survey respondents were to be non-students 18 years old or older, willing to answer all items, with no more than two members from any one extended family. No college faculty members were allowed to be surveyed. Of the approximately 55 students completing the course, 31 students completed this extra-credit assignment. Of the 242 adults surveyed, 240 provided a sufficient set of answers to survey questions to calculate test scores. Among the 240 adults with test scores, 215 provided usable information on the variables that were included in the regression analysis (described later).

It should be observed that each of the 25 adults excluded from the regression analysis failed to answer one of the survey items that were used to create the explanatory variables. Using the answers provided by those who did answer a particular question, the 25 excluded adults were nearly identical to the 215 adults who completed the entire survey with regard to age, gender and income. They were about 20 percentage points less likely to be married or have children. They were about six percentage points more likely to have taken an economics course and 15 percentage points more likely to have taken a personal finance course in high school, and had roughly the same number of college economics courses, on average. As would be expected of a sub-sample of survey respondents who chose not to answer all of the test items (a requirement in the directions for the survey responses to be useful), these 25 adults scored lower on the Financial Fitness for Life (FFFL) test by about 8 percentage points than the 215 with complete tests.

The test portion of the survey included all items on the FFFL high school test (Walstad and Rebeck, 2005). The reader is encouraged to consult the *Financial Fitness for Life: High School Test Examiner's Manual* for a discussion of the validity and reliability of the exam, and for a list of items and their associated item statistics. The manual also provides information on the norming sample of high school students whose results are presented in this chapter for comparison.

This instrument is a standardized test for measuring the achievement of high school students in courses that use the FFFL curriculum materials. This standardization process means that items were carefully written and revised, reviewed by content experts, field tested with students and subject to statistical analysis before being included in the final version of the test. Detailed test results, both overall and for each item, are reported for the large sample of school students who participated in the final test administration. The 50 items on the test are evenly distributed across five content themes: (1) the economic way of thinking; (2) income; (3) saving; (4) spending and credit; and (5) money management. The answers to these 50 items were used to compute the total test score and sub-scores for each of the five content areas.

Although the test was developed for a particular curriculum, the content for the test items was prepared so that the test would be suitable as a general measure of student achievement in most high school courses teaching personal finance. In fact, the FFFL test manual shows the distribution of the FFFL test items across five major categories listed in national content standards for personal finance (income; money management; spending and credit; saving; and investing) as developed by the Jump$tart Coalition for Personal Financial Literacy. In addition, some of the items focus on economic concepts and decision making as related to personal finance, so that the test manual also reports how items are distributed across national content standards in economics as developed by the Council for Economic Education. Our review of item content for the test manual showed that among the 50 items, 29 can be classified as primarily ones that focus on personal finance topics. The other 21 items can be classified primarily as items covering basic economic concepts or decision making as related to personal finance. This classification differs somewhat from the one used in the FFFL manual (tables 2 and 3, pp. 6–7). The main change for this study is that five items originally listed as personal finance were reclassified as economics and seven items originally listed as economics were switched to personal finance. We switched seven items from economics to personal finance, such as those about interest rates (compounding, rule of 72) and loans (annual percentage rate (APR), non-payment), because they were written in terms of consumer economics. We moved five items from personal finance to economics, such as those related to economic decision making (saving for the future or investment criteria) because the choice or outcome had costs and benefits. The net effect of the changes was minor. Previously, the split for personal finance and economic items was 28 to 22, but now the split is 29 to 21.

This separation of FFFL test items into a personal finance score and an economic score is not meant to suggest a typical course in personal finance taught in high school would not currently include content about an item we coded as 'economics.' The reason for the separation is to reveal the importance, if any, of incorporating economics elements into a personal finance curriculum. We used the two distinctions to create a 'personal finance' score composed of 29 items and an 'economics' score based on 21 items. Using our sample of 240 adults, the KR-20 reliability estimate for the scores determined by the entire 50-item FFFL exam was .88. Fewer items will reduce an estimated reliability, but our sub-set of economics items and sub-set of personal finance items appeared to provide satisfactory internal reliability for both score categories. The reliability for the test with 21 economics items was .70. The reliability for the test with 29 personal finance items was .84.

The other portion of the survey asked questions about the demographics and education of a respondent. From the demographic items we obtained information on a respondent's gender, age, income level, marital status, whether or not they had children and homeownership. The education items asked about the highest level of educational attainment (not a high school graduate, high school graduate only, some college attendance and college graduate). The education items also asked respondents whether they had taken a high school course in economics or personal finance, or both. Among those respondents who had attended college a question was asked about how many college courses in economics they had taken.

14.3 ADULT AND HIGH SCHOOL STUDENT COMPARISONS

Table 14.1 provides the average total scores of the adults surveyed and also their average scores across the five content areas. For comparison, the scores of the high school FFFL norming sample are included in the table. The adults in our sample had an average overall score of 33.70 (67 percent correct). This adult score is significantly greater than either the overall score of 27.84 (56 percent correct) for the high school students who had been taught using the FFFL materials, and the overall score of 22.34 (45 percent correct) for the high school students who had not received any instruction with FFFL materials.

Most high schools are likely to have a mix of students who have been taught some economics and personal finance. Our prior work with high school transcript data from the US Department of Education for the year in which these data were collected (2005) shows that 44 percent of 2005 high school graduates had taken a separate course in economics, either basic or college level (Walstad and Rebeck, 2012). Another 6–7 percent took a separate course in personal finance (for example, consumer economics and consumer education). Combining these percentages suggests that about half of US high school graduates that year took either an economics course or a personal finance course. We can use the test data from the FFFL-instructed group as a rough proxy for the average scores for all high school students with coursework in personal finance and economics and the test data from the non-FFFL group as a rough proxy

Table 14.1 Scores by FFFL theme

Theme		Adults[a] (*n* = 240)	High School With FFFL[b] (*n* = 524)	High School Without FFFL[b] (*n* = 335)
Entire Test (50 items)				
	Mean	33.70	27.84	22.34
	S.D.	(8.15)	(8.72)	(6.52)
1. Economic Way of Thinking (10 items)				
	Mean	6.63	6.38	5.33
	S.D.	(1.65)	(2.01)	(1.74)
2. Income (10 items)				
	Mean	7.59	6.42	5.22
	S.D.	(2.04)	(2.24)	(2.09)
3. Saving (10 items)				
	Mean	5.61	4.42	3.54
	S.D.	(2.18)	(2.02)	(1.61)
4. Spending/Credit (10 items)				
	Mean	6.35	5.32	3.79
	S.D.	(2.18)	(2.36)	(1.76)
5. Money Management (10 items)				
	Mean	7.52	5.30	4.47
	S.D.	(2.02)	(2.37)	(2.17)

Notes:

a. Non-student (or university faculty) adults, Upper Midwest, Spring 2005.
b. 2003–04 High School Norming.

for the average scores for all high school students without personal finance or economics coursework. Weighting the two groups equally would produce an estimate of 25.09 (or 50 percent correct) for the overall score for high school students with and without personal finance and economics coursework. This result indicates that the average high school student knows about a third less than the average adult in our sample, so apparently adults gain more knowledge of personal finance and economics after high school.

The test scores in Table 14.1 also reveal that the average knowledge of adults in our sample is greater than the average knowledge of high school students for each of the five content categories. The differences, however, are not consistent across the five content categories. In percentage terms, adult knowledge of 'money management,' a category consisting primarily of personal finance concepts such as net worth, the basics of checking accounts and types of insurance, is over 20 percentage points greater than that of high school students who had completed the FFFL curriculum. For the categories 'income,' 'saving' and 'spending and credit,' the difference is roughly 10 percentage points. These categories consist of both economics and personal finance items. Adults had only slightly greater knowledge than did high school students of the 'economic way of thinking.' This category consists of topics related to decision making such as strategies for improving one's financial life, cost-benefit analysis, alternatives given up when making decisions and the steps of effective decision making. This difference between the two groups is only 2.5 percentage points.

Table 14.2 presents the percentage of adults who answered each item correctly, along with the percent correct for the two high school samples. As would be expected given the overall scores differences, adults answered more items correctly than high school students. Of the 50 total items, adults had higher item percent correct scores on 41 (82 percent). What Table 14.2 shows in more detail with the item percent correct scores than was shown with the average scores in Table 14.1 is the item variation by theme. The most variation in whether adults or high school students have higher or lower item percent correct scores is shown within the economic way of thinking theme. That variation is reduced substantially for almost all items for the income, saving and spending/credit themes with adults showing higher item percent correct scores. In the case of the money management items, adults score higher than high school students on all items.

Of the 29 personal finance items, adults had higher percent correct scores on 26 (91 percent). Of the 21 economics items, adults had higher percent correct scores on 15 (71 percent). The 20 percentage point difference in personal finance compared with economics scores suggest that for adults life experiences after high school tend to increase knowledge of personal finance substantially more than those life experiences increase knowledge of economics. This extrapolation is speculative of course because it assumes that the high school group's achievement on the FFFL exam is similar to what the adults would have achieved had they also been tested when they were high school students, but it is roughly suggestive of what is likely to be found or expected if an exact comparison could be made.

Table 14.2 FFFL item percent correct

Item	Item Type	Adults (*n* = 240)	High School With FFFL (*n* = 524)	High School Without FFFL (*n* = 335)
Theme 1: Economic Way of Thinking				
1	E-work hours and wealth	0.51	0.58	0.17
2	E-saving decision	0.93	0.94	0.88
3	E-opportunity cost-buying	0.13	0.30	0.14
4	E-benefits and costs	0.91	0.82	0.80
5	E-scarcity and resources	0.44	0.40	0.31
6	E-choices and consequences	0.81	0.80	0.83
7	E-opportunity cost-school	0.90	0.84	0.78
8	E-scarcity and choice	0.79	0.62	0.56
9	E-human resource	0.77	0.52	0.38
10	E-decision-making steps	0.45	0.56	0.47
		0.66	0.64	0.53
Theme 2: Income				
11	PF-job application	0.85	0.76	0.68
12	PF-networking	0.71	0.52	0.39
13	PF-job interview	0.81	0.65	0.46
14	E-Entrepreneurs	0.93	0.86	0.76
15	E-Human capital	0.73	0.54	0.42
16	E-Demand increase	0.63	0.56	0.49
17	E-Job market	0.56	0.71	0.57
18	PF-Gross and net pay	0.75	0.54	0.42
19	PF-FICA contributions Finance	0.72	0.50	0.37
20	PF-Net pay calculation Finance	0.90	0.78	0.66
		0.76	0.64	0.52
Theme 3: Saving				
21	E-opportunity cost-savings	0.29	0.32	0.23
22	PF-compound interest	0.43	0.33	0.23

Item	Item Type	Adults ($n = 240$)	High School With FFFL ($n = 524$)	High School Without FFFL ($n = 335$)
23	E-saving decision	0.72	0.44	0.32
24	E-rule of 72	0.45	0.34	0.25
25	PF-market price risk	0.67	0.44	0.48
26	PF-liquidity risk	0.38	0.36	0.30
27	E-risk and reward	0.72	0.69	0.51
28	E-inflation and real return	0.40	0.22	0.20
29	PF-common stock	0.73	0.55	0.48
30	E-investment decision	0.84	0.73	0.54
		0.56	0.44	0.35
Theme 4: Spending/Credit				
31	PF-purpose of credit	0.70	0.75	0.61
32	E-loans and voluntary trade	0.79	0.63	0.51
33	PF-creditworthiness	0.31	0.34	0.16
34	PF-credit bureau	0.61	0.40	0.27
35	PF-loans and interest	0.83	0.64	0.57
36	PF-loan payment and time	0.65	0.53	0.44
37	PF-APR and loan cost Finance	0.65	0.46	0.36
38	PF-credit card liability	0.25	0.48	0.16
39	PF-pyramid scheme	0.83	0.67	0.48
40	PF-payday loans	0.75	0.44	0.24
		0.64	0.53	0.38
Theme 5: Money Management				
41	PF-disposable income	0.59	0.42	0.37
42	PF-net worth	0.79	0.41	0.34
43	E-saving and income decision	0.70	0.61	0.44
44	PF-debit cards	0.82	0.62	0.50
45	PF-checkbook entry	0.95	0.69	0.59
46	PF-liability insurance	0.87	0.60	0.56
47	PF-collision coverage	0.73	0.44	0.37
48	PF-insurance deductible Finance	0.92	0.61	0.56

Item	Item Type	Adults (*n* = 240)	High School With FFFL (*n* = 524)	High School Without FFFL (*n* = 335)
49	PF-comprehensive coverage Finance	0.43	0.35	0.25
50	PF-whole life insurance Finance	0.73	0.55	0.49
		0.75	0.53	0.45

Note: Item types were coded into one of two categories: Economics (E) or Personal Finance (PF).

Table 14.3 presents the sub-scores achieved by each group on the 29 personal finance items and 21 economics items. The average percent correct scores for adults were remarkably similar for the personal finance sub-test (68 percent correct) and the economics sub-test (66 percent correct). This result indicates that personal finance and economics items were about equally challenging for the adults. That conclusion does not hold for high school students either with FFFL instruction or without it. For either group there is about an 8 point difference between the personal finance score and the economics score. High school students score significantly better on the economics items than the personal finance items. Why this outcome occurs is a mystery, but it may arise from more exposure to economics either directly through formal coursework or indirectly through exposure to economics instruction in other courses. Remember too that about 44 percent of high school graduates have taken a separate course in economics compared with only about 6–7 percent of high school graduates who took a personal finance course. It is likely that the typical high school student has received more economics instruction than personal finance instruction.

Table 14.3 Percent scores on financial sub-test and economics sub-test

	Adults (*n* = 240)	High School With FFFL (*n* = 524)	High School Without FFFL (*n* = 335)
Personal Finance Items (29 items)	68.16 (18.26)	52.26 (18.97)	41.47 (14.34)
Economics Items (21 items)	66.37 (15.77)	60.41 (18.32)	49.13 (15.15)

The interesting issue is what happens after high school. Here the adult and high school data are most telling, especially when compared with the FFFL group. The average score of 68 percent correct for adults on personal finance items is a sizable 16 percentage points greater than the average score achieved from the high school group taught with the FFFL curriculum. By contrast, the average score of 66 percent correct for adults is only 6 percentage points greater than the average achieved by that same group of FFFL high school students. Apparently adults gain a substantial amount of knowledge and understanding of personal finance from life experiences after high school that helps them close the gap. For economics, however, the change in knowledge or understanding after high school is relatively limited, so the gap closing is minimal. This conclusion also holds for high school students without FFFL instruction. Although the gap is quite large for both groups, the differential is 27 percentage points in favor of adults on personal finance, but only 17 percentage points for economics.

14.4 FACTORS INFLUENCING ADULT SCORES

The findings from Tables 14.1, 14.2 and 14.3 suggest that adults learn both personal finance and economics after high school, but larger gains are seen in personal finance. Seemingly unrelated regression (SUR) analysis was used to investigate the factors associated with adult understanding of personal finance and economics and to compare the relative effects of these factors on each type of knowledge. Demographic variables such as gender, age, income and level of educational attainment are factors that are associated with high achievement in many subject areas. It seems reasonable that each of these characteristics might influence understanding of both personal finance and economics. Other factors included in our estimation are likely to have a more direct influence specifically on personal finance or economics knowledge. Those adults who are married, have children or own a home, on average, face more personal finance-related situations. Similarly, if an adult had taken a formal personal finance course in high school, he or she might have a greater knowledge of personal finance than adults who had not taken personal finance in high school. High school economics, on the other hand, might increase the knowledge of economics and effective decision making, as would the number of college economics courses taken.

Two equations were estimated in the SUR analysis. The first one used the percent correct score on the personal finance items as the dependent variable and the second one used the percent correct score on the economics items as the dependent variable. As for the set of explanatory variables, the ones that are expected to influence personal finance knowledge may also influence economics knowledge, and vice versa. Accordingly, each equation included the same set of explanatory variables to capture the effects of gender, age, income, marital status, children, homeownership, and high school and college course-taking on each type of knowledge. The benefit of SUR in this chapter is that it provides a simple approach to test whether the effects of the explanatory variables are individually or jointly equal across equations.

Table 14.4 reports the SUR results. The set of explanatory variables explained 26 percent of the variance in the adults' knowledge of personal finance and 22 percent of the variance in adults' knowledge of economics. Gender (FEMALE) has no statistically significant influence on either score. This outcome was not unexpected as the high school data showed only a minor difference in the overall test scores of high school students between males and females, so apparently this relationship continues to hold into adulthood. The results also show that being married or having children has no consequential effect on either knowledge outcome. Other variables, however, are important and significant. On average, each ten years of age adds about 2.5 percentage points to the personal finance score of adults. Age has a slightly smaller effect on economics knowledge, with each ten years adding about 2 percentage points to the economics test score of adults. The level of education also matters. Relative to adults who did not attend college, adults who attended or completed college have higher average scores. Some college (SOME COLLEGE) increases personal finance scores by about 8.6 percentage points and economics scores by about 7.5 percentage points. College graduates (COLLEGE GRADUATE) score about 10.3 percentage points higher on the personal finance items than adults not attending college, and about 8.1 percentage points higher on the economics items. Income too is associated with higher test scores. Adults earning an income over $70,000 (INCOME > $70K) score about 8.2 percentage points higher on the personal finance items than those earning less, and about 6.1 percentage points higher on the economics items. Homeownership increases knowledge of personal finance by about 9.7 percentage points. The effect of homeownership on economics knowledge is smaller and insignificant. Using a cross-equation Wald test, a test of the null hypothesis that the coefficient on HOMEOWNER is not larger in the financial knowledge equation was rejected at the 0.05 level.

Table 14.4 SUR results

Variable	Dependent Variable FINANCIAL KNOWLEDGE SCORE (%)	ECONOMICS KNOWLEDGE SCORE (%)
GENDER	–0.948	–0.064
(47%)	(0.416)	(0.032)
AGE	0.268*	0.188*
(Mean = 38.60; S.D. = 13.67)	(2.479)	(1.974)
SOME COLLEGE	8.594*	7.518*
(32%)	(2.526)	(2.527)
COLLEGE GRADUATE	10.274**	8.109**
(44%)	(3.011)	(2.718)
INCOME > $70K	8.221**	6.144*
(17%)	(2.638)	(2.255)
MARRIED	–1.430	–1.027
(61%)	(0.471)	(0.387)
CHILDREN	0.685	0.649
(64%)	(0.216)	(0.234)
HOMEOWNER	9.684**	5.469
(71%)	(2.860)	(1.848)
HIGH SCHOOL PERS FINANCE	–1.056	–2.197
(45%)	(0.496)	(1.181)
HIGH SCHOOL ECONOMICS	6.309	7.652*
(10%)	(1.463)	(2.029)
COLLEGE ECONOMICS COURSES	0.854	1.893**
(Mean = 1.00; S.D. = 1.82)	(1.376)	(3.489)
CONSTANT	43.181	47.719
N	*215*	*215*
Chi-square (df = 11)	*93.025***	*73.787***
Adj. R^2	*0.264*	*0.215*

Note: Absolute value of t-statistics in parentheses. * $p < 0.05$, ** $p < 0.01$ two-tailed test.

The two factors we expected to have a larger effect on knowledge of economics – having taken economics in high school (HIGH SCHOOL ECONOMICS), and the number of college courses taken in economics (COLLEGE ECONOMICS COURSES) – each have estimated coefficients that are larger for the economics equation than the financial knowledge equation, and each are statistically significant in the economics equation. Having taken economics in high school increases the score on the economics items by about 7.7 percentage points, while each additional college course taken in economics increases the economics score by about 1.9 percentage points. Neither economics course-taking variable, however, had a statistically significant influence on personal finance knowledge. A Wald test rejected the hypothesis that the coefficients on these economics course-taking variables were not jointly larger in the economics equation. Also, taking a personal financial course in high school does not raise personal finance or economics scores. The lack of a relationship between a course in personal finance in high school and the personal finance score indicates that such courses may not have a lasting effect.

What the SUR results suggest is that for each variable expected to influence both knowledge of personal finance and economics, slightly larger effects were found on knowledge of personal finance. These differences, however, were small, but nevertheless consistently larger in the personal finance equation. For those variables expected to have a larger influence on personal finance knowledge, homeownership appears to have a sizable influence, but a smaller and insignificant influence on economics knowledge. Both economics course-taking variables that were expected to have a larger influence on economics knowledge than personal finance knowledge show the expected outcome, with economics coursework significantly increasing economics scores but not personal finance scores. In closing this section of the chapter, it is observed that no significant influence was found for high school economics when coded as 1 for any adult having taken economics in high school. It is likely that a college course in economics overrides any effect of the high school course for those adults who had college economics. We coded HIGH SCHOOL ECONOMICS as a 1 only for those adults who had not attended college.

14.5 CONCLUSION

Knowledge of economics and personal finance are often considered complementary. An understanding of the economic way of thinking, combined with knowledge of personal finance, can help people make wiser financial decisions. This chapter has explored the factors that influence adult knowledge of personal finance, on the one hand, and economics, on the other hand. We sampled adults with a previously developed and reliable standardized test of economics and personal finance and conducted a background survey. Results of this study indicate that the production of economics and effective decision-making knowledge is quite separate from the production of personal finance knowledge. We found that age, income and general education after high school are associated with greater understanding of both economics and personal finance, but while personal finance knowledge is affected by certain life experiences, such as owning a home, knowledge of economics is not. As would be expected, formal study in economics increased economic knowledge, but such coursework did not significantly increase knowledge of personal finance.

An implication from our study is that preparing adults to handle their financial and economic world requires combined education of both personal finance and economics. One type of knowledge will not substitute for the other and how the two types of knowledge complement each other for adults is not fully understood. What is important to recognize is that personal financial education that focuses almost exclusively on facts and relationships will not provide a sufficient set of tools or a complete foundation to use when making the vast array of financial decisions that adults encounter over a lifetime and that can be directly or indirectly influenced by economic forces such as markets and government policy. Our results suggest that knowledge of economics and decision-making skills grow with age, but without formal study of economics an adult will have less knowledge of how the economy works and how markets and decision making affect economic outcomes. We think this outcome will adversely affect adults in their personal financial decisions because knowledge of economics helps adults better understand those decisions. Personal finance programs and materials that are economics-based will better prepare adults to conduct sound financial planning and decision making.

15. Success in the economics major: is it path dependent?

Carlos J. Asarta, Roger B. Butters and Andrew Perumal

15.1 INTRODUCTION

The economics profession has consistently demonstrated an interest in increasing the number of students exposed to economics, providing students with a quality education and identifying the key determinants of student success in the economics curriculum. Several strategies have been recommended, and include implementing an applied approach rather than a theoretical approach (Okoye, 2011), exposing students to economics as early as possible in their undergraduate careers (Fournier and Sass, 2000), assigning popular professors to principles courses (Becker, 1997; Margo and Siegfried, 1996), modifying the curriculum to make economics more accessible to a broader range of students (Bartlett, 1995) and presenting material in a way that is relevant and interesting to students (Siegfried and Raymond, 1984).

Economics departments have also demonstrated the desire to improve the quality of economics education by using formal assessment plans and department reviews by outside economists (Kasper, 2005; Myers et al., 2011). Furthermore, several researchers have explored how to improve the quality of the economics curriculum. Okoye (2011) argued that the economics curriculum should be designed to reflect the diverse needs of all economics majors, not just those who will go on to complete graduate degrees. Hoyt (2003) indicated that economics departments should focus on relevant economic content, active learning techniques and examples based on current events and everyday life to make the study of economics a fulfilling social science. Some have suggested implementing honors thesis requirements or senior projects to enhance the value of the economics major (Elliott et al., 1998; Siegfried, 2001). Others have argued that improving the economics curriculum does not require 'radical' changes (Elzinga, 2001; McMillin, 2003; Siegfried and Sanderson, 2003).

Additionally, researchers have attempted to identify the key determinants of student success in the economics curriculum. Some of the variables examined include mathematical ability, grade point average (GPA), attendance, choice of textbook, class size, instructional quality, learning medium, prior economic knowledge, attitudes, personality and relatability (Arias and Walker, 2004; Grove et al., 2006; Lagerlof and Seltzer, 2009; Marburger, 2006; Pyne, 2007; Ramsett et al., 1973; Rask and Bailey, 2002; Swope and Schmitt, 2006).

Yet, even with all this attention devoted to improving the quality of the curriculum, increasing the number of students exposed to economics and identifying the determinants of student performance, Hansen (2001) concluded that in order to be successful in economics, students must be able to access and command existing knowledge, and then apply it to create new knowledge. Given the importance of existing knowledge in the creation of new knowledge, examining the way undergraduate students approach the economics curriculum is relevant and important. Specifically, are students who follow the traditional approach of principles–intermediate–advanced courses more proficient in economics than students who follow other learning paths? Is there a sequence that seems to be more effective at creating knowledge than others?

Siegfried et al. (1991, p. 202) eloquently captured the fundamental reason behind our interest in exploring the importance of course order and sequencing:

> The economics major is a helix – plowing the same ground repeatedly at progressively greater depth. It goes beyond a simple accumulation of exposure to successively more topics. Basic principles introduced in beginning courses are reinforced and refined in intermediate theory courses and then rediscovered and extended in elective courses.

To address the question of course sequencing, we examine the academic transcripts and demographic characteristics of 359 economics majors who graduated from a large Midwestern university between August 1999 and December 2010. Our goal is to determine whether or not following a principles–intermediate–advanced sequence of economics courses has a significant impact on the overall performance of students graduating with an economics degree. We find that success in the economics major is path dependent, and identify predictors of path choice. To our knowledge, the economics education literature has not approached the question of sequencing before, perhaps due to the enforcement of course prerequisites at most institutions of higher education. Additionally, our research provides a more accurate picture of what determines the overall performance of economics majors in upper division economics courses.

15.2 THE ECONOMICS MAJOR

The Department of Economics at the University of Nebraska–Lincoln (UNL) is administratively housed in the College of Business. Unlike many universities, however, undergraduate students can complete an economics degree either in the College of Business (BS degree) or in the College of Arts and Sciences (AS degree). The Business College is the third largest college within the university, and its undergraduate business students must complete a minimum of 120 credit hours and have at least a 2.5 cumulative grade point average to graduate.

The Arts and Sciences College is the largest college within the university. Its students are required to complete a minimum of 125 credit hours and have a 2.0 or higher cumulative grade point average to graduate. When compared to BS degrees, AS degrees have lower entry and graduation cumulative GPA requirements, but a higher credit hour completion requirement due to a foreign language component that all students need to satisfy prior to graduation. Completion of BS and AS economics majors averaged approximately 22 and 19 graduates per year, respectively, between the years 2000 and 2010 (Asarta and Butters, 2012). Both peaked in 2010, showing a gain in interest and popularity for the economics degree. As a proportion of their means, BS and AS economics degrees have experienced a positive trend at the university since the year 2000. National data show a similar growth pattern for economics degrees over the same sample period (US Department of Education, 2010).

A striking characteristic of the economics program examined in our study is that students are not required to complete the major in a fixed sequence once a basic core of three courses is completed. These courses are principles of macroeconomics, principles of microeconomics and statistics. Statistics requires only sophomore standing and the completion of introductory calculus as prerequisites, while principles courses are open to first year students meeting minimum credit hour requirements. Students are strongly encouraged to complete at least one of the intermediate theory courses prior to enrolling in upper division field courses. However, no barriers exist to prevent them from registering for advanced courses without having first completed an intermediate theory course. As a result, we are able to investigate whether or not success in the economics major is path dependent. More formally, do students who follow the recommended principles–intermediate–advanced path perform better in upper division field courses than students who elect to follow a less strict educational program?

15.3 DATA AND DESCRIPTIVE STATISTICS

Data were obtained with the permission of the Institutional Review Board and collected from computerized student transcript records. Descriptive statistics for our sample of 359 economics majors are presented in Table 15.1. We measure performance in upper division economics courses using the variable *Econ400 GPA,* which is the weighted-average grade, expressed numerically, for all advanced level economics courses completed by each student in our sample. This variable serves as a metric of success in the major and mastery of the economics curriculum. Average course grades are calculated using a scale of 0 to 4 points, with an 'F' letter grade receiving 0 points and an 'A/A+' letter grade earning 4 points. Overall, the students' average grade in upper division courses is 3.18, which is equivalent to a 'B' letter grade.

The variables *Race, Residency* and *Gender* are indicator variables that take the value of 1 if the student is Caucasian, a resident of Nebraska or male, respectively. We find that all three are broadly similar, with approximately 78 percent of the students in our sample being Caucasian, 76 percent residents and 71 percent male. The low proportion of female students (29 percent) is consistent with the steadily declining trend of female undergraduates completing economics majors in the United States over the past decade. Siegfried (2010) found that the percentage of undergraduate economics degrees completed by women declined from a peak of 34 percent in 2003 to 30 percent in 2009.

Age is a student's age, in months, at the time of matriculation into the university and has a mean value of 228 months, or 19.1 years. *ACT Composite* is the composite score on the American College Testing (ACT) aptitude test. In our sample, the average ACT score is 22.4. Although we have more disaggregated ACT measures for these students, for parsimony we only report the composite score. Our coefficient estimates were not sensitive to using disaggregated ACT measures. Additionally, while the majority of students complete the ACT aptitude test prior to attending the university, there are a number of students who, for diverse reasons (for example, foreign students), complete only the Scholastic Assessment Test (SAT). We use the correspondence table

Table 15.1 Descriptive statistics

	Mean	S.D.	Min	Max	*N*
Econ400 GPA	3.182	0.618	0.75	4	359
Race	0.777	0.416	0	1	359
Residency	0.757	0.429	0	1	359
Gender	0.713	0.452	0	1	359
Age	227.602	17.901	190	364	359
ACT Composite	22.373	9.913	0	35	359
AS Major	0.440	0.497	0	1	359
Time in Major	32.905	12.902	0	112	359
Transfer Courses	0.251	0.434	0	1	359
Transfer Credits	9.887	24.593	0	192	359
Off Path	0.426	0.495	0	1	359
On Path	0.574	0.495	0	1	359
Strict	0.359	0.480	0	1	359
Semi-strict	0.214	0.411	0	1	359
Principles and Intermediate Grades					
P. Macro	3.305	0.730	0	4	359
P. Micro	3.417	0.723	0	4	359
P. Macro (A/B Letter Grades)	0.833	0.374	0	1	359
P. Micro (A/B Letter Grades)	0.861	0.347	0	1	359
Int. Macro	3.227	0.730	0	4	355
Int. Micro	3.265	0.768	0.667	4	352
Field Course Grades					
History	3.089	0.700	1.333	4	97
Institutional	3.036	0.849	0	4	102
International	3.322	0.619	1	4	270
Labor	3.154	0.765	0	4	121
Money and Banking	2.583	0.856	0	4	150
Public Finance	3.000	0.782	0.667	4	89
Quantitative	3.400	0.830	0	4	68
Regional	3.247	0.695	0	4	54

developed by Dorans (1999) to transform SAT scores into equivalent composite ACT scores. This transformation was only necessary for data collected prior to 2005 and is not available for the different SAT sub-scores. Equivalent composite ACT and SAT scores were available in student transcripts beginning in 2005 and follow the concordance table developed by the College Board (2009).

AS Major is an indicator variable that takes the value of 1 if the student completed the economics major within the College of Arts and Sciences. The location of an economics department, and by default its effect on the economics curriculum, has been debated in the literature. For example, Siegfried and Bidani (1992) concluded that the location of an economics department has a minimal impact on the curriculum. On the other hand, Dean and Dolan (2001) concluded that location has a significant impact on a program's characteristics. Graduates from the College of Arts and Sciences account for 44 percent of all economics majors. The remaining 56 percent completed their degree in the College of Business. *Time in Major* represents the number of months between the time a student first took principles of macroeconomics or microeconomics and their last economics course. In our sample, 25 percent of students transferred courses from outside institutions as represented by the variable *Transfer Courses*. For estimation, we use the actual number of credit hours transferred, *Transfer Credits*. Students transferred an average of 10 credit hours.

We divide our student cohort into two distinct groups depending on the extent to which they followed the recommended sequence, or path, of courses in the economics major. *Off Path* includes students who completed at least one advanced level economics course before completing any intermediate theory course. *On Path* includes students who completed at least one intermediate theory course before enrolling in advanced economics classes. The latter is the strongly suggested, and recommended, sequence of courses for economics majors. In our sample, 43 percent of students fall into the *Off Path* category, while 57 percent of students are classified as *On Path*. We further disaggregate the *On Path* students into two sub-groups. Students in the *Strict* group completed all intermediate theory courses before taking an advanced level course, and account for 36 percent of students in our sample. Students included in the *Semi-strict* group completed only one intermediate theory course before enrolling in advanced level courses, and comprise 21 percent of students in the sample.

The variables *P. Macro, P. Micro, Int. Macro* and *Int. Micro* represent the performance of students in principles and intermediate economics courses and are calculated using a scale of 0 to 4 points, with an 'F' letter grade receiving 0 points and an 'A/A+' grade earning 4 points. We use several ability measures because using a single ability variable tends to result in very large differences in the estimates of learning outcomes (Grove et al., 2006). Overall, students performed best in principles of microeconomics and worst in intermediate macroeconomics. Additionally, two indicator variables, *P. Macro (A/B Letter Grades)* and *P. Micro (A/B Letter Grades)*, were created to account for students who completed principles of economics courses with an 'A' or 'B' level letter grade (value of 1). There were 83 percent of students completing principles of macroeconomics, and 86 percent completing principles of microeconomics, with an 'A' or 'B' level letter grade. Given that a 'B' level letter grade is the average grade earned by economics majors in these two classes, these variables identify students who performed at, or above average in principles courses.

Finally, we measure the performance of students in advanced level courses for each of the major fields of study offered by the economics department. These variables were created following the procedure used to calculate *Econ400 GPA*. Of the eight major areas offered, students performed best in the quantitative economics courses, and worst in the money and banking classes.

15.4 ESTIMATION AND RESULTS

We estimate the significance of path dependence on student success in the economics major using the following education production function:

$$Econ400\ GPA_i = F(D_i, M_i, P_i) \qquad (15.1)$$

where *Econ400 GPA* is a function of student demographic characteristics, *D*, major-specific characteristics, *M*, and chosen path, *P*. Results are presented in Table 15.2.

We begin by estimating a baseline model that relates demographic and major-specific variables to performance in the economics major without considering the extent to which students adhered to the recommended path. The baseline results indicate that race, residency, age, college and the number of credits transferred from other institutions have no significant effect on student performance in upper division courses. These results are robust across specifications. However, the coefficient on student gender (Male = 1) is both negative and highly significant, suggesting that female students outperform their male peers in upper division coursework. This is true for every specification of the model and

Table 15.2 Regression results

	(1) Baseline	(2) Off Path	(3) Off Path	(4) Off Path	(5) Off Path
Race	–0.071	–0.066	0.005	–0.034	0.007
	(0.090)	(0.089)	(0.078)	(0.081)	(0.075)
Residency	–0.011	–0.002	–0.023	0.003	–0.015
	(0.084)	(0.084)	(0.073)	(0.076)	(0.070)
Gender	–0.235***	–0.237***	–0.178***	–0.174***	–0.153***
	(0.070)	(0.069)	(0.060)	(0.063)	(0.058)
Age	–0.023	–0.021	–0.019	–0.020	–0.019
	(0.018)	(0.018)	(0.016)	(0.016)	(0.015)
Age^2	0.000	0.000	0.000	0.000	0.000
	(0.000)	(0.000)	(0.000)	(0.000)	(0.000)
ACT Composite	0.017***	0.016***	0.006	0.006	0.002
	(0.004)	(0.004)	(0.003)	(0.004)	(0.003)
AS Major	–0.043	–0.033	–0.035	0.026	0.001
	(0.063)	(0.063)	(0.054)	(0.057)	(0.053)
Time in Major	–0.010***	–0.010***	–0.007***	–0.007***	–0.006***
	(0.002)	(0.002)	(0.002)	(0.002)	(0.002)
Transfer Credits	–0.001	–0.001	–0.001	–0.001	–0.001
	(0.001)	(0.001)	(0.001)	(0.001)	(0.001)
Off Path		–0.144**	–0.095*	–0.099*	–0.079
		(0.062)	(0.054)	(0.056)	(0.052)
P. Macro			0.412***		0.315***
			(0.038)		(0.041)
P. Micro				0.366***	0.220***
				(0.041)	(0.043)
Constant	5.902**	5.679**	4.272*	4.586**	3.945*
	(2.512)	(2.499)	(2.176)	(2.264)	(2.103)
N	359	359	359	359	359
R^2	0.114	0.124	0.338	0.283	0.383

Note: Standard errors in parentheses. * $p<0.10$, ** $p<0.05$, *** $p<0.01$.

is a significant deviation from previous research in economics education (Butters and Asarta, 2011). There are two other variables, *Time in Major* and *ACT Composite*, which significantly impact student performance in upper division economics courses. The positive significance of the *ACT Composite* variable is consistent with past research in economics education (Ballard and Johnson, 2004; Barr and Carr, 1980; Becker, 1997; Wetzel, O'Toole, and Millner, 1991; Yang and Raehsler, 2005). The negative and significant coefficient on *Time in Major*, however, seems to suggest that the longer students take to complete the economics major, the less likely they are to succeed in the upper level economics curriculum. This finding may be indicative of human capital depreciation.

Next, we introduce dummy variables to measure the effect of the chosen path on student success. In Model 2, the *Off Path* coefficient is negative and significant indicating that, at the most basic level, success within the major is path dependent and that there is measurable value in completing at least one intermediate economics theory class prior to enrolling in advanced courses. In Models 3 and 4 we introduce the variables *P. Macro* and *P. Micro*, the students' grades in principles of macroeconomics and microeconomics. In each of these specifications, the coefficients on the grade and *Off Path* variables are positive and significant. However, in Model 5, where we include the grade for both principles of macroeconomics and microeconomics, the grade variables remain positive and significant but the coefficient on *Off Path* becomes insignificant.

At first glance, our results seem to indicate that there is a significant advantage to following the suggested course path for students majoring in economics. However, at a more fundamental level, performance in the principles of economics sequence is a better predictor of performance in upper division classes than course sequencing. Indeed, this is a result we would almost expect. Students who do well in foundational economics courses likely have the academic and reasoning skills that will enable them to excel in the major.

Although this finding may be true in a global sense, within the economics major itself, there are areas of specialization that differ from one another in terms of difficulty and quantitative rigor. This effect is compounded further by the fact that some courses in the major are actively marketed to non-economics majors as interdisciplinary electives. We address this issue by extending our analysis and performing a field-by-field estimation. The results are presented in Table 15.3. The first column in the table denotes the subfield for which the model is estimated, and the second provides the model specification (from Table 15.2). For parsimony, we report only the coefficients for the *Off Path*, *P. Macro* and *P. Micro* variables.

Table 15.3 Regression results by economics subfield

	Model	*Off Path*	*P. Macro*	*P. Micro*	Constant	*N*	Adj. R^2
History	(2)	–0.166			–0.088	97	0.175
		(0.135)			(9.698)		
	(5)	–0.221*	0.519***	–0.012	–9.631	97	0.374
		(0.119)	(0.106)	(0.086)	(8.640)		
Institutional	(2)	–0.172			10.523*	102	0.142
		(0.164)			(5.403)		
	(5)	–0.128	0.168	0.394***	5.556	102	0.288
		(0.150)	(0.110)	(0.118)	(5.061)		
International	(2)	–0.188**			4.767	270	0.098
		(0.073)			(2.989)		
	(5)	–0.110*	0.340***	0.131**	3.773	270	0.317
		(0.064)	(0.050)	(0.052)	(2.605)		
Labor	(2)	–0.134			–0.730	121	0.162
		(0.135)			(5.968)		
	(5)	–0.037	0.292***	0.373***	0.224	121	0.391
		(0.117)	(0.084)	(0.102)	(5.104)		
Money and Banking	(2)	–0.297**			7.261	150	0.137
		(0.138)			(5.311)		
	(5)	–0.297**	0.253**	0.164*	5.307	150	0.202
		(0.133)	(0.108)	(0.095)	(5.140)		
Public Finance	(2)	–0.388**			6.899	89	0.094
		(0.166)			(6.513)		
	(5)	–0.284**	0.433***	0.191*	7.024	89	0.392
		(0.137)	(0.103)	(0.109)	(5.402)		
Quantitative	(2)	0.094			10.528	68	0.249
		(0.209)			(12.249)		
	(5)	0.147	0.447***	0.068	6.528	68	0.344
		(0.197)	(0.167)	(0.193)	(11.731)		

	Model	*Off Path*	*P. Macro*	*P. Micro*	Constant	*N*	Adj. R^2
Regional	(2)	–0.451**			13.259	54	0.167
		(0.182)			(11.979)		
	(5)	–0.361*	0.306**	0.050	9.839	54	0.230
		(0.180)	(0.139)	(0.126)	(11.705)		

Note: Standard errors in parentheses. * $p<0.10$, ** $p<0.05$, *** $p<0.01$. For parsimony, only the coefficients on the *Off Path, Principles of Macroeconomics* and *Principles of Microeconomics* variables are reported.

For the Institutional, Labor and Quantitative areas, performance in the principles of macroeconomics and microeconomics courses tends to be the dominant determinant of performance at the advanced level. The *Off Path* variable is insignificant for these three areas of study. However, fields such as History, International, Money and Banking, Public Finance and Regional economics require both good performance at the principles level and adherence to the course sequencing recommended to students.

From an advisory viewpoint, these results suggest that completing coursework in intermediate theory either before, or concurrent with, advanced coursework (*On Path*) may or may not be essential depending on two factors: (1) what is the student's intended field of study? and (2) how well did the student perform in principles of economics? If the student performed well in principles of economics there may be no need to adhere to the suggested course sequence depending on the field of study. However, we find that as a general rule, students electing to stay on the recommended path perform better in advanced economics classes than students who do not.

In an effort to understand which student characteristics predict path choice, we estimate a logit model using demographic and major characteristics, as well as student grades in principles of economics. Results are reported in Table 15.4. Estimated coefficients for Model 6 indicate that none of our variables are significant predictors of path choice. We extend our analysis by replacing the overall grade variables in principles with dummy variables taking a value of 1 if a student's grade was in the 'A' or 'B' level letter grade, and 0 otherwise. While the *P. Macro (A/B Letter Grades)* dummy variable is both positive and significant in Model 7, the variable *P. Micro (A/B Letter Grades)* is insignificant in Model 8. This indicates that students who perform well in principles of macroeconomics are more likely to stay on path, but that the same is not true for students who perform well in principles of microeconomics.

As a robustness check, we include both dummy variables in Model 9 and find, once again, that only the coefficient on *P. Macro (A/B Letter Grades)* is significant. The fact that the *P. Micro (A/B Letter Grades)* coefficient is insignificant may very well be the result of the sequential nature of these two classes. Given that the grade in principles of macroeconomics is a significant determinant of whether or not a student follows the recommended path, and given that students in our sample generally take principles of microeconomics after macroeconomics, the decision to adhere to the path is most likely based on the first grade earned, before a student completes the second principles course.

These findings, together with those in the previous models, present us with several interesting results. First, grades in principles of economics courses are a good predictor of performance in advanced economics coursework. Second, adhering to the outlined course sequence (*On Path*) is also a strong predictor of performance in upper division coursework. Finally, whether or not students follow the recommended sequence is largely dependent on how they do in principles of macroeconomics, generally their first course in the major. Again, from an advisory standpoint, this suggests that although it may be acceptable to advise a student with high grades in principles to deviate from the suggested course sequence, the principles–intermediate–advanced sequence is still preferred.

As a final extension, we note that our definition of 'On Path' students actually consists of two distinct groups: those who completed all intermediate coursework prior to completing advanced courses (*Strict*) and those who completed only one intermediate course prior to engaging in upper division coursework (*Semi-strict*). Once students complete their first intermediate class, they can then choose to complete the second intermediate course or immediately begin upper division coursework. In an effort to better understand the reasons for choosing the semi-strict path over the strict path, we use logit analysis on two sub-samples of our economics majors. The sub-samples are for students who took intermediate macroeconomic theory before intermediate microeconomic theory, and vice versa. We hypothesize that a student's intermediate course grade will significantly influence the student's path choice. We base our hypothesis on findings by Calkins and Welki (2006), who showed that successful performance in economics classes increases the likelihood of students pursuing an economics degree. Our dependent variable is dichotomous, taking a value of 1 if the student followed the semi-strict path and 0 if the student followed the strict path.

Table 15.4 Logit results: predicting the decision of path choice

	(6) On Path	(7) On Path	(8) On Path	(9) On Path
Race	–0.098	–0.109	–0.136	–0.109
	(0.320)	(0.320)	(0.319)	(0.320)
Residency	–0.260	–0.257	–0.258	–0.258
	(0.302)	(0.302)	(0.301)	(0.303)
Gender	0.122	0.090	0.068	0.091
	(0.249)	(0.248)	(0.246)	(0.248)
Age	–0.060	–0.057	–0.062	–0.057
	(0.066)	(0.066)	(0.066)	(0.066)
Age^2	0.000	0.000	0.000	0.000
	(0.000)	(0.000)	(0.000)	(0.000)
ACT Composite	0.003	0.007	0.011	0.007
	(0.016)	(0.015)	(0.015)	(0.015)
AS Major	–0.242	–0.270	–0.249	–0.267
	(0.225)	(0.223)	(0.226)	(0.228)
Time in Major	–0.010	–0.009	–0.011	–0.009
	(0.008)	(0.008)	(0.008)	(0.008)
Transfer Credits	–0.004	–0.004	–0.004	–0.004
	(0.004)	(0.004)	(0.004)	(0.004)
P. Macro	0.161			
	(0.175)			
P. Micro	0.198			
	(0.180)			
P. Macro (A/B Letter Grades)		0.619**		0.614**
		(0.297)		(0.305)
P. Micro (A/B Letter Grades)			0.176	0.023
			(0.329)	(0.341)
Constant	7.438	7.561	8.460	7.558
	(8.956)	(8.938)	(8.900)	(8.939)
N	359	359	359	359
Pseudo R^2	0.023	0.024	0.016	0.024
LLR	–239.324	–239.016	–241.055	–239.014

Note: Standard errors in parentheses. * $p < 0.10$, ** $p < 0.05$, *** $p < 0.01$. LLR is the logarithm of the likelihood ratio.

Results of the logit estimation are presented in Table 15.5. In addition to the variables used in estimating Equation (15.1), we include the grades that students received in intermediate macroeconomics and microeconomics, as well as an interactive variable for whether or not the course was the first intermediate course taken. It is important to note that the sum of the sample sizes in the two models exceeds the overall sample size of 359 students. This is due to the fact that students following the strict path are used in both regressions when making comparisons against students who completed either intermediate macroeconomics or intermediate microeconomics first.

While we find that transfer credits do not play a role in determining grades in higher level economics courses, we now discover that the more credit hours students transfer, the more likely they are to choose the strict path. Furthermore, we find that doing well in the intermediate theory courses, irrespective of which course it is, has a positive and significant impact on a student's choice to follow a semi-strict path. In short, students who excel in their first intermediate course are more likely to move quickly through the major by immediately enrolling in advanced courses. In a similar fashion, students who are less successful in their first intermediate course proceed cautiously through the major.

15.5 CONCLUSION

The lack of prerequisites for advanced level economics courses at a major Midwestern university provides a unique opportunity to investigate whether or not course sequence affects student performance in upper division economics classes. Our research finds that the longer students take to complete the major the lower their grades are in advanced courses, that performance in principles of macroeconomics and microeconomics are strong predictors of performance later in the major, and that, contrary to previous research in economic education, female students tend to outperform their male peers in upper division economics courses. We extend our investigation by estimating regressions for subfields in economics and show that following the principles–intermediate–advanced course sequence can be a significant predictor of grades in advanced coursework for certain fields but not others. We find that performance in principles of economics courses remains a robust predictor of success regardless of the field of advanced study.

Given that the choice of course sequencing can be a significant determinant of student success, we estimate a logit model to determine the predictors of path choice. For our general 'On Path' students, their

Table 15.5 Logit results: predicting strict versus semi-strict path choice

	(1) Strict	(2) Semi-strict
Race	–0.464	–0.435
	(0.454)	(0.450)
Residency	0.326	0.588
	(0.450)	(0.449)
Gender	0.043	0.123
	(0.357)	(0.358)
Age	0.134	0.092
	(0.106)	(0.097)
Age^2	–0.000	–0.000
	(0.000)	(0.000)
ACT Composite	–0.001	–0.010
	(0.023)	(0.023)
AS Major	–0.082	–0.039
	(0.320)	(0.322)
Time in Major	0.009	0.004
	(0.015)	(0.016)
Transfer Credits	–0.020**	–0.020*
	(0.010)	(0.010)
Int. Macro	0.014	
	(0.229)	
Int. Macro 1st	0.337***	
	(0.092)	
Int. Micro		0.157
		(0.239)
Int. Micro 1st		0.284***
		(0.094)
Constant	–19.744	–14.372
	(14.353)	(13.319)
N	204	203
Pseudo R^2	0.081	0.071
LLR	–124.207	–124.659

Note: Standard errors in parentheses. * $p < 0.10$, ** $p < 0.05$, *** $p < 0.01$. LLR is the logarithm of the likelihood ratio.

grade in principles of macroeconomics is the only significant predictor of path choice. We further disaggregate the 'On Path' group into students who strictly followed the recommended course sequence and students who completed only one intermediate course prior to enrolling in advanced courses. We find that students who excel in their first intermediate theory course are more likely to immediately enroll in advanced courses, while other students are likely to proceed more cautiously.

This research has direct practical applications to advising students. As a general rule, economics students should be advised to follow the recommended sequence of coursework. High performing students in principles and intermediate courses, however, may be able to customize their path depending on their chosen field of study. As such, when advising economics students, counselors should ascertain their grades in principles and intermediate courses, discuss intended fields of study and evaluate the pros and cons of following the recommended course sequencing. In short, the skilled advisor will take the time to assess the student's capabilities, understand her educational goals and then make recommendations based on the findings discussed above.

16. Economic literacy and policy perceptions during the financial crisis

Paul W. Grimes, Kevin E. Rogers and William D. Bosshardt*

16.1 INTRODUCTION

Most of the economic education research literature is classroom oriented. Most empirical studies tend to focus on student learning, pedagogy and content. Although the issues surrounding the long-term retention of economic knowledge have been discussed for at least 50 years (Saunders, 1971, 1980; Stigler, 1963), only recently have researchers turned their attention to the impact of economic education on personal outcomes observed long after the student leaves the classroom. Examples of this new stream of investigation include a series of articles by Allgood et al. (2004, 2010, 2011), which analyses the long-term effects of economic understanding on civic behavior, labor market experiences and personal financial decisions. In another study, Grimes et al. (2009) explore the influence of economic education on banking and consumer experiences. Extending on this prior work, we examine how investments in economic human capital influence perceptions concerning the causes of the recent financial crisis and resulting Great Recession. Using the results of a national survey that included a short quiz over basic economic concepts, we are able to distinguish between perceived and revealed economic understanding. The results indicate that economic literacy influenced the survey respondents' opinions concerning the financial crisis and public policy options. Those with relatively high levels of economic human capital were more likely to blame the mortgage industry for the crisis and prefer reducing the role of government as a solution to the resulting economic problems. Our survey methodology and analysis of the empirical results are presented and discussed in the following sections.

16.2 SURVEY

Building on previous national studies of economic understanding, we conducted a national survey to capture consumer experiences and perceptions surrounding the financial crisis and ensuing recession. In collaboration with the Gallup Organization, Walstad and Larsen (1992) demonstrated how an abbreviated quiz on economic relationships and current events can be incorporated into a survey and used to measure the basic economic understanding of adults. Our survey emulates this technique as well as capturing a measure of each respondent's attainment of formal economic education. Each respondent identified the completion of any economics, personal finance and business courses during their formal educational experience.

Officially, the US economy entered a recessionary phase during December 2007. The financial crisis occurred during the fall of 2008, with the recession ending in June 2009 (NBER, 2010). Our data were collected one year later, during March and April 2010, by the Survey Research Laboratory of the Social Science Research Center at Mississippi State University. Telephone interviews with adult respondents were conducted using a simple random sample of telephone numbers from households throughout the nation. The household telephone numbers were selected using random-digit-dialing (RDD) sampling procedures. The sample includes households with unlisted numbers, cell numbers and land-line numbers. The sampling error for the total dataset (binomial response option with a 50/50 split) is no larger than +/– 3.5 percent at a 95 percent confidence interval.

The final sample included 1408 households from all 50 states and the District of Columbia. Table 16.1 provides an overview of the sample's basic characteristics. The respondents' demographic characteristics reflect those expected for a national telephone survey. More than half of the respondents were female and two-thirds were married or living with a partner. Nearly one in every three of the households surveyed had children living at home. The average respondent's age was slightly more than 54 years and the racial distribution is consistent with national figures, with minorities slightly under-represented (US Department of Commerce, 2012). Approximately 60 percent of the sample reported household incomes below $80,000, with a like percentage reporting ownership of a savings account. Interestingly, the data indicate a relatively high incidence of civic engagement, with 92 percent of the survey respondents reporting that they voted in the 2008 presidential election. Interestingly, this voter participation rate is significantly higher than the 64 percent of all voting-age citizens that voted that year (US Department

Table 16.1 Sample profile (total surveyed 1408)

Respondent Characteristic	*N*	Value
Male	1408	42.3%
Race:		
White	1379	83.1%
Black		11.0%
Asian		1.2%
Native American		1.0%
Hispanic	1406	3.8%
Mean Age in Years	1372	54.3 (14.9)
Marital Status:		
Married	1402	63.9%
Single, Living with Partner		2.8%
Single, Living Alone		12.1%
Divorced		10.3%
Widow		9.6%
Separated /Don't know		1.2%
Households with Children at Home	1402	29.6%
Geographic Location:		
Urban	1408	25.6%
Suburban		54.8%
Rural		19.7%
Household Income:		
Less than $20,000	1408	10.7%
$20,001 to $40,000		18.0%
$40,001 to $60,000		17.2%
$60,001 to $80,000		13.3%
$80,001 to $120,000		16.1%
Greater than $120,000		11.5%
Not Known		2.5%
Refused		10.7%
Savings /Investment Instruments Owned:		
Savings Account at Bank or Financial Institution	1366	72.0%
401(k) or Similar Retirement Account		54.0%
IRA or Roth IRA Account		40.4%
Non-retirement Stocks, Bonds or Mutual Funds		35.6%
Life Insurance Policies		62.4%
Voted in 2008 National Elections	1307	92.1%

Table 16.1 continued

Respondent Characteristic	*N*	Value
Educational Attainment:		
Less than High School Degree	1401	5.9%
High School Degree		25.2%
Some College		17.9%
Associates or Technical Degree		11.1%
Bachelors Degree		23.4%
Graduate Degree		16.5%
Economics Score Category – Gallup Quiz:		
Low (0, 1 or 2 out of 7)	1399	33.0%
Middle (3 or 4 out of 7)		37.6%
High (5, 6 or 7 out of 7)		29.4%

Note: ( ) indicates standard deviation. Variations in *N* reflect respondents' refusal to answer specific questions. For income, refused observations are presented as a separate category.

of Commerce, 2012). As expected, a vast majority of the respondents reported completion of high school and/or additional educational attainment beyond the secondary level. Taken together, the characteristics reported in Table 16.1 indicate that the survey captured a generally representative sample of American households, and that the resulting data are appropriate to analyse the questions under investigation.

Given that the primary motivation for this study was to examine the impact of economic education on a person's perceptions and opinions concerning the financial crisis and public policy, Table 16.2 summarizes the economic education background of the survey participants. As shown in the last column, 36.2 percent of all respondents reported completing no formal economics courses; an almost identical 36.5 percent of respondents reported taking an undergraduate college course as their highest level of formal economics training. The prevalence of economics in the American college curriculum is seen in the fact that 70.4 percent of those in the sample with a Bachelors degree had completed at least one undergraduate economics course. Of those with only a high school diploma, less than half, only 43.1 percent, reported completing an economics course. This is consistent with the historic distribution of economics course mandates across state curriculums at the secondary school level (Grimes, 2012).

Table 16.2 Highest economics course taken by educational attainment

Highest Economics Course Taken	Less than High School Degree (%)	High School Degree (%)	Bachelors Degree (%)	Graduate (%)	Overall Population (%)
None	76.6	56.9	18.3	20.4	36.2
High School	13.4	43.1	11.3	6.9	20.7
Undergraduate			70.4	32.5	36.5
Graduate				40.3	6.6

16.3 ECONOMIC LITERACY AND EDUCATION

Table 16.3 provides two perspectives on the economic literacy of the survey respondents. The top panel of the table reports how the respondents rated their own level of economic understanding, from poor to excellent; the bottom panel of the table reports the percentage of correct responses to seven basic economic questions taken from the Gallup survey noted above. The Gallup Quiz questions included in our survey and derived from Walstad and Larsen (1992) are reproduced in the Appendix. The resulting data are reported for the full sample and broken down by the level of formal economic education reported by each respondent – no formal economic education, only studied economics in high school, studied economics in college and studied economics in graduate school.

The vast majority, approximately 79 percent, of the full sample rated their economic knowledge as fair to good. Overall, 55 percent rated their understanding as good or excellent. Those who had studied economics at the college level were much more likely to rate their understanding as good relative to those whose only formal exposure to economics was in high school – 53.2 percent versus 36.6 percent. Likewise, those with high school economics were more confident in their understanding relative to those with no formal economics education, although the gap was much smaller. The same patterns were seen for those respondents rating their understanding as excellent.

The Gallup questions were designed to measure actual economic literacy across seven basic areas of knowledge. For the full sample, the proportion answered correctly was near 50 percent for most questions, with the average being 3.3 questions out of seven. However, two outliers

Table 16.3 Perceived and revealed economic literacy

	Full Sample	No Economics	With High School Economics	With Undergraduate Economics	With Graduate Economics
	N = 1393	*N* = 501	*N* = 290	*N* = 509	*N* = 93
Self-perceived Economics Understanding:					
Excellent	11.8%	7.2%	10.7%	14.3%	25.8%
Good	43.2%	35.9%	36.6%	53.2%	48.4%
Fair	36.1%	42.7%	42.1%	28.3%	24.7%
Poor	8.9%	14.2%	10.7%	4.1%	1.1%
Average Score (out of 7)	3.3	2.8	3.0	3.9	4.3
Correct Response to Basic Question Concerning:					
Measurement of Economic Growth (GDP)	45.6%	34.2%	37.1%	57.7%	68.8%
Definition of Federal Government Deficit (Spending, Taxes)	49.7%	39.5%	44.6%	59.8%	65.2%
Identify Institution Responsible for Monetary Policy (The Fed)	43.5%	33.9%	36.0%	52.9%	67.7%
Example of Fiscal Policy (Taxes)	23.9%	20.6%	24.7%	25.8%	29.0%
Indentify Primary Determinant of Wages (Productivity)	54.7%	52.3%	51.9%	58.5%	55.4%
Erosion of Purchasing Power (Inflation)	55.8%	48.9%	55.5%	60.2%	68.8%
Market Determination of Prices (Supply and Demand)	62.5%	52.1%	54.1%	75.0%	76.3%

Note: *N* varies slightly down the columns as some questions were refused.

were observed – the percentage correctly answering the fiscal policy question was well below this mark, at just less than 24 percent, and the percentage correctly answering the supply and demand question was above the mark, at almost 63 percent. Table 16.3 shows that the level of revealed economic literacy was positively correlated with the level of reported economic education. The percentage of correct responses for the high school only subsample was consistently higher than those for the no economics subsample for all but one of the seven questions. The subsample that studied economics in college scored higher on all seven questions than those with only high school economics.

Perhaps the most interesting aspect of the data reported in Table 16.3 is the apparent difference between perceived and revealed economic knowledge and understanding. A sense of 'false confidence' is evident in the fact that even though significant numbers of respondents at all levels of economics education reported a good or excellent understanding, most questions were correctly answered less than 60 percent of the time.

16.4 PERCEPTIONS OF THE CAUSES AND SOLUTIONS TO THE CRISIS AND RECESSION

The survey asked each respondent about perceived causes and solutions to the financial crisis and ensuing recession. Specifically, the survey asked, 'Where do you place responsibility for the current economic crisis?' The possible responses are found in Table 16.4, which reports the means for each answer. The respondents' choices were not mutually exclusive – any or all of the agents listed could be identified as accountable. The response most often given was 'Wall Street and the large banks,' followed by 'former President Bush,' 'the US Congress' and 'the mortgage industry.' Community banks were listed less than half as frequently as any other possible response. Interestingly, the Federal Reserve and President Obama – who was about a year into office at the time of the survey – were also held relatively faultless.

Of course, our interest is to determine whether economic knowledge and understanding influenced these responses. The number of correctly answered Gallup Quiz questions was summed for each survey respondent. As noted earlier, these scores ranged from 0 to 7, with an average of 3.3. In addition to the overall mean for each possible response, Table 16.4 shows the breakdown for those scoring 2 or below (the low group) and those scoring 5 or higher (the high group) on the Gallup Quiz. These two groups represent the bottom and top third of the score distribution for the overall sample.

Table 16.4 Who respondents held responsible for crisis

Response	Mean (%)	Mean of Low Economics Knowledge (%)	Mean of High Economics Knowledge (%)
Of the 1305 who responded with some blame:	Who Placed Responsibility on:	Who Placed Responsibility on:	Who Placed Responsibility on:
Wall Street and the large banks	59.7	56.3	62.5
Community banks	16.3	17.6	13.9
The mortgage industry	42.7	34.1	48.9
The US Congress	46.3	46.6	50.4
The Federal Reserve System	26.6	25.4	28.2
Former President Bush	47.7	54.1	37.5
President Obama	25.0	29.0	22.9
Of the total 1408 surveyed:			
None of the above	3.5		
Don't Know/Not Sure	3.3		
Refused entire question	0.5		

As seen in Table 16.4, economic knowledge did impact who was held responsible for the crisis. Those who had a high score on the economics test (top third) were more likely to blame the mortgage industry for the crisis than those who scored low. Furthermore, those with low levels of revealed economics understanding were relatively more likely to hold former President Bush responsible for the crisis.

In terms of policy solutions to the recession, the survey asked respondents 'To solve the financial crisis policymakers must:' The possible responses are given in Table 16.5, which also reports the means for each answer. Again, the results are presented for the overall sample and broken down across low and high scoring groups.

Most answers received about 40 percent support – except for 'increasing government spending,' which only 16 percent of the respondents believed was a viable solution. Recall that the survey was conducted one year after the primary fiscal stimulus, which was not successful in bringing down the unemployment rate.

Table 16.5 Respondents' opinions on solutions to problems

Response	Mean	Mean of Low Economics Knowledge	Mean of High Economics Knowledge
Of the 1276 who identified at least one solution:	Who Thought Action Was a Solution: (%)	Who Thought Action Was a Solution: (%)	Who Thought Action Was a Solution: (%)
Maintain low interest rates	37.0	40.3	33.2
Increase government spending to stimulate the economy	16.0	17.3	16.8
Reduce federal taxes to stimulate the economy	37.4	36.4	41.4
Reduce the role of government so the private sector can rebound	39.6	35.4	45.0
Increase government regulation on banks and Wall Street	43.1	40.0	44.0
Place limit on CEO pay	42.7	50.9	27.9
Of the total 1408 surveyed:			
None of the above	4.9		
Don't Know/Not Sure	4.0		
Refused entire question	0.4		

In terms of solutions, high economic knowledge respondents tended to favor lower interest rates relatively less (probably realizing that interest rates were already historically low). Reducing taxes and reducing government spending were two solutions that also increased in popularity with higher economic knowledge (reflecting free market attitudes), although increased regulation of Wall Street was also more popular. Finally, the biggest observed difference was on the limits on Chief Executive Officer (CEO) pay. While 50 percent of low economic knowledge respondents thought this was a good idea, only 28 percent of high economic knowledge respondents did.

In sum, economic knowledge appears correlated with people's perceptions about the crisis and policy responses. Those with relatively higher levels of revealed economic understanding tended to select more free market-oriented responses. One final interesting point concerns the respondents who answered 'Don't Know' to the responsibility and policy questions. Those so responding had substantially lower scores on the economic knowledge test – only a 2.00 average (out of 7) for those who did not know where to place responsibility, and 1.67 for those who did not know if any of the solutions were appropriate. So, those who said they don't know, probably did not know.

16.5 REGRESSION RESULTS

A series of probit equations was estimated to further examine the relationship between economics education and the respondents' views on blame and solutions to the financial crisis and Great Recession. Specifically, the equations took the following general form:

Respondent's Opinion = *f* (*Economics Courses*, *Economics Test Score*, *Educational Attainment*, *Household Income*, *Household Demographics*, *Location*)

The empirical specification for each of the variables representing the independent elements included in the model is found in Table 16.6. Table 16.7 presents the marginal effects derived from the probit results for where the survey respondents placed blame for the financial crisis.

Table 16.6 Specifications of independent variables by category

Variable	Specification
Economics Courses	
High School	Highest level economics course completed was in high school = 1; Otherwise = 0
College	Highest level economics course completed was in college = 1; Otherwise = 0
Graduate School	Highest level economics course completed was in graduate school = 1; Otherwise = 0
Economics Score	
Low	Respondent scored 2 or less on Gallup Quiz = 1; Otherwise = 0
Middle	Respondent scored 3 or 4 on Gallup Quiz = 1; Otherwise = 0
High	Respondent scored 5 to 7 on Gallup Quiz = 1; Otherwise = 0

Variable	Specification
Educational Attainment	
High School Graduate	Highest educational level completed was high school diploma = 1; Otherwise = 0
Some College	Highest educational level completed less than Bachelors degree = 1; Otherwise = 0
College Graduate	Highest educational level completed was bachelor degree = 1; Otherwise = 0
Postgraduate Degree	Highest educational level completed was Masters or higher degree = 1; Otherwise = 0
Household Income	
Income 1	Less than $20,000 = 1; Otherwise = 0
Income 2	$20,001 to $40,000 = 1; Otherwise = 0
Income 3	$40,001 to $60,000 = 1; Otherwise = 0
Income 4	$60,001 to $80,000 = 1; Otherwise = 0
Income 5	$80,001 to $120,000 = 1; Otherwise = 0
Income 6	Greater than $120,000 = 1; Otherwise = 0
Not Known	Respondent did not know household income = 1; Otherwise = 0
Refused	Respondent refused to report household income = 1; Otherwise = 0
Demographics	
Household Size	Number of family members living at the same residence
Married	Respondent was married or living with partner = 1; Otherwise = 0
Black	Respondent was African-American = 1; Otherwise = 0
Male	Respondent was male = 1; Otherwise = 0
Age	Age of respondent in years
Location	
Urban	Household located in US Census defined urban area = 1; Otherwise = 0
Suburban	Household located in US Census defined suburban area = 1; Otherwise = 0
Rural	Household located in US Census defined rural area = 1; Otherwise = 0

Examination of Tables 16.6 and 16.7 does not reveal clear patterns of blame across successive levels of investment in economic human capital. However, the statistically significant negative marginal effects for Wall Street, community banks and President Bush indicate that those with formal economics education experiences were less likely to place blame on these agents, holding all else constant. Survey respondents who had taken a college economics course were more likely to blame the US Congress and President Obama, *ceteris paribus*.

In terms of economic literacy as revealed through the Gallup Quiz, those with middle and high scores were 6–8 percent more likely to blame the mortgage industry than those with low scores, all else being the same. Those with relatively high scores were also less likely to blame community banks, the US Congress and President Bush.

The results in Table 16.7 also show that those with formal education beyond high school, and those with relatively high household incomes, were more likely to hold the mortgage industry accountable for the financial crisis and recession when compared to those with lower levels of educational attainment and income. Also, higher levels of educational attainment were correlated with a lower likelihood of blame being placed on President Obama, *ceteris paribus*. Demographically, African-American respondents were statistically less likely to assign blame to any of the options except President Bush. In fact, holding all else constant, African-Americans were 20 percent more likely to blame President Bush relative to their cohorts from other racial backgrounds.

Table 16.8 presents the marginal effects for which solutions the survey respondents believed should be taken (keeping in mind this survey was done in the spring of 2010). Certainly no significant consensus was apparent as to whether fiscal or monetary policy was the best approach to solving the effects of the financial crisis and recession. Furthermore, no consensus was found as to whether increasing government spending or decreasing taxes was a better policy. However, market restrictions were not favored by those with formal economics coursework, holding everything else constant. This is seen in the positive and statistically significant marginal effects for the high school, college and graduate school economics course variables. In a similar manner, those with graduate coursework in economics were less likely to favor additional banking regulation, *ceteris paribus*. Those with formal training in economics and those with high scores on the Gallup Quiz were also less likely to advocate for limits on CEO compensation.

Table 16.7 Marginal effects from probit equation: the blame game

Variable	Wall Street and Large Banks	Community Banks	Mortgage Industry	US Congress	Federal Reserve	President Bush	President Obama	None
Economics Courses								
High School	–0.091**	–0.062**	–0.039	0.030	–0.041	–0.067*	0.003	–0.007
College	–0.025	–0.022	–0.046	0.085**	0.001	–0.044	0.049*	–0.013
Graduate School	–0.135*	–0.062	–0.069	–0.021	–0.097	–0.140**	0.041	–0.011
Economics Score								
Middle	0.022	0.001	0.066**	–0.062*	0.003	–0.009	–0.041	–0.025**
High	0.040	–0.043*	0.083**	–0.005	0.033	–0.127***	–0.029	–0.035**
Educational Attainment								
High School Graduate	0.001	–0.024	0.066	0.005	0.014	–0.026	–0.012	0.009
Some College	0.026	–0.049	0.124*	–0.076	–0.002	–0.009	–0.094*	0.001
College Graduate	0.064	–0.079*	0.145*	–0.095	–0.039	–0.041	–0.189***	–0.002
Postgraduate Degree	0.108	–0.099*	0.150*	0.083	–0.048	0.105	–0.227***	0.015

Variable	Wall Street and Large Banks	Community Banks	Mortgage Industry	US Congress	Federal Reserve	President Bush	President Obama	None
Household Income								
Income 2	0.080*	0.017	0.048	0.033	–0.019	–0.012	0.005	–0.016
Income 3	0.060	0.021	0.130**	0.138**	0.037	–0.004	0.038	0.004
Income 4	–0.014	0.063	0.152**	0.142**	0.038	–0.033	–0.001	–0.001
Income 5	0.025	0.040	0.144**	0.075	0.004	–0.018	0.005	0.019
Income 6	0.119*	0.088*	0.164**	0.100*	0.028	–0.027	0.018	0.019
Not Known	0.059	0.038	0.059	0.074	–0.019	–0.067	0.086	–0.006
Refused	0.101*	0.084*	0.213***	0.160**	0.112*	0.071	0.094*	0.014
Demographics								
Household Size	0.001	–0.010	0.003	0.006	–0.002	–0.009	0.007	–0.003
Married	–0.020	0.005	–0.018	0.008	0.031	–0.047	0.026	–0.009
Black	–0.177***	–0.058*	–0.092**	–0.195***	–0.132***	0.203***	–0.272***	–0.011***
Male	–0.095***	–0.002	–0.052*	0.034	–0.027	–0.0184	–0.023	0.029***
Age	0.001	–0.001	–0.002*	–0.001	–0.002*	–0.002*	–0.001	–0.001**
Location								
Suburban	0.028	–0.004	–0.040	–0.028	–0.009	–0.050*	–0.008	0.002
Rural	0.032	–0.074**	–0.058	0.013	–0.022	–0.052	–0.035	–0.003

Note: Statistical significance, two-tailed test: *$p < 0.15$; **$p < 0.05$; ***$p < 0.01$.

Table 16.8 Marginal effects from probit equation: the solution game

Variable	Maintain Low Interest Rates	Increase Government Spending	Reduce Federal Taxes	Reduce Role of Government	Increase Bank Regulation	Limit CEO Compensation
Economics Courses						
High School	–0.009	–0.007	–0.089**	0.090***	–0.024	–0.075**
College	–0.001	0.012	0.018	0.084**	–0.034	–0.056*
Graduate School	–0.028	–0.049	0.037	0.136**	–0.140**	–0.077
Economics Score						
Middle	–0.022	–0.026	–0.015	–0.007	0.034	–0.019
High	–0.040	–0.006	0.054	0.037	0.029	–0.191***
Educational Attainment						
High School Graduate	0.023	0.057	0.104*	0.089	0.043	0.027
Some College	0.018	0.013	0.052	0.115*	0.057	0.047
College Graduate	0.023	0.037	0.039	0.116*	0.139*	0.006
Postgraduate Degree	–0.024	0.147***	–0.086	–0.066	0.273***	0.096

Variable	Maintain Low Interest Rates	Increase Government Spending	Reduce Federal Taxes	Reduce Role of Government	Increase Bank Regulation	Limit CEO Compensation
Household Income						
Income 2	–0.061	–0.056	–0.051	–0.041	0.058	0.002
Income 3	–0.048	–0.063*	0.007	–0.043	0.070	0.022
Income 4	–0.084	–0.031	0.009	–0.040	0.084	0.038
Income 5	–0.006	–0.035	0.026	–0.003	0.043	0.016
Income 6	–0.150**	–0.030	–0.014	–0.018	–0.007	–0.092
Not Known	–0.115	0.002	–0.011	0.032	–0.056	–0.137
Refused	0.005	–0.045	0.010*	0.064	0.020	0.083
Demographics						
Household Size	0.022*	0.002	0.024**	0.014	–0.010	0.002
Married	0.026	–0.035	–0.009	0.068**	–0.034	–0.006
Black	0.010	0.085***	0.046	–0.250***	0.095**	0.073*
Male	–0.029	0.023	0.044*	0.041*	–0.075***	–0.069***
Age	0.001	–0.001	0.003**	0.002**	0.001	–0.002
Location						
Suburban	–0.021	–0.037*	–0.010	–0.003	–0.024	0.014
Rural	–0.032	–0.011	–0.026	0.041	–0.010	0.009

Note: Statistical significance: $^{*}p < 0.15$; $^{**}p < 0.05$; $^{***}p < 0.01$.

Taken together, the results shown in Table 16.8 provide an indication that economic literacy is correlated with favorable opinions toward public policies with a free market orientation. This finding is consistent with the results of studies examining the opinions of professional and academic economists (Alston et al., 1992; Fuller and Geide-Stevenson, 2003). It would not be surprising that those who design the curriculums and teach the courses tend to pass along their views and opinions in addition to knowledge and understanding. Thus, formal economics coursework at the high school level and above appears to transmit to students a predisposition for evaluating public policy from the same market perspective that dominates the viewpoint of professional economists today.

16.6 CONCLUSION

Our national survey of American households found that a substantial proportion of adults have taken formal courses in economics as part of their overall educational experience, regardless of their level of educational attainment. However, the data indicate a false confidence in the self-perception of economic knowledge as revealed by the results of a short test on basic economic concepts and principles.

Survey respondents with relatively high test scores, as well as those with higher incomes, tended to place blame for the financial crisis and recession on the mortgage industry. Those who had completed formal economics coursework at the college level, *ceteris paribus*, tended to place responsibility on the US Congress and President Obama. The probit results also indicate that those with formal economics education at any level favor a reduced role of government in the economy as a solution to the recessionary problems. Economic literacy appears to be associated with favorable opinions regarding market-oriented public policies toward the financial crisis and recession.

Overall, the analysis presented here arguably provides a glimpse into the long-term effects of economics education. Our measures of personal investments in economic human capital are limited by the nature of the survey. The results suggest that the relationship between formal coursework in economics and revealed economic understanding is not necessarily linear or direct. More research is needed to refine measures of economic human capital and to unravel its impact on the formation of personal perceptions and preferred policy prescriptions.

NOTE

* Financial support for this project was provided by an Excellence in Economic Education sub-grant from the Council for Economic Education through funding from the United States Department of Education Office of Innovation and Improvement.

APPENDIX

The following seven questions derived from Walstad and Larsen's (1992) work constituted the Gallup Quiz included in our survey.

1. Economic growth is measured by a change in which of the following?
   - The money supply
   - The Producer Price Index
   - The Gross Domestic Product
   - The balance of payments
   - Don't know
2. There is a deficit in the Federal budget when
   - Government spending is greater than tax revenues
   - US imports are greater than US exports
   - The total demand for money is greater than the total supply of money
   - Don't know
3. Who sets monetary policy in the USA?
   - The President
   - Congress
   - The Federal Reserve
   - The US Treasury
   - Don't know
4. What is an example of fiscal policy?
   - A change in Federal income tax rates
   - A change in the discount rate
   - A change in the prime rate
   - Don't know
5. Which of the following is most likely to improve the wages of American workers?
   - An increase in stock market prices
   - An increase in business inventories
   - An increase in productivity
   - An increase in interest rates
   - Don't know
6. The purchasing power of people's income is most affected by the
   - Inflation rate
   - Trade deficit
   - Balance of payments
   - Don't know

7. The prices of most products in a competitive market are determined by
   - The government
   - Business monopolies
   - Supply and demand
   - The consumer price index
   - Don't know

17. The effects of legalized cheating in the economics classroom

Joel M. Potter and John L. Scott

17.1 INTRODUCTION

Using a classroom experiment, we seek to find the upper bound of grade improvements from cheating by removing the stigma from the activity and by allowing extensive access to others' answers. To remove the stigma, we attempted a value-neutral experiment in which students worked a quiz without collaboration, then switched papers and took ample time to rework the quiz using their partners answers. We found modest effects given the generous experimental opportunities for cheating. Further, the data paint a picture of the internal processes of apparent cheating that the researchers did not expect – the apparent cheating might not even be said to be cheating in the traditional sense. In brief, students do not appraise partners' answers as correct or incorrect and strategically change their answers based on this information.

In the following section, we review the literature on cheating. We discuss our experiment and then discuss the data gleaned from the experiment. After that, we present our results and in the final section, we offer a summary of our work.

17.2 LITERATURE REVIEW

An extensive literature on student cheating assumes that cheating unfairly benefits cheaters and that instructors should curtail the behavior. Some studies investigate self-reported cheating using anonymous student surveys (Burrus et al., 2007; Bunn et al., 1992; Caudill and Mixon, 2005; Grimes and Rezek, 2005; Mixon, 1996; Taylor, 2009). Other research investigates factors associated with cheaters who are detected by allowing students to self-grade assignments (Nowell and Laufer, 1997; Tittle and Rowe, 1973). Van der Ark et al. (2008) attempt to detect 'copier-source' pairs on a multiple choice exam while Hetherington and Feldman (1964) use classroom 'spies' to detect cheating.

Analysing data from 12 separate principles of economics classes, Kerkvliet and Sigmund (1999) test how effective the methods used by teachers actually are at reducing cheating. They hypothesize that a student's expected class grade, number of credit hours and major grade point average (GPA) requirements influence the benefits of cheating. These factors were statistically insignificant in explaining self-reported cheating. Harmon and Lambrinos (2008) use data from two online principles of economics courses to indirectly study cheating. One final exam was proctored while the other exam was not proctored. Using exam score as the dependent variable and GPA as the independent variable (cheating was an omitted variable in their model), they ran separate regressions for the proctored and non-proctored finals. There were 24 observations for the non-proctored final and 38 observations for the proctored final. The non-proctored exam model had an R-squared of 0.008, while the proctored exam had an R-squared of 0.4972. Harmon and Lambrinos (2008) conclude that the relatively low R-squared for the non-proctored exam was caused by an increase of cheating.

Our study is the first to quantify the benefits of cheating on an instructor-graded exam. By explicitly allowing students to copy from their neighbor on a multiple choice exam, we directly observe the effects of legalized cheating. Using this experimental design, we answer the following questions: How much do students increase their grade by cheating from their neighbor? Do all students benefit from this behavior? What is the micro-process of cheating?

In order for cheating to truly benefit a particular student on a multiple choice exam, the student must identify a higher ability student and then copy answers. However, research has shown that individuals often have a distorted view of their own strengths and weaknesses. 'For nearly any subject and socially desirable dimension … most people see themselves as better than average' (Myers, 1998, p. 440). In a study on self-assessment for a macroeconomics exam, Grimes (2002, p. 17) states, 'clearly, the ability of students to monitor what has and has not been learned establishes the basis for choosing between alternative study strategies and effort expenditures.' This ability also relates to a student that is potentially going to cheat. Grimes (2002) also found that although 70.36 percent of macroeconomics students surveyed immediately after a test expected a better score than their performance on their previous test, only 52.17 percent of students actually did better. Nowell and Alston (2007) find that economics students with lower GPAs exhibit overconfidence. While investigating self-recognized competence, Kennedy et al.

(2002) discover that poorer students overestimated their own ability, while better students underestimated their own ability. The 'better than average' effect has also been observed by Stinson and Zhao (2008), Alicke et al. (1995), Brown and Gallagher (1992) and Weinstein (1980).

17.3 EXPERIMENTAL DESIGN

In the first round of our experiment, our control, we gave a ten-question multiple choice quiz to two sections of microeconomics students. Students were under the impression that their performance on the first round would be graded. To discourage cheating during the control round, two professors actively proctored the ten-minute quiz. Students marked their answers on answer sheets and on the test form. The experimenters then collected the answer sheets and passed out fresh answer sheets, asking students to duplicate their answers using their test forms, so that they would have a perfect record of their first round answers. Each student switched the marked test forms with an adjacent student, but retained their own duplicate answer sheets. Students then had five minutes in which they were free to change the answers on their duplicate answer sheets, using the information on the adjacent students' marked test forms. However, when the experimenters began round two they informed students that only the round two results would be recorded, giving students high marginal gains from using their partner's answers. The experimenters attempted to say as little as possible during the process, other than read basic instructions, so as not to use value-laden terms like 'cheating.' All instructions were run as a PowerPoint presentation throughout the experiment in order to minimize experimenter commentary and student talking.

17.4 AGGREGATE RESULTS

From round one to round two, the average score increased from 49.2 percent to 56.5 percent. The purpose of this chapter is to explain what caused this 7.3 percentage point gain. The traditional explanation is that students accurately appraise some of their partners' answers as being better than their own, and copy those better answers. This chapter finds that copying partners' correct answers did not cause the gain. Rather, the increase in average score is explained by the structure of the test, coupled with a heuristic that the data imply that students use.

The heuristic that the data imply is that, *ceteris paribus*, the fact that a partner has a different answer triggers the student to change an answer. This differs from the traditional view in that our student, on average, does not accurately appraise a partner's answer as being correct before changing to match the partner. Our results show that, *ceteris paribus*, if a student's partner has a different answer, the student is much more likely to change their answer than when their partner has the identical answer. Having different answers creates doubt, and the increased doubt increases the probability of change. However, this effect is lessened, although still significant, when the student originally has the correct answer – a priori, a student with a correct answer is, on average, more certain compared to the same student with an incorrect answer, *ceteris paribus*.

This stands in opposition to the 'better than average' effect (Myers, 1998). The 'better than average' effect predicts that students would be overly optimistic in their own answers; hence, students would tend to ignore the information provided by their partners' answers. However, we find that students are pessimistic when their answers differ from their partners' answers. In addition, students cannot discern whether their partner is correct or incorrect; rather, it appears that students change answers because they are pessimistic when their answer differs than their partner's answer.

If students are unskilled at appraising partners' answers, why did our second round performance increase by 7.3 percentage points? The overall gain in grades comes about because students tend to hold onto correct answers and to change incorrect answers – and in changing an incorrect answer, the student does not profit from taking the specific information from the partner, but, on average, the student gains from changing an incorrect answer. Table 17.1 contains the distribution of answers to each question.

We now detail how the data support our assertion. After round one, there are five possible outcomes that can occur for each student's answer to each question. These are:

wrong_partnercorrect: the student has the wrong answer while their partner has the correct answer

correct_partnerwrong: the student has the correct answer and their partner has the wrong answer

sameandwrong: the student and their partner have the same wrong answer

Table 17.1 Summary of answer distribution: round one

	1	2	3	4	5
Question 1	70[a]	7	14	5	–
Question 2	12	20	22[a]	7	35
Question 3	14	12	54[a]	16	–
Question 4	14	62[a]	16	4	–
Question 5	15	26	35[a]	20	–
Question 6	30[a]	3	10	43	10
Question 7	26	2	2	66[a]	–
Question 8	21	26[a]	4	43	2
Question 9	6	15	58[a]	15	2
Question 10	36	5	5	3	47[a]

Note: a. Correct answer.

differentandwrong: the student and their partner have different answers, both of which are wrong

rightright: the student and their partner both have the correct answer.

The multiple choice framework is analytically attractive because of the discrete number of choices for each problem. Given our design, a student can either increase or decrease their score by changing his or her answer. There are three states of nature in which a student can be wrong on round one, and thus increase the score on round two – *wrong_partnercorrect*, *differentandwrong* and *sameandwrong*. There are two ways a student can decrease his or her score from round one to round two – *rightright* and *correct partnerwrong*. The possibilities *rightright* and *sameandwrong* are similar because both students have the same round one answer; hence, a student cannot expect to gain from his or her partner's answer in these cases.

Further, Table 17.2 shows that students with correct answers are more likely to change their answers if their partner has a different (wrong) answer, compared to the situation in which they have the same wrong answer. Finally, if both students have correct answers, *rightright*, students are highly unlikely to change – this happened for only one student on one question.

Table 17.2 The raw success of cheating

	Mean	Opportunities	Number of Changes	Overall Change in Score
wrong_partnercorrect	0.204	196	102	+98
differentandwrong	0.145	139	64	+9
correct_partnerwrong	0.209	201	44	–44
sameandwrong	0.161	155	15	+10
rightright	0.280	269	1	–1
Total	1	960	226	+72

There were 226 changes from round one to round two. Out of these 226 changes, the aggregate score increased by 72 (a 31.9 percent success rate). The only way to gain from the traditional sense of cheating is when the student is wrong and the partner is correct, *wrong_partnercorrect*. However, there were 44 occasions where a student was initially correct, but then changed his or her answer (thereby reducing his or her score).

17.5 HOW DO STUDENTS DECIDE WHEN TO CHANGE ANSWERS?

Cheating is accomplished through a student changing an answer. In this section, we explore the determinants of change. There were 226 changes from round one to round two (960 possible changes). Change occurred in 23.5 percent of the sample – a sizable amount. In Table 17.3, we begin to make our case that copying another student's answers does not yield a positive expected value.

Regression I controls for student fixed effects (Chamberlain, 1980), while regression II does not. However, regression II's coefficients may be interpreted as probability changes in the dependent variable that are caused by changes in the associated independent variables. Both regressions use dummy variables to control for question effects. A student is more likely to change their wrong answer when it is different from their partner's (that is, *wrong_partnercorrect* or *differentandwrong*) compared to *sameandwrong* (the reference case). This gives evidence that student behavior depends on the influence of the partner's round one answer. However, the coefficients of *wrong_partnercorrect* and *differentandwrong* are not statistically different at usually cited levels of significance.

Students are just as likely to change in response to a partner's incorrect answer as they are to change in response to a partner's correct answer. Hence, the data show that students do not seem to be able to discriminate between correct answers of a partner and incorrect answers of a partner.

Table 17.3 Under which conditions do students change answers?

	I Xtlogit	II dprobit
correct_partnerwrong	1.278*** (0.382)	0.128*** (0.049)
wrong_partnercorrect	2.191*** (0.365)	0.397*** (0.062)
differentandwrong	2.177*** (0.373)	0.369*** (0.067)
rightright	–3.397*** (1.062)	–0.209*** (0.028)
Question dummies	Yes	Yes
Student fixed effects	Yes	No
Pseudo R^2	–	0.2548
Observations	810[a]	960

Notes: The reference dummy is *sameandwrong*. Standard errors are in parentheses. *** p 0.01.

a. 150 observations (from 15 students) were dropped because those students did not change any of their round 1 answers.

Further, Table 17.3 shows that students with correct answers are more likely to change their answers if their partner has a different (wrong) answer, compared to the situation in which they have the same wrong answer. This indicates that students who are correct, but differ from their partner, are more likely to change their answers, to their detriment, compared to the situation in which the students agree on a wrong answer. However, the coefficient is lower on *correct_partnerwrong* than those on *wrong_partnercorrect* and *differentandwrong*, indicating that students are less likely to change their answers when they are correct than when they are incorrect. Finally, if both students have correct answers, *rightright*, students are highly unlikely to change – this happened for only one student on one question.

In Table 17.4 we focus on how likely a student with a correct answer is to change his or her answer to an incorrect partner's answer. To focus on this change, we include only observations in which the students had different answers. The dprobit coefficient in regression IV indicates that students who are correct are 24.7 percent less likely than students who are incorrect to change an answer to a partner's incorrect answer. Regression IV also reiterates that students who are incorrect are no more likely to change to a partner's correct answer than they are to change to a partner's incorrect answer.

Table 17.4 Focus on the effect of being correct

	III Xtlogit	IV dprobit
correct_partnerwrong	–0.929*** (0.297)	–0.247*** (0.049)
wrong_partnercorrect	–0.172 (0.279)	0.058 (0.054)
Question dummies	Yes	Yes
Student fixed effects	Yes	No
Pseudo R^2	–	0.060
Observations	432	536

Note: This sample excludes observations where the student and partner had the same answer. The reference group is *differentandwrong*. Standard errors are in parentheses.
*** p 0.01.

The estimations in Table 17.5 recast the data to get at the heart of our hypothesis – that students do not directly gain from copying the answers of others. Regression V shows that a student is more likely to change his or her answer if it is *different* than his or her partner's answer, holding constant the student's answer, his or her partner's answer, question effects and individual fixed effects. This includes any unique effects his or her partner has on his or her decision to change – such as the student's appraisal of the partner as either competent or incompetent. A student who was correct on round one, Cora1, is less likely to change his or her answer. Finally, other things equal, the decision for the student to change an answer does not depend on the correctness of his or her partner's answer; that is, a student improves because the partner's answer happens to be different, and not because the student has appraised that the partner is correct.

Table 17.5 Which factors influence students to change answers?

	V Xtlogit	VI dprobit
different	2.758*** (0.307)	0.307*** (0.024)
Cora1	–1.319*** (0.265)	–0.199*** (0.026)
Pcora1	–0.371 (0.252)	–0.007 (0.027)
Question dummies	Yes	Yes
Psuedo R^2	–	0.2514
Observations	810[a]	960

Notes: Cora1 is the student's round one answer (1 if correct and 0 if incorrect). Pcora1 is the partner's round one answer (1 if correct and 0 if incorrect). Standard errors are in parentheses. *** p 0.01.

a. 150 observations (from 15 students) were dropped because those students did not change any of their round one answers.

This completes our demonstration that copying another student's correct answer does not directly benefit a student.

17.6 SUMMARY AND CONCLUSION

Compared to round one performance, the class average on round two increased by 7.3 percentage points. Our experiment was generous in giving opportunities to cheat. Each had five unconstrained minutes to evaluate a partner's answers. In the typical classroom situation, where the ability to view another's paper is constrained by the possibility that the professor will spot the cheater, and by the possibility that other students will complain about such blatant cheating as existed in our experiment, students would be less likely to be able to share as much information. Further, by using neutral language in the experiment, we attempted to remove the stigma of taking answers from another, creating a classroom dynamic that should be seen as no more unethical than assigned group work. Hence, we view the improvement of three-quarters of one letter grade as an upper bound on cheating by copying answers.

Although this result appears to confirm that cheating (that is, copying) from a neighbor boosts grades, we find that the increase is largely explained as an artifact of multiple choice questions and a heuristic used by students in selecting answers when cheating. Students with correct answers are somewhat more likely to hold to those answers when given the opportunity to cheat. Students with incorrect answers are more likely to change their answers when given the opportunity to cheat, and changing an incorrect answer can only yield gains. However, given that students cannot distinguish between correct and incorrect answers that a partner gives, they gain not by copying answers that they appraise as correct but merely by changing a wrong answer to another answer.

18. Instructor attractiveness and institutional choice in economics: a decomposition approach

Trellis G. Green, Franklin G. Mixon, Jr and Len J. Treviño

18.1 INTRODUCTION

Since the beginning of 2005, the already expansive literature on the impact of beauty on various economic and non-economic outcomes has grown by leaps and bounds (for example, see Green et al., 2005; Hamermesh, 2006, 2011; Hamermesh and Abrevaya, 2012; Hamermesh and Parker, 2005; Mixon and Caudill, 2013; Mixon and Smith, 2013; Salter et al., 2012). As pointed out by Green et al. (2005), a recent trend in empirical research has shown that student evaluations of college instructors are positively related to student perceptions of instructor beauty or attractiveness. This finding is compelling, particularly given that college and university administrators often use student evaluations of teaching as a proxy for an instructor's teaching effectiveness when determining merit raises and other job-related rewards.

This chapter advances academic research that has examined the impact of attractiveness on teaching evaluations by extending the work of Green et al. (2005), who examined the role that attractiveness plays in professors' occupational choices, particularly as they relate to institutional affiliations (that is, liberal arts versus research-oriented institutions). Following Green et al. (2005), we investigate whether attractive or good-looking instructors are more or less likely than their less attractive counterparts to seek and retain employment with liberal arts institutions, where the focus on teaching is greater, as opposed to research-oriented institutions. To do so, we employ, as do Green et al. (2005), the large sample of student evaluations data in Smith (2005). Our study differs, however, from that of Green et al. (2005) in terms of empirical strategy. This study employs a Blinder-type decomposition approach, which has been used in seminal studies to examine the presence or absence of gender- and race-related wage discrimination. In our study, the prospective university faculty member is discriminating in his or her choice of employer or institutional setting, depending upon that prospective faculty member's looks or attractiveness.

18.2 THEORETICAL FOUNDATION

The model developed in Green et al. (2005) is based on an adaptation of the standard wage model of beauty (see Biddle and Hamermesh, 1998; Hamermesh and Biddle, 1994; Hamermesh et al., 2002) to higher education. That adaptation appears in Equation (18.1):

$$W_{ij} = a_j X_i + b_j \theta_i + c_j Z_i + \epsilon_i \qquad (18.1)$$

In Equation (18.1), W_{ij} is the wage of professor *i* teaching at university *j*. Wage rates reflect marginal productivity, *ceteris paribus*, and professors are assumed to choose that university setting offering the highest full wage (Green et al., 2005, p. 58). Each professor is endowed with a vector of standard productivity-enhancing characteristics, X_i, which are related to teaching, research and service, the standard activities of those in the professorate. Professors are perceived by their students as being attractive, unattractive or neither. These perceptions are reflected as $\theta_i > 0$, $\theta_i < 0$ and $\theta_i = 0$, respectively (Green et al., 2005, p. 58).[1] Professor *i*'s wages may be affected by students' perceptions through the teaching evaluation process. Professor *i*'s institutional setting Z_i is likely to also be an integral part of wage determination, given that market incentives influence occupational choice (Green et al., 2005, p. 58).

Green et al. (2005, p. 58) partition the professor's productivity matrix, X, into $(X_T|X_R|X_S)$ for teaching, research and service activities, respectively. This partitioning is shown in Equation (18.2):

$$X_T = \theta[Q_T(\theta_T)] \Rightarrow \theta_T>0 \quad X_R = \theta[Q_R(\theta_R)] \Rightarrow \theta_R=0$$
$$X_S = \theta[Q_S(\theta_S)] \Rightarrow \theta_S=? \qquad (18.2)$$

Green et al. (2005, p. 58) indicate that, in practice, productivity measurement in these three diverse academic areas can be proxied with indices of performance quality, such as those denoted by Q_T, Q_R and Q_S, respectively. These indices represent how university administrators often seek to index teaching productivity with formalized student evaluations of teaching, while research and service productivity are indexed by documenting the quality and quantity of one's publications and by university, professional and community service activities, respectively. Substantial research shows that attractiveness is positively and significantly related to a professor's teaching performance as measured by student evaluations of teaching (for example, Boex, 2000; Felton et al., 2004; Hamermesh and Parker, 2005; Smith, 2005).[2]

Given that our study re-examines that of Green et al. (2005), we explore the effect of perceived attractiveness on the occupational choice of professor *i*. In doing so, we focus our analysis on the X_T component of the academic productivity matrix in Equation (18.2) above, wherein Q_T represents information of teaching performance from a formal student teaching evaluation instrument. Information from this instrument is used to proxy performance with quality-enhancing factors such as teaching clarity and helpfulness.[3] Next, variable θ_T is an indicator of a professor's attractiveness as perceived by students (Green et al., 2005, p. 59). One would expect a sorting or self-selection process to occur, wherein attractive professors select universities where the economic return to attractiveness is greatest, *ceteris paribus*. The economic return, which comes in the form of financial rewards from university administration, is likely to be greatest in universities emphasizing teaching, the one activity in Equation (18.2) above exhibiting a positive return to attractiveness, over the other academic activities (Green et al., 2005, p. 59).

Following Green et al. (2005, p. 59), the institutional dichotomy employed in this study separates liberal arts universities, which emphasize teaching, from research-oriented universities. What is modeled here is the tendency of professor *i* to select employment with a liberal arts university. That tendency, although a continuous variable, is latent. What can be observed, however, is whether professor *i* maintains employment with a liberal arts university. That variable, LIBARTS, is a dichotomous variable, equal to 1 if professor *i* is employed with a liberal arts university, and 0 otherwise. Thus, the empirical occupational choice model described here is given in Equation (18.3),

$$\text{Prob}(LIBARTS=1) = \frac{e^{\alpha+\delta Q_{Ti}+\beta\theta_{Ti}}}{1+e^{\alpha+\delta Q_{Ti}+\beta\theta_{Ti}}} \tag{18.3}$$

where professor *i*'s institutional setting is explained by perceived teaching quality, Q_{Ti}, and perceived attractiveness, θ_{Ti}.

18.3 DATA AND EMPIRICAL STRATEGY

As in Green et al. (2005), data for the empirical tests explained below come from Smith (2005), and were originally compiled from the popular website, ratemyprofessors.com. Individual faculty represent the unit of observation, where only those faculty receiving ratings from ten or more students (at the time of the data compilation) were included in the sample.[4] Teaching quality, Q_{Ti}, is proxied by indicators of teaching effectiveness taken from ratemyprofessors.com. There, respondents rate their professors, each in terms of teaching clarity and helpfulness, on a scale of 1 (that is, least clear; least helpful) to 5 (that is, most clear; most helpful). The average of these two scores for each professor, QUALITY, is included to capture Q_{Ti} in Equation (18.3) above. Attractiveness, θ_{Ti}, is proxied by ATTRACTIVENESS, a dummy variable equal to 1 if professor *i* is rated as attractive/good-looking by more than 14.5 percent of student raters, and 0 otherwise. This particular percentage (ratio) was chosen because it denotes a statistically significant proportion of students who rate a given professor as attractive. This aspect of our empirical approach differs from that in Green et al. (2005).

Following Green et al. (2005, p. 59), it is expected that an aptitude for high-quality teaching would, *ceteris paribus*, create a tendency for professor *i* to seek/secure employment at a liberal arts university, given that teaching is the primary source of advancement in such an institutional setting. Thus, one expects that QUALITY will be positively related to Prob(*LIBARTS* =1). A positive relationship between ATTRACTIVENESS and *LIBARTS* in Equation (18.3) above would provide support for our hypothesis, and that in Green et al. (2005), that attractive or good-looking professors tend to secure employment at liberal arts institutions, where the returns to effective teaching often dominate those from other activities. As stated previously, and shown in Equation (18.2) above, it is professor *i*'s teaching activities that are positively impacted by attractiveness.

This study differs from Green et al. (2005) in ways beyond construction of the regressor for professor attractiveness. Our empirical strategy follows that from seminal studies of wage discrimination, whether based on gender or race, in the labor economics literature (for example, Blinder, 1973; Flanagan, 1974; Oaxaca, 1973). This strategy includes a variation of the decomposition technique used in these and other studies to measure wage discrimination. In our case, however, the dummy variable for professor attractiveness is used to partition our sample into subsamples, with one for attractive professors and another for unattractive professors. Following Jackson and Lindley (1989), for the sub-sample of attractive professors, Equation (18.4) is established,

$$\overline{P}^{A} = a^{A} + b^{A}\overline{Q}^{A} \tag{18.4}$$

wherein *a* and *b* are estimates of traditional regression model parameters α and β, respectively, while the superscript *A* denotes that the results refer to the sub-sample of attractive professors and the bar superscripts denote sample means for *P* and *Q*, the probability of securing employment at a liberal arts institution and professor *i*'s teaching effectiveness, respectively. For the sub-sample of unattractive professors, the superscript in Equation (18.4) is changed to *UA*, as in

$$\overline{P}^{UA} = a^{UA} + b^{UA}\overline{Q}^{UA} \tag{18.5}$$

Under the assumption that the probability of choosing a liberal arts employment setting for attractive professors, $\overline{P}^{A}$, responds to changes in teaching effectiveness the same way as the probability of choosing a liberal arts employment setting for unattractive professors, $\overline{P}^{UA}$, responds to changes in teaching effectiveness, the mean probability of choosing a liberal arts employment setting for attractive professors is given by

$$\overline{P}^{H} = a^{UA} + b^{UA}\overline{Q}^{A} \tag{18.6}$$

The total difference in mean probabilities can be expressed as the sum of the endowment effect and the residual difference. The residual difference is, in our decomposition approach, the counterpart to the traditional measure of the extent of wage discrimination in labor markets. In our case, it is the difference between the total difference in mean probabilities and the endowment effect, which is that portion of the total difference that is explained by differences in teaching effectiveness (QUALITY) across attractive and unattractive professors. For this study, the probability expressed in Equation (18.7),

$$\text{Prob}(\mathit{LIBARTS}=1) = \frac{e^{\alpha+\delta Q_{Ti}}}{1+e^{\alpha+\delta Q_{Ti}}} \tag{18.7}$$

is estimated using data from the sub-sample of unattractive professors. Having produced an estimate for Equation (18.7) using the unattractive-only sub-sample, $\overline{Q}^{UA}_{Ti}$ and $\overline{Q}^{A}_{Ti}$ are each substituted for $\overline{Q}_{Ti}$ in order to measure the endowment effect. This effect is then subtracted from the total difference in probabilities in order to obtain the residual difference in probabilities, which in our case is a measure of the effect of professor attractiveness on the choice of institutional setting (that is, a liberal arts or research-oriented university). These tests and others are explored in more detail in the following section.

18.4 EMPIRICAL RESULTS

The variables, along with their descriptions, that are used in this study are included in Table 18.1. Also included in Table 18.1 are summary statistics (that is, means and standard deviations) for those variables.

Table 18.1 Variable descriptions and summary statistics

Variables	Description	Summary Statistics
LIBARTS	Dummy variable equal to 1 for faculty at liberal arts institutions, and 0 otherwise.	0.086 (0.280)
ATTRACTIVENESS	Dummy variable equal to 1 for faculty rated as attractive/good-looking by more than 14.5 percent of student raters, and 0 otherwise.	0.132 (0.339)
QUALITY	Average rating of overall quality of each faculty, based on student ratings of clarity and helpfulness of each faculty.	3.490 (0.956)

Note: The summary statistics above are means (standard deviations).

As shown in Table 18.1, about 8.6 percent of the 2986 faculty, for a total of 257 faculty, included in our overall sample are affiliated with liberal arts institutions. In terms of teaching effectiveness, the average quality rating, in terms of teaching clarity and helpfulness, across the faculty is 3.49 (out of 5). Lastly, about 13.2 percent, or 394 faculty, are considered attractive or good-looking by student raters.

Before turning to the decomposition tests, we first explore maximum likelihood logit estimates of the probability expressed above in Equation (18.3). These results, which are based on our full sample of 2986 professors, are shown in Table 18.2.

The first set of results in Table 18.2 is based on a restricted version of Equation (18.3), including only ATTRACTIVENESS on the right-hand side. There, professor attractiveness is shown to be both positively and significantly (at the 0.01 level) related to the probability of choosing a faculty affiliation with a liberal arts university. The second set of results

Table 18.2 Maximum likelihood logit results

Variables	(1)	(2)
Constant	–2.454*	–3.021*
	(–33.72)	(–10.95)
ATTRACTIVENESS	0.546*	0.400*
	(3.27)	(2.24)
QUALITY		0.165*
		(2.17)
N	2986	2986
Model χ^2	9.801*	54.218*

Note: The numbers in parentheses are *t*-values. * denotes p = 0.05.

includes both ATTRACTIVENESS and QUALITY on the right-hand side. In each case, the regressor is both positively and significantly (at the 0.05 level) related to the probability of choosing a faculty affiliation with a liberal arts university. These results are consistent with the hypotheses in Green et al. (2005) and in this study.

Turning to the decomposition approach, a simple logit regression specification indicates that attractive professors exhibit a 0.05 (that is, 5 percentage points) greater probability of affiliating with a liberal arts university – where the returns to teaching and, thus, the returns to attractiveness are greater – than their unattractive counterparts. This difference, the total difference, is significant at the 0.001 level based on a χ^2 (1 dfe) statistic of 10.701. This result is shown in column one of Table 18.3.

Table 18.3 Decomposition tests

Total Difference	Endowment Effect	Residual Difference
+0.050*	+0.010	+0.040*
[χ^2_{1dfe} = 10.701]		[χ^2_{2dfe} = 6.320]

Note: * denotes significance at the 0.05 level or better.

Estimation of Equation (18.7), using only the sub-sample unattractive professors, provides the regression estimates needed to compute the probabilities expressed in Equations (18.5) and (18.6). The difference in these probabilities constitutes the endowment effect, showing how much of the total difference is explained by differences in teaching endowments (that is, teaching effectiveness) across attractive and unattractive professors. Our estimate of the endowment effect is 0.01 (that is, 1 percentage point), which is only 20 percent of the total difference described above. Thus, the residual difference, which is the difference in the probabilities of affiliating with a liberal arts university that is due to attractiveness, is 0.04 (that is, 4 percentage points), or 80 percent of the total difference in this case. The residual difference is treated stochastically, following a χ^2 distribution with two degrees of freedom. The test statistic (that is, χ^2 with 2 dfe) is obtained from a traditional likelihood ratio test based on logit regressions employing the full sample, where the restricted model includes only QUALITY, while the unrestricted model includes both QUALITY and ATTRACTIVENESS along with an interaction term (that is, QUALITY × ATTRACTIVENESS). As indicated in Table 18.3, the residual difference is significant at the 0.042 level based on a χ^2 (2 dfe) statistic of 6.320. That is, the residual difference, which is the difference in the probabilities of affiliating with a liberal arts university that is due to instructor attractiveness, is statistically significant.

18.5 CONCLUDING COMMENTS

As in Green et al. (2005), this study posits that attractive or good-looking university faculty are, *ceteris paribus*, more likely to be employed by liberal arts institutions. This follows from the simple fact that teaching effectiveness is often the primary determinant of faculty advancement at liberal arts universities, as opposed to research-oriented universities, and that attractiveness has been shown to enhance students' evaluations of their instructors, the primary metric for determining teaching effectiveness. Findings from a Blinder-type decomposition approach used herein support that hypothesis. In fact, we find that 80 percent of the difference between the probability that an attractive professor holds an appointment with a liberal arts institution and that same probability for his or her unattractive counterpart stems from differences in how students, and perhaps others, perceive their physical attractiveness. By pinpointing this division in the probability difference, this study both supports and extends that of Green et al. (2005) and others.

NOTES

1. See Hamermesh and Biddle (1994) and Hartfield and Sprecher (1986) for work on the empirical consistency of perceived attractiveness (θ) at a point in time.

2. The positive relationship between attractiveness and teaching performance, $\theta_T > 0$, is referred to as the 'fox effect' (Green et al., 2005, p. 58). As indicated in Green et al. (2005, p. 64), some studies have also shown the existence of a 'halo effect,' where attractive professors can partly avoid the damaging consequences of classroom (exam) rigor that often motivate their less attractive counterparts to implement less rigorous classroom standards (Boex, 2000; Bosshardt and Watts, 2001; Felton et al., 2004; Krautmann and Sander, 1999; Mixon and Smith, 2013; Smith, 2005).
3. For more on this, see Green et al. (2005, p. 59) and also Hamermesh and Parker (2005), who point out that, regardless of the statistical evidence or one's beliefs about whether student evaluations have any relation to pedagogical productivity, evaluations by students are part of what universities use in their evaluation of faculty teaching performance. In fact, in decisions involving the compensation of faculty, university administrators often link economic rewards with formal student evaluations.
4. For a school with hundreds of faculty with ten or more ratings, a random subset (of up to 200 faculty) was chosen from that school. The final sample includes 2986 faculty observations. It is worth noting that ratemyprofessors.com is freely accessible, allowing any visitor to rate a particular professor. As such, the data used in this study are not generated in a traditional scientific manner. Thus, all are urged to proceed with caution as we delve into the empirical analysis.

19. Do clickers enhance student performance in economics?

Joel M. Potter and John L. Scott

19.1 INTRODUCTION

Clickers, also known as 'personal response systems,' resemble television remote controls. Students use clickers to respond to multiple choice questions that the instructor asks verbally or with multimedia assistance. Each student in class has a clicker, which transmits responses to a USB receiver attached to the professor's computer. At the instructor's discretion, the clicker software on the computer may display the frequency distribution of answers to students. The clicker software may also build a grade book and export student grades to spreadsheet files that the professor can merge with other grade files.

The instructor may use clickers to take attendance, to anonymously poll students without recording grades, to intersperse lectures with questions, to review material or to give regular quizzes. Managing the clicker software requires a fixed expenditure of the instructor's time, but may free the professor from the variable expenditure of time associated with grading quizzes, recording grades or taking roll; hence, clickers are time efficient in large sections. Clickers sell for $20 to $50 each and may be resold.

Research on clickers has largely focused on student attitudes. For example, Ghosh and Renna (2009) examine clicker use in undergraduate economics courses. Although they did not test for the impact of clickers on grades, their students had positive attitudes about their use of clickers. Using pedagogical techniques suggested by Ghosh and Renna (2009), we test whether clickers improve student performance.

The non-economics studies that measure how clickers influence student performance have, with one exception, either compared averages or used bivariate statistical tests on different sections of a course. The exception is Morling et al. (2008), which used MANOVA and does not yield the sensitivity measure of a regression coefficient; hence, the study did not measure how much of an impact clickers had on grades.

We use an experimental design that yields stronger controls than we have found in the literature. Unlike previous studies, we use multiple regression; hence, we derive measures of how sensitive grades are to clicker use, rather than simply testing whether clicker use affects grades. In the following section of this chapter, we review the literature on clickers, paying special attention to research that attempts to measure whether clickers affect grades. We describe our experiment and data set and then discuss our statistical technique and results. Finally, we offer conclusions.

19.2 RESEARCH ON CLICKERS

We direct readers who desire a rich explanation of the use of clickers to Elliott (2003), who provides an excellent discussion of the use of clickers in promoting active learning. Most research on clickers focuses on student attitudes toward the learning device. The study by Chaplain and Morgan (2008) is typical. They find that students see clickers as (1) being easy to use; (2) increasing the enjoyment of lectures; (3) encouraging attendance; and (4) increasing confidence. They find that students preferred clicker use to traditional methods of quizzing and monitoring attendance. Students view Chaplain and Morgan's method of interspersing questions with the lecture as solving the problem of students not being actively engaged in PowerPoint lectures and, in general, not being able to concentrate for more than 20–30 minutes. Students appreciated the way that clickers broke the lecture into smaller parts, encouraged students to focus on the material and, through frequency distributions of the answers, reassured them that they were not alone in their imperfect understanding of the subject matter.

Herreid (2006) asserts that in large sections of general biology, clickers 'dramatically' increase attendance, increase the course's value to students, raise performance on critical thinking questions and raise grades. Herreid provides measurements of improvements in attendance – attendance increases from around 50 percent to around 90 percent – however, he does not provide measurements of improvements in grades or measurements of other improvements.

Dill (2008) finds that clickers do not enhance learning in brief instruction sessions in libraries. Dill recognizes that the test students took to measure learning was not graded and that this lack of incentive may drive her result. She makes the allowance that prolonged use of clickers in a course may enhance grades, but warns that '[s]imply layering technology onto instruction will likely not yield any significant improvements in student learning' (Dill, 2008, p. 529).

Reay et al. (2008), like other researchers, find that students enjoy clickers. They perform pre-tests and post-tests in large section physics courses and compare education gains from sections where clickers are used with sections where clickers are not used. They perform *t*-tests on the various sections, but variations in treatment of the sections cloud their pre-test/post-test results. However, they find that on test questions that are similar to clicker questions students in clicker classes perform substantively and statistically significantly better. In particular, they find that students in sections that used clickers correctly saw a 22–26 percent standardized gain over students in sections that did not use clickers. The standardized gain is not the typical increase that we discuss in grade improvement. A 25 percent standardized gain does not mean that a student advances from a 50 percent to a 75 percent – but that a student advances from correctly answering ten questions to correctly answering 12.5 questions in sections with clicker use.

Morling et al. (2008) use MANOVA to control for the differences in treatment of students who took different exams in courses under different professors, some of whom used clickers and some of whom did not. They find that clickers affect performance in a statistically significant, but minor, way. The only inferences that their readers can draw regarding the magnitude of the effect of clickers on performance come from examination of test averages in clicker and non-clicker sections.

19.3 EXPERIMENT AND DATA

We collected data from two sections of Principles of Microeconomics in which 64 students took the first test. The same professor taught both sections. At the time of the experiment, the professor had used clickers for two years in multiple sections. He had been trained in the use of clickers by the Center for Teaching and Learning Excellence at the University of North Georgia, and he had written a practical guide for clicker installation and use for the faculty of the Mike Cottrell College of Business at the University of North Georgia. Students took a graded multiple choice exam that related to material covered by the textbook, lectures and online homework. The exam covered two chapters where students had access to a clicker: supply/demand and elasticity. Ten exam questions related to the supply and demand chapter and ten questions related to the elasticity chapter.

In one section, we used clickers only during the supply and demand lectures; in the other section, we used clickers only during the elasticity lectures. When clickers were used in class, students answered a total of five multiple choice questions that were interspersed throughout the PowerPoint slides. When the question appeared, students were given time to read and answer the question. The professor read each question and the accompanying answers aloud twice in order to reduce the likelihood that students would miss a question due to errors in reading comprehension. After time had elapsed, students were shown a histogram that indicated how much support each of the multiple choice answers had garnered. The class then discussed why the correct answers were correct and why the incorrect answers were incorrect. Since the incorrect answers often incorporated common misconceptions, students were given clear prompting and discussion that should dispense with those misconceptions and focus students on the logic of the concept involved in the question.

Ghosh and Renna (2009) provide practical advice for administering clickers in the Principles of Economics classroom. Our procedures were consistent with the advice of Ghosh and Renna (2009) in the following ways. We did (1) use questions that focused on a single concept; (2) use questions that engaged students in higher-order thinking; (3) formulate multiple choice questions that included students' most common misconceptions; (4) use questions that signaled core concepts; (5) not use questions that were too easy or too hard; and (6) not grade questions, but gave extra points for each correct answer. We did not, however, post the questions, as Ghosh and Renna suggest, although we allowed students enough time to copy the questions and answers in their class notes.

Summary statistics for the control variables and the dependent variable are shown in Table 19.1. Our fixed-effects model hypothesizes that student performance depends on student characteristics, clicker use, attendance, homework grades and a chapter dummy:

$$\begin{aligned} Correct_{ij} = a_i + b_1 Clicker_{ij} + b_2 Attendance_{ij} + b_3 Homework_{ij} + \\ b_4 Chapter_{ij} + e_{ij},\ i = 1,\ldots, n \text{ and } j = 1,2 \end{aligned} \tag{19.1}$$

The dependent variable, *Correct*, represents the number of questions that student i answered correctly on chapter j material, while a_i is a student-specific effect that is unique to individual i. Our independent variable of interest is a dummy variable, *Clicker*, which is equal to 1 if student i used a clicker when chapter j was presented in class; *Clicker* is equal to 0 if student i did not use a clicker when chapter j was presented in class. Because of our experimental design, the mean of *Clicker* is 0.5.

Table 19.1 Summary statistics (n = 128)

Variable	Mean	S.D.	Min	Max
Correct	0.644	0.182	0.2	1
Clicker	0.5	0.502	0	1
Attendance	0.761	0.332	0	1
Homework	0.539	0.318	0	1

Attendance is the percentage of classes that student i attended when chapter j material was presented. *Homework* is the percentage of online homework questions that student i answered correctly on chapter j material. *Chapter* is a chapter dummy variable that is equal to 1 for the elasticity material and equal to 0 for the supply/demand material. Given that we estimate a fixed-effects model, we are only able to obtain estimates that have variation within students (that is, *Clicker*, *Attendance*, *Homework* and *Chapter*). Thus, we are not able to estimate how a factor like grade point average (GPA) influences the dependent variable because GPA is constant for student i across chapter j = 1 and j = 2. However, all effects that lack within-variation – such as GPA and unobserved student characteristics – are still controlled for through the use of our fixed-effects approach given that we have observations on the same students' performances on the different chapters. By using a fixed-effects approach, we are able to estimate how clicker access influences student i's score on chapter j relative to student i's average score (controlling for attendance, homework score, specific chapter effects and specific student effects). These controls are essential for finding the true effect of clickers on performance.

19.4 STATISTICAL RESULTS

Our empirical results are reported in Table 19.2.

Table 19.2 Empirical results

Variable	Coefficient
Clicker	–0.055 (0.283)
Attendance	–0.412 (0.708)
Homework	0.004 (0.069)
Chapter	–1.440* (0.281)
Constant	7.476* (0.648)
n	128
R^2 – within	0.343

Note: The numbers in parentheses are standard errors. * denotes significance at the 1 percent level.

As indicated in Table 19.2, clickers did not significantly affect performance on the exam. The point estimate of the clicker coefficient is negative. The only statistically significant coefficient is the dummy variable that captures chapter-specific effects; other things being equal, we estimate that a given student correctly answered 1.44 fewer elasticity questions than supply/demand questions. This result provides evidence that the elasticity portion of the exam was relatively more difficult than the supply/demand portion.

19.5 CONCLUSIONS

Students enjoy clickers. Professors state that clickers keep students' attention and break up monotony. Previous research has shown scant support for the hypothesis that clickers affect classroom performance – either no effect or minute effects were found. Also, some previous research on performance was confounded by problems with the execution of the experiments. Using a technique that takes account of the complex interactions of the relevant variables, in this chapter, we find no support for the hypothesis that clickers improve performance.

Bibliography

Adkins, R. and M. Newsome (2006), 'Designing the economics curriculum: a survey of the use of "big ideas" and proficiencies', *Journal of Economics and Finance Education*, **5**(2), 7–16.

Ali, M.M., H.W. Cecil and J.A. Knoblett (2001), 'The effects of tax rates and enforcement policies on taxpayer compliance: a study of self-employed taxpayers', *Atlantic Economic Journal*, **29**(2), 186–202.

Alicke, M.D., M.L. Klotz, D.L. Breitenbecher, T.J. Yurak and D.S. Vredenburg (1995), 'Personal contact, individuation, and the better-than-average effect', *Journal of Personality and Social Psychology*, **68**(5), 804–25.

Allgood, S., W. Bosshardt, W. van der Klaauw and M. Watts (2004), 'What students remember and say about college economics years later', *American Economic Review*, **94**(2), 259–65.

Allgood, S., W. Bosshardt, W. van der Klaauw and M. Watts (2010), 'Is economics coursework, or majoring in economics, associated with different civic behaviors?', University of Nebraska, Department of Economics Working Paper.

Allgood, S., W. Bosshardt, W. van der Klaauw and M. Watts (2011), 'Economics coursework and long-term behavior and experiences of college graduates in labor markets and personal finance', *Economic Inquiry*, **49**(3), 771–94.

Allingham, M.G. and A. Sandmo (1972), 'Income tax evasion', *Journal of Public Economics*, **1**(3), 323–38.

Alm, J. and M. Yunus (2009), 'Spatiality and persistence in U.S. individual income tax compliance', *National Tax Journal*, **62**(1), 101–24.

Alm, J., B. Jackson and M. McKee (1992), 'Institutional uncertainty and taxpayer compliance', *American Economic Review*, **82**(4), 1018–26.

Alm, J., G.H. McClelland and W.D. Schulze (1999), 'Changing the social norm of tax compliance by voting', *Kyklos*, **52**(1), 141–71.

Alston, R.M., J.R. Kearl and M.B. Vaughn (1992), 'Is there a consensus among economists in the 1990's?', *American Economic Review*, **82**(2), 203–9.

Anderson, G.M. (1991), 'The 1946 voter revolt against government regulation', *The Freeman: Ideas on Liberty*, **41**(2), 52–6.

Arias, J.J. and D.M. Walker (2004), 'Additional evidence on the relationship between class size and student performance', *Journal of Economic Education*, **35**(4), 311–29.

Arnold, R.A. (2011), *Economics*, Mason, OH, USA: South-Western.

Asarta, C.J. and R.B. Butters (2012), 'The discouraged-business-major hypothesis revisited: could economics be the encouraged-business-major?', *Journal of Economic Education*, **43**(1), 19–32.

Austen, J. (1813), *Pride and Prejudice*, London, UK: Penguin Classics.

Bade, R. and M. Parkin (2011), *Foundations of Economics*, Boston, MA, USA: Addison-Wesley.

Bajaj, V. and J. Yardley (2012), 'Scandal poses a riddle: will India ever be able to tackle corruption?', *New York Times*, 15 September.

Baldry, J.C. (1987), 'Income tax evasion and the tax schedule: some experimental results', *Public Finance/Finances Publiques*, **42**(2), 357–83.

Ballard, C.L. and M.F. Johnson (2004), 'Basic math skills and performance in an introductory economics class', *Journal of Economic Education*, **35**(1), 3–23.

Barnes, D.W. and L.A. Stout (1992), *Cases and Materials on Law and Economics*, St Paul, MN, USA: West Group.

Barr, S.Z. and G.D. Carr (1980), 'Improving economic understanding in junior college economics principles courses', *Community/Junior College Research Quarterly*, **4**(3), 219–24.

Bartlett, R.L. (1995), 'Attracting "otherwise bright students" to Economics 101', *American Economic Review*, **85**(2), 362–6.

Bauman, Y. (2003), 'Mankiw's ten principles of economics, translated', *Annals of Improbable Research*, **9**(1), 2.

Bauman, Y. (2009), '*Economic Inquiry*: the new home of economics humor!', available at http://standupeconomist.com/economic-inquiry-the-new-home-of-economics-humor/.

Bauman, Y. (2013), 'The world's first and only stand-up economist', available at http://www.standupeconomist.com.

Baumol, W.J. and W.E. Oates (1988), *The Theory of Environmental Policy*, Cambridge, UK: Cambridge University Press.

Bawley, D. (1982), *The Subterranean Economy*, New York, NY, USA: McGraw-Hill.

Becker, G.S. (1996), 'Not-so-dismal scientist', *Business Week*, 21 October, 19.

Becker, W.E. (1997), 'Teaching economics to undergraduates', *Journal of Economic Literature*, **35**(3), 1347–73.

Becker, W.E. (2001), 'How to make economics the sexy social science', *Chronicle of Higher Education*, 7 December, B10–B11.

Becker, W.E. (2003), 'Undergraduate choice: sexy or non-sexy', *Southern Economic Journal*, **70**(1), 219–23.
Becker, W.E. (2004), 'Economics for a higher education', *International Review of Economics Education*, **3**(1), 52–62.
Becker, W.E. and M. Watts (1996), 'Chalk and talk: a national survey of teaching undergraduate economics', *American Economic Review*, **86**(2), 448–54.
Becker, W.E. and M. Watts (1999), 'How departments of economics evaluate teaching', *American Economic Review*, **90**(2), 344–9.
Becker, W.E. and M. Watts (2000), *Teaching Economics to Undergraduates: Alternatives to Chalk and Talk*, Cheltenham, UK and Northampton, MA, USA: Edward Elgar.
Becker, W.E. and M. Watts (2001), 'Teaching economics at the start of the 21st century: still chalk and talk', *American Economic Review*, **91**(2), 446–51.
Becker, W.E. and M. Watts (2008), 'A little more than chalk and talk: results from a third National Survey of Teaching Methods in Undergraduate Economics Courses', *Journal of Economic Education*, **39**(3), 273–86.
Becker, W.E., M. Watts and S.R. Becker (2006), *Teaching Economics: More Alternatives to Chalk and Talk*, Cheltenham, UK and Northampton, MA, USA: Edward Elgar.
Bergstrom, T.C. and J.H. Miller (1999), *Experiments with Economic Principles: Microeconomics*, Boston, MA, USA: Irwin McGraw-Hill.
Biddle, J.E. and D.S. Hamermesh (1998), 'Beauty, productivity, and discrimination: lawyers' looks and lucre', *Journal of Labor Economics*, **16**(1), 172–201.
Bischof, G., A. Pelinka and D. Stiefel (2000), *The Marshall Plan in Austria*, Piscataway, NJ, USA: Transaction Publishers.
Blackwell, C. (2010), 'A meta-analysis of incentive effects in tax compliance experiments', in J. Alm, J. Martinez-Vazquez and B. Torgler (eds), *Developing Alternative Frameworks for Explaining Tax Compliance*, New York, NY, USA: Routledge, pp. 97–112.
Blinder, A.S. (1973), 'Wage discrimination: reduced form and structural estimates', *Journal of Human Resources*, **8**(4), 436–55.
Bloom, B.S. (1956), *Taxonomy of Educational Objectives: The Classification of Educational Goals*, New York, NY, USA: D. McKay Co.
Blundell, J. (2000), 'Foreword', in A. Pollard (ed.), *Readings 53: The Representation of Business in Literature*, London, UK: Institute of Economic Affairs, p. viii.
Boettke, P.J. (1993), 'The collapse of communism in the USSR: cold war victory or cold war illusions?', in J.E. Payne and A.P. Sahu (eds),

Defense Spending and Economic Growth, Boulder, CO, USA: Westview Press, pp. 187–201.

Boex, L.F. (2000), 'Attributes of effective economics instructors: an analysis of student evaluations', *Journal of Economic Education*, **31**(3), 211–27.

Bogart, W.T. (1995), 'Looking backward at feasible socialism: using Bellamy to teach Schumpeter', *Journal of Economic Education*, **26**(4), 352–6.

Bohanon, C. and M.A. Vachris (2012), 'Economics and literature: the gains from trade', in G. Hoyt and K.M. McGoldrick (eds), *The International Handbook on Teaching and Learning Economics*, Cheltenham, UK and Northampton, MA, USA: Edward Elgar, pp. 223–33.

Bosshardt, W. and M. Watts (2001), 'Comparing student and instructor evaluations of teaching', *Journal of Economic Education*, **32**(1), 3–17.

Boyes, W. and M. Melvin (2011), *Economics*, Mason, OH, USA: South-Western.

Bransford, J.D., A.L. Brown and R.R. Cocking (2000), *How People Learn: Brain, Mind, Experience, and School: Expanded Edition*, Washington, DC, USA: National Academy Press.

Bray, M. and J. Leape (2008), 'Writing for economists: embedding the development of writing skills in economics courses', available at http://78.158.56.101/archive/economics/projects/mini/bray_writing.htm. (accessed 12 March 2013).

Brown, J.D. and F.M. Gallagher (1992), 'Coming to terms with failure: private self-enhancement and public self-effacement', *Journal of Experimental Social Psychology*, **28**(1), 3–22.

Bunn, D.N., S.B. Caudill and D.M. Gropper (1992), 'Crime in the classroom: an economic analysis of undergraduate student cheating behavior', *Journal of Economic Education*, **23**(3), 197–207.

Burrus, R.T., K. McGoldrick and P.W. Schumann (2007), 'Self-reports of student cheating: does a definition of cheating matter?', *Journal of Economic Education*, **38**(1), 3–16.

Butters, R.B. and C.J. Asarta (2011), 'Gender and economic understanding in U.S. high schools', *Journal of Economics and Finance Education*, **10**(1), 37–40.

Caballe, J. and J. Panades (1997), 'Tax evasion and economic growth', *Public Finance/Finances Publiques*, **52**(2), 318–40.

Calabresi, G. (1970), *The Cost of Accidents*, New Haven, CT, USA: Yale University Press.

Calkins, L.N. and A. Welki (2006), 'Factors that influence choice of major: why some students never consider economics', *International Journal of Social Economics*, **33**(8), 547–64.

Camerer, C.F. (2003), *Behavioral Game Theory*, Princeton, NJ, USA: Princeton University Press.

Caplan, B. (2007), '*Atlas Shrugged* and public choice: the obvious parallels', in E.W. Younkins (ed.), *Ayn Rand's* Atlas Shrugged*: A Philosophical and Literary Companion*, Burlington, VT, USA: Ashgate, pp. 215–24.

Carleton, J. (2011), 'Lots of green is at stake in the San Francisco spat', *Wall Street Journal*, available at http://online.wsj.com/article/SB10001424052702303654804576343763766328484.html (accessed 14 July 2011).

Carson, C. (1984), 'The underground economy: an introduction', *Survey of Current Business*, **64**(1), 24–35.

Carson, S.W. (1949), *The Third Man*, Films on Liberty and the State, Ludwig von Mises Institute, available at http://www.mises.org/content/film.asp#Third (accessed 12 March 2013).

Carter, K. (1993), 'The place of story in the study of teaching and teacher education', *Educational Researcher*, **22**(1), 5–18.

Carter, K. and W. Doyle (1996), 'Personal narrative and life history in learning to teach', in J.P. Sikula, T.J. Buttery and E. Guyton (eds), *Handbook of Research on Teacher Education*, 2nd edn, New York, NY, USA: Macmillan, pp. 120–42.

Case, K.E., R.C. Fair and S.C. Oster (2012), *Principles of Economics*, Boston, MA, USA: Prentice Hall.

Caudill, S.B. and F.G. Mixon, Jr (1994), 'Cartels and the incentive to cheat: evidence from the classroom', *Journal of Economic Education*, **25**(3), 267–9.

Caudill, S.B. and F.G. Mixon, Jr (2005), 'Analyzing misleading discrete responses: a logit model based on misclassified data', *Oxford Bulletin of Economics and Statistics*, **67**(1), 105–13.

Cebula, R.J. (2001), 'Impact of income-detection technology and other factors on aggregate income tax evasion: the case of the United States', *Banca Nazionale del Lavoro Quarterly Review*, **54**(4), 401–15.

Cebula, R.J. (2004), 'Income tax evasion revisited: the impact of interest rate yields on tax-free municipal bonds', *Southern Economic Journal*, **71**(2), 418–23.

Cebula, R.J. (2008), 'Does the public's job approval rating of the U.S. President influence the degree of federal personal income tax evasion?', *Public Finance/Finances Publiques*, **55**(1–2), 48–63.

Cebula, R.J. and C. Coombs (2009), 'Do government spending-induced federal budget deficits "crowd out" tax compliance in the U.S.?', *Tax Notes*, November, 30, 1007–12.

Chamberlain, G. (1980), 'Analysis of covariance with qualitative data', *Review of Economic Studies*, **47**(1), 225–38.

Chamlee-Wright, E. (2011), 'Cultivating the economic imagination with *Atlas Shrugged*', *Journal of Economics and Finance Education*, **10**(2), 41–53.
Chaplain, D. and B. Morgan (2008), 'Making the case for personal response systems: evidence from small microeconomics courses', *Journal of Economics*, **34**(2), 83–91.
Cho, K. and C.D. Schunn (2007), 'Scaffolded writing and rewriting in the discipline: a web-based reciprocal peer review system', *Computers and Education*, **48**(3), 409–26.
Cho, K., C.D. Schunn and R. Wilson (2006), 'Validity and reliability of scaffolded peer assessment of writing from instructor and student perspectives', *Journal of Educational Psychology*, **98**(4), 891–901.
Cizek, G.J. (1999), *Cheating on Tests: How to Do It, Detect It, and Prevent It*, London, UK: Routletdge.
Cizek, G.J. (2003), *Detecting and Preventing Classroom Cheating: Promoting Integrity in Assessment*, Thousand Oaks, CA, USA: Corwin Press.
Clotfelter, C.P. (1997), *On the Third Hand: Wit and Humor in the Dismal Science*, Ann Arbor, MI, USA: University of Michigan Press.
Clotfelter, C.T. (1983), 'Tax evasion and tax rates: an analysis of individual returns', *Review of Economics and Statistics*, **65**(2), 363–73.
Coase, R.H. (1960), 'The problem of social cost', *Journal of Law and Economics*, **3**(1), 1–44.
Coase, R.H. (1988), *The Firm, the Market, and the Law*, Chicago, IL, USA: University of Chicago Press.
Colander, D.C. (2006), *The Stories Economists Tell: Essays on the Art of Teaching Economics*, New York, NY, USA: McGraw-Hill.
Colander, D.C. (2010), *Economics*, Boston, MA, USA: McGraw-Hill.
College Board (2009), *ACT and SAT Concordance Tables. Research Notes 40*, available at http://professionals.collegeboard.com/data-reports-research/cb/act-sat-concordance (accessed 1 May 2011).
Connelly, R. (2004), 'A note on income tax evasion', *Atlantic Economic Journal*, **32**(2), 157.
Cornes, R. and T. Sandler (1996), *The Theory of Externalities, Public Goods, and Club Goods*, Cambridge, UK: Cambridge University Press.
Coté, J. (2010), 'America's Cup: big S.F. fundraising push', *San Francisco Chronicle*, available at http://www.sfgate.com/cgi-bin/article.cgi?f=/c/a/2010/09/28/BAV61FKTG8.DTL&tsp=1 (accessed 15 August 2011).
Cotti, C. and M. Johnson (2012), 'Teaching economics using historical novels: Jonathan Harr's *The Lost Painting*', *Journal of Economic Education*, **43**(3), 269–81.

Cowen, P.S. (1984), 'Film and text: order effects in recall and social inferences', *Educational Communication and Technology*, **32**(3), 131–44.

Cowen, T. (2005), 'Is a novel a model?', available at http://www.gmu.edu/centers/publicchoice/faculty%20pages/Tyler/Model.pdf (accessed 12 March 2013).

Cowen, T. (2008a), *Discover Your Inner Economist: Use Incentives to Fall in Love, Survive Your Next Meeting, and Motivate Your Dentist*, New York, NY, USA: Plume.

Cowen, T. (2008b), 'Is a novel a model?', in S.J. Peart and D.M. Levy (eds), *The Street Porter and the Philosopher: Conversations on Analytical Egalitarianism*, Ann Arbor, MI, USA: University of Michigan Press, pp. 319–37.

Cox, D. (1984), 'Raising revenue in the underground economy', *National Tax Journal*, **37**(3), 283–8.

Coyne, C.J. and P.T. Leeson (2011), 'An Austrian inquiry into the wealth of nations: incorporating Austrian economics into economic development', *Journal of Economics and Finance Education*, **10**(2), 54–69.

Crisp, A.M. and F.G. Mixon, Jr (2012), 'Pony distress: using ESPN's 30FOR30 films to teach cartel theory', *Journal of Economics and Finance Education*, **11**(1), 15–26.

Dalton, A. (2011), 'Frustrated with obstructed views, Larry Ellison buys neighbor's $40 million home', available at http://sfist.com/2011/05/31/frustrated_with_obstructed_views_la.php (accessed 12 August 2011).

Das-Gupta, A. (1994), 'A theory of hard-to-get groups', *Public Finance/Finances Publiques*, **49**(1), 28–39.

Davies, P. and J. Mangan (2008), 'Threshold concepts in economics: implications for teaching, learning and assessment', *The Handbook for Economic Lecturers*, Bristol, UK: Economics Network of the Higher Education Authority.

De Mesquita, B.B. (2001), *The Trial of Ebeneezer Scrooge*, Columbus, OH, USA: Ohio State University Press.

De Soto, H. (2003), *The Mystery of Capital: Why Capitalism Triumphs in the West and Fails Everywhere Else*, New York, NY, USA: Basic Books.

Dean, D.H. and R.C. Dolan (2001), 'Liberal arts or business: does the location of the economics department alter the major?', *Journal of Economic Education*, **32**(1), 18–35.

Dickens, C. (1843), *A Christmas Carol*, reprinted in *Christmas Books* (1997), Oxford, UK: Oxford University Press.

Dickens, C. (1850), *David Copperfield*, reprinted in *The Oxford Illustrated Dickens* (1997), Oxford, UK: Oxford University Press.

Dickens, C. (1853), *Bleak House*, reprinted in *The Oxford Illustrated Dickens* (1997), Oxford, UK: Oxford University Press.
Dickens, C. (1854), *Hard Times*, reprinted in *The Oxford Illustrated Dickens* (1997), Oxford, UK: Oxford University Press.
Dickens, C. (1857), *Little Dorrit*, reprinted in *The Oxford Illustrated Dickens* (1997), Oxford, UK: Oxford University Press.
Dill, E. (2008), 'Perspective on… do clickers improve library instruction? Lock in your answers now', *Journal of Academic Librarianship*, **34**(6), 527–9.
Ding, L., N. Reay, A. Lee and L. Bao (2008), 'Effects of testing conditions on conceptual survey results', *Physics Education Research*, **4**(1), 1–6.
Dixit, A. (2005), 'Restoring fun to game theory', *Journal of Economic Education*, **36**(3), 205–19.
Dixit, A. (2012), 'An option value problem from *Seinfeld*', *Economic Inquiry*, **50**(2), 563–5.
Dorans, N.J. (1999), *Correspondences Between ACT and SAT I Scores*, College Board Research Report 99-1, ETS Research Report 99-2, New York, NY, USA: College Entrance Examination Board.
Doyle, W. (1997), 'Heard any really good stories lately? A critique of the critics of narrative in educational research', *Teaching and Teacher Education*, **13**(1), 93–9.
Dubner, S.J. and S.D. Levitt (2005), *Freakonomics: A Rogue Economist Explores the Hidden Side of Everything*, London, UK: Allen Lane.
Dynan, K.E., D.W. Elmendorf and D.E. Sichel (2006), 'Can financial innovation help to explain the reduced volatility of economic activity', *Journal of Monetary Economics*, **53**(1), 123–50.
Dynan L. and T. Cate (2008), 'The impact of writing assignments on student learning: should writing assignments be structured or unstructured?', *International Review of Economics Education*, **8**(1), 64–86.
Dynan, L., T. Cate and K. Rhee (2008), 'The impact of learning structures on students' readiness for self-directed learning', *Journal of Education for Business*, **84**(2), 96–100.
Easterly, W. (2002), *The Elusive Quest for Growth: Economists' Adventures and Misadventures in the Tropics*, Cambridge, MA, USA: MIT Press.
Elliott, C. (2003), 'Using a personal response system in economics teaching', *International Review of Economics Education*, **1**(1), 80–6.
Elliott, D., J. Meisel and W. Richards (1998), 'The senior project: using the literature of distinguished economists', *Journal of Economic Education*, **29**(4), 312–20.
Elzinga, K.G. (2001), 'Fifteen theses on classroom teaching', *Southern Economic Journal*, **68**(2), 249–57.

Erard, B. and J.S. Feinstein (1994), 'The role of moral sentiments and audit perceptions in tax compliance', *Public Finance/Finances Publiques*, **49**(1), 70–89.

Falkinger, J. (1988), 'Tax evasion and equity: a theoretical analysis', *Public Finance/Finance Publiques*, **43**(3), 388–95.

Feige, E.L. (1994), 'The underground economy and the currency enigma', *Public Finance/Finances Publiques*, **49**(1), 119–36.

Feinstein, J. (1991), 'An econometric analysis of income tax evasion and its detection', *RAND Journal of Economics*, **22**(1), 14–35.

Felton, J., J. Mitchell and M. Stinson (2004), 'Web-based student evaluations of professors: the relations between perceived quality, easiness, and sexiness', *Assessment and Evaluation in Higher Education*, **29**(1), 91–108.

Ferrato, L. (2011a), 'Pacific heights: Larry Ellison buys house next door for $40m, shrubbery fracas settled', available at http://sf.curbed.com/archives/2011/05/31/pacific_heights_larry_ellison_buys_house_next_door_for_40m_shrubbery_fracas_settled.php (accessed 12 August 2011).

Ferrato, L. (2011b), 'Billionaire Larry Ellison hedges bets, buys $40 million pad', available at http://homes.yahoo.com/news/billionaire-larry-ellison-hedges-bets-buys-40-million-163919381.html (accessed 13 February 2013).

Flanagan, R.J. (1974), 'Labor force experience, job turnover, and racial wage differentials', *Review of Economics and Statistics*, **56**(4), 521–9.

Fournier, G.M. and T.R. Sass (2000), 'Take my course, "please": the effects of the principles experience on student curriculum choice', *Journal of Economic Education*, **31**(4), 323–39.

Frank, R. (1999), *Luxury Fever: Money and Happiness in an Era of Excess*, Princeton, NJ, USA: Princeton University Press.

Frank, R.H. (2006), '*The Economic Naturalist* writing assignment', *Journal of Economic Education*, **37**(1), 58–67.

Frank, R.H. (2007), *The Economic Naturalist: In Search of Explanations for Everyday Enigmas*, New York, NY, USA: Basic Books.

Frank, R.H. and B.S. Bernanke (2011), *Principles of Economics*, Boston, MA, USA: McGraw-Hill.

Fryer, R., J. Goeree and C. Holt (2005), 'Experience-based discrimination: classroom games', *Journal of Economic Education*, **36**(2), 160–70.

Fuller, D. and D. Geide-Stevenson (2003), 'Consensus among economists: revisited', *Journal of Economic Education*, **34**(4), 369–87.

Gahramanov, E. (2009), 'The theoretical analysis of income tax evasion revisited', *Economic Issues*, **14**(1), 35–41.

Geerling, W. (2012), 'Bringing the "dismal science" to life: teaching economics through multimedia', *International Review of Economics Education*, **11**(2), 81–90.

Ghent, L.S., A. Grant and G. Lesica (2010), 'The economics of *Seinfeld*', available at http://www.yadayadayadaecon.com/(accessed 22 June 2011).

Ghent, L.S., G.D. Mateer and M.A. Stone (2011), 'TV for economics', *Journal of Economic Education*, **42**(2), 207.

Ghent, L.S., G.D. Mateer and M.A. Stone (2013), 'TV for economics', available at http://tvforecon.blogspot.com/ (accessed 12 March 2013).

Ghosh, S. and F. Renna (2009), 'Using electronic response systems in economics classes', *Journal of Economic Education*, **40**(4), 354–65.

Gleason, J. and L.J. Van Scyoc (1995), 'A report on the economic literacy of adults', *Journal of Economic Education*, **26**(3), 203–10.

Green, T.G., F.G. Mixon, Jr and L.J. Treviño (2005), 'Have you seen the new econ prof? Beauty, teaching, and occupational choice in higher education', in F.G. Mixon, Jr (ed.), *Shaping the Learning Curve: Essays on Economic Education*, New York, NY, USA: *i*Universe, pp. 57–67.

Greene, G. (1949), *The Third Man*, Internet Movie Database, available at http://imdb.com/title/tt0041959/ (accessed 12 March 2013).

Greenlaw, S. (2003), 'Using writing to enhance student learning in undergraduate economics', *International Review of Economics Education*, **1**(1), 61–70.

Gregory, P.R. and R.C. Stuart *(*2001*), Russian and Soviet Economic Performance and Structure*, 7th edn, New York, NY, USA: Addison Wesley.

Grimes, P.W. (2002), 'The overconfident principles of economics student: an examination of a metacognitive skill', *Journal of Economic Education*, **33**(1), 15–30.

Grimes, P.W. (2012), 'Economic education in American elementary and secondary schools', in G.M. Hoyt and K.M. McGoldrick (eds), *International Handbook on Teaching and Learning Economics*, Cheltenham, UK and Northhampton, MA, USA: Edward Elgar, pp. 259–72.

Grimes, P.W. and J.P. Rezek (2005), 'The determinants of cheating by high school economics students: a comparative study of academic dishonesty in the transitional economies', *International Review of Economics Education*, **4**(2), 23–45.

Grimes, P.W., K.E. Rogers and R.J. Smith (2009), 'High school economic education and access to financial services', *Journal of Consumer Affairs*, **44**(2), 317–35.

Grove, W.A., T. Wasserman and A. Grodner (2006), 'Choosing a proxy for academic aptitude', *Journal of Economic Education*, **37**(2), 131–47.

Hall, J.C. (2005), 'Homer economicus: using *The Simpsons* to teach economics', *Journal of Private Enterprise*, **20**(2), 165–76.

Hall, J.C. and R.A. Lawson (2008), 'Using music to teach microeconomics', *Perspectives on Economic Education Research*, **4**(1), 23–36.

Hall, J.C., R.A. Lawson, G.D. Mateer and A. Rice (2008), 'Teaching private enterprise through tunes: an abecedarium of music for economists', *Journal of Private Enterprise*, **23**(2), 157–66.

Hall, J.C., R.A. Lawson and G.D. Mateer (2013), 'From Abba to Zeppelin, Led', available at http://www.divisionoflabour.com/music/author_archives/dirk_mateer/ (accessed 12 March 2013).

Hamermesh, D.S. (1992), 'The young economist's guide to professional etiquette', *Journal of Economic Perspectives*, **6**(1), 169–79.

Hamermesh, D.S. (2005), 'An old male economist's advice to young female economists', *CSWEP Bulletin*, Winter, 12–13.

Hamermesh, D.S. (2006), 'Changing looks and changing "discrimination": the beauty of economists', *Economics Letters*, **93**(3), 405–12.

Hamermesh, D.S. (2011), *Beauty Pays: Why Attractive People are More Successful*, Princeton, NJ, USA: Princeton University Press.

Hamermesh, D.S. and J. Abrevaya (2012), 'Beauty is the promise of happiness?', Unpublished manuscript.

Hamermesh, D.S. and J.E. Biddle (1994), 'Beauty and the labor market', *American Economic Review*, **84**(5), 1174–94.

Hamermesh, D.S. and A.M. Parker (2005), 'Beauty in the classroom: professors' pulchritude and putative pedagogical productivity', *Economics of Education Review*, **24**(4), 369–76.

Hamermesh, D.S., X. Meng and J. Zhang (2002), 'Dress for success – does primping pay?', *Labour Economics*, **9**(3), 361–73.

Hamlen, W.A., Jr (2000), 'The economics of *Animal Farm*', *Southern Economic Journal*, **66**(4), 942–56.

Hammock, M.R., A.R. Luccasen and K.M. Thomas (2011), 'Teaching macroeconomics principles using animated cartoons', *American Economist*, **56**(1), 1–10.

Hansen, W.L. (2001), 'Expected proficiencies for undergraduate economics majors', *Journal of Economic Education*, **32**(3), 231–42.

Hansen, W.L., M.K. Salemi and J.J. Siegfried (2002), 'Promoting economic literacy in the introductory economics course – use it or lose it: teaching literacy in the economics principles course', *American Economic Review: Papers and Proceedings*, **92**(2), 473–7.

Harmon, O.R. and J. Lambrinos (2008), 'Are online exams an invitation to cheat?', *Journal of Economic Education*, **39**(2), 116–25.

Hartfield, E. and S. Sprecher (1986), *Mirror, Mirror ...: The Importance of Looks in Everyday Life*, Albany, NY, USA: State University of New York Press.

Hartl, R.F. and A. Mehlmann (1982), 'The Transylvanian problem of renewable resources', *R.A.I.R.O. Operations Research*, **16**(4), 379.

Hartley, J.E. (2001), 'The great books and economics', *Journal of Economic Education*, **23**(2), 147–59.

Hastings, J.S., B. Madrian and W.L. Skimmyhorn (2012), 'Financial literacy, financial education and economic outcomes', National Bureau of Economic Research (NBER) Working Paper No. 18412.

Hawes, D. (2000), *Who's Who in Dickens*, 2nd edn, London, UK: Routledge.

Heckman, J.J. (2010), 'The effect of prayer on God's attitude toward mankind', *Economic Inquiry*, **48**(1), 234–5.

Herreid, C.F. (2006), '"Clicker" cases: introducing case study teaching into large classrooms', *Journal of College Science Teaching*, **36**(2), 43–7.

Hetherington, E.M. and S.E. Feldman (1964), 'College cheating as a function of subject and situational variables', *Journal of Educational Psychology*, **55**(4), 212–18.

Hickman, M. (2011), 'Billionaire magnate Larry Ellison settles with neighbors in bizarre tree lawsuit', available at http://www.forbes.com/sites/eco-magnate-larry-ellison-settles-with-neighbors-in-bizarre-tree-lawsuit/ (accessed 13 February 2013).

Hilgert, M.A., J.M. Hogarth and S.G. Beverly (2003), 'Household financial management: the connection between literacy and behavior', *Federal Reserve Bulletin*, July, 309–22.

Horwitz, S.G. (2011), 'Austrian economists and liberal arts colleges as a complementary capital combination', *Journal of Economics and Finance Education*, **10**(2), 31–40.

Hoyt, G.M. (2003), 'How to make economics the fulfilling social science', *Southern Economic Journal*, **70**(1), 201–6.

Huston, S.J. (2010), 'Measuring financial literacy', *Journal of Consumer Affairs*, **44**(2), 296–316.

Jackson, J.D. and J.T. Lindley (1989), 'Measuring the extent of wage discrimination: a statistical test and a caveat', *Applied Economics*, **21**(4), 515–40.

Jensen, G.S. (2003), 'A good country', *The Atlantic Monthly*, **291**(4), 93–101.

Kasper, H. (2005), 'Peer to peer: right and wrong lessons for department reviews', *Journal of Economic Education*, **36**(2), 185–97.

Katz, D. (1973), 'Faculty salaries, promotions, and productivity at a large university', *American Economic Review*, **63**(3), 469–77.

Kaun, D. (1984), 'Faculty advancement in a nontraditional university environment', *Industrial and Labor Relations Review*, **37**(4), 592–606.

Kennedy, E.J., L. Lawton and E.L. Plumlee (2002), 'Blissful ignorance: the problem of unrecognized incompetence and academic performance', *Journal of Marketing Education*, **24**(3), 243–52.

Kerkvliet, J. and C.L. Sigmund (1999), 'Can we control cheating in the classroom?', *Journal of Economic Education*, **30**(4), 331–43.

Kish-Goodling, D.M. (1998), 'Using *The Merchant of Venice* in teaching monetary economics', *Journal of Economic Education*, **29**(4), 330–9.

Kjar, S.A. (2009), 'Using *The Sims* to teach Mengerian economics', in F.G. Mixon, Jr and R.J. Cebula (eds), *Expanding Teaching and Learning Horizons in Economic Education*, New York, NY, USA: Nova Science, pp. 191–8.

Klepper, S., D. Nagin and S. Spurr (1991), 'Tax rates, tax compliance, and the reporting of long term capital gains', *Public Finance/Finances Publiques*, **46**(2), 236–51.

Kornai, J. (1992), *The Socialist System: The Political Economy of Communism*, Princeton, NJ, USA: Princeton University Press.

Krautmann, A.C. and W. Sander (1999), 'Grades and student evaluations of teachers', *Economics of Education Review*, **18**(1), 59–63.

Krugman, P.R. (2008), 'Economics: the final frontier', *New York Times*, 11 March, available at http://krugman.blogs.nytimes.com/2008/03/11/economics-the-final-frontier/.

Krugman, P.R. (2010), 'The theory of interstellar trade', *Economic Inquiry*, **48**(4), 1119–23.

Kvam, P.H. (1996), 'Using exam scores to estimate the prevalence of classroom cheating', *The American Statistician*, **50**(3), 238–42.

Lagerlof, J. and A.J. Seltzer (2009), 'The effects of remedial mathematics on the learning of economics: evidence from a natural experiment', *Journal of Economic Education*, **40**(2), 115–36.

Landsburg, S.E. (2004), 'What I like about Scrooge: in praise of misers', *Slate*, 9 December, 1–2, available at http://www.slate.com/id/2110817/.

Lawson, R. (2006), 'Teaching economics principles with comic strips', *Journal of Private Enterprise*, **22**(1), 168–76.

Lawson, R., J. Hall and G.D. Mateer (2008), 'From Abba to Zeppelin, Led: using music to teach economics', *Journal of Economic Education*, **39**(1), 107.

Ledbetter, M. (2004), 'A comparison of BEA estimates of personal income and IRS estimates of adjusted gross income', *Survey of Current Business*, **84**(4), 8–22.

Leijonhufvud, A. (1973), 'Life among the Econ', *Western Economic Journal*, **11**(3), 327–37.

Levitt, S.D. (2007a), 'This is what happens to people who listen to too much AC/DC', available at http://www.freakonomics.com/2007/08/20/this-is-what-happens-to-people-who-listen-to-too-much-acdc/.

Levitt, S.D. (2007b), 'There is hope for economics: the AC/DC paper was a joke', available at http://www.freakonomics.com/2007/08/21/there-is-hope-for-economics-the-acdc-paper-was-a-joke/.

Lewis, J. (2000), 'Dancing on a tight rope: the beginning of the Marshall Plan', in G. Bischof, A. Pelinka and D. Stiefel (eds), *The Marshall Plan in Austria*, Piscataway, NJ, USA: Transaction Publishers, pp. 138–55.

Long, J.E. and J. Gwartney (1987), 'Income tax avoidance: evidence from individual tax returns', *National Tax Journal*, **40**(4), 517–32.

Luccasen, R.A. and M.K. Thomas (2010), 'Simpsonomics: teaching economics using episodes of *The Simpsons*', *Journal of Economic Education*, **41**(2), 136–49.

Lusardi, A. and O.S. Mitchell (2007), 'Baby boomer retirement security: the roles of planning, financial literacy, and housing wealth', *Journal of Monetary Economics*, **54**(1), 205–24.

Lyman, F.T. (1987), 'Think-pair-share: an expanding teaching technique', *MAA-CIE Cooperative News*, **1**(1), 1–2.

Mankiw, N.G. (2011), *Principles of Economics*, Mason, OH, USA: South-Western.

Mankiw, N.G. (2012), *Principles of Economics*, Mason, OH, USA: South-Western.

Marburger, D.R. (2006), 'Does mandatory attendance improve student performance?', *Journal of Economic Education*, **37**(2), 148–55.

Margo, R.A. and J.J. Siegfried (1996), 'Long-run trend in economics Bachelor's degrees', *Journal of Economic Education*, **27**(4), 326–36.

Mateer, G.D. (2004), *Economics in the Movies*, Mason, OH, USA: South-Western.

Mateer, G.D. (2005), *Economics in the Movies*, Mason, OH, USA: South-Western.

Mateer, G.D. (2009), 'Recent film scenes for teaching introductory economics', in F.G. Mixon, Jr and R.J. Cebula (eds), *Expanding Teaching and Learning Horizons in Economic Education*, New York, NY, USA: Nova Science, pp. 165–72.

Mateer, G.D. (2011), 'Teaching economics with YouTube', available at http://www.youtube.com/dmateer (accessed 22 June 2011).

Mateer, G.D. (2012), 'Using media to enhance teaching and learning', available at http://serc.carleton.edu/media/index.html.

Mateer, G.D. (2013), http://www.dirkmateer.com.

Mateer, G.D. and H. Li (2008), 'Movie scenes for economics', *Journal of Economic Education*, **39**(3), 303.
Mateer, G.D. and A. Rice (2007), 'Using flash to create synchronized lyrics and music to teach economics', *Perspectives on Economic Education Research*, **3**(1), 53–64.
Mateer, G.D. and E.F. Stephenson (2011), 'Using film clips to teach public choice economics', *Journal of Economics and Finance Education*, **10**(1), 28–36.
Mateer, G.D., L.S. Ghent and M. Stone (2011), 'TV for economics', *Journal of Economic Education*, **42**(2), 207.
McAfee, R.P. (1983), 'American economic growth and the voyage of Columbus', *American Economic Review*, **73**(4), 735–40.
McCloskey, D. (2010), *The Bourgeois Dignity: Why Economics Can't Explain the Modern World*, Chicago, IL, USA: University of Chicago Press.
McConnell, C.R., S.L. Brue and S.M. Flynn (2012), *Economics: Principles, Problems, and Policies*, Boston, MA, USA: McGraw-Hill.
McEachern, W.A. (1990), 'Introduction', *The Teaching Economist*, **1**(1), 1–5.
McEachern, W.A. (2010), *Micro Econ*, Mason, OH, USA: South-Western.
McGough, L.J., S.J. Reynolds, T.C. Quinn and J.M. Zenilman (2005), 'Which patients first? Setting priorities for antiretroviral therapy where resources are limited', *American Journal of Public Health*, **95**(7), 1173–80.
McMillin, W.D. (2003), 'Is the economics major dying and, if so, will changes in teaching technology and course content save it?', *Southern Economic Journal*, **70**(1), 206–9.
Miller, B. and M. Watts (2011), 'Oh, the economics you'll find in Dr. Seuss!', *Journal of Economic Education*, **42**(2), 147–67.
Miron, J.A. and J. Zwiebel (1995), 'The economic case against drug prohibition', *Journal of Economic Perspectives*, **9**(4), 175–92.
Mixon, F.G., Jr (1996), 'Crime in the classroom: an extension', *Journal of Economic Education*, **27**(3), 195–200.
Mixon, F.G., Jr (2001), 'Cartel (in)stability on *Survivor* island', *Journal of Education for Business*, **77**(2), 89–94.
Mixon, F.G., Jr (ed.) (2005), *Shaping the Learning Curve: Essays on Economic Education*, New York, NY, USA: *i*Universe.
Mixon, F.G., Jr (2010), 'More economics in the movies: discovering the modern theory of bureaucracy from scenes in *Conspiracy* and *Valkyrie*', *Journal of Economics and Economic Education Research*, **11**(1), 101–13.

Mixon, F.G., Jr and S.B. Caudill (2013), 'Campus competition and co-ed allure: an institution-level analysis of collegiate dating markets', *Economics Bulletin*, **33**(1), 442–53.

Mixon, F.G., Jr and R.J. Cebula (eds) (2009), *Expanding Teaching and Learning Horizons in Economic Education*, Hauppage, NY, USA: Nova Science.

Mixon, F.G., Jr and K. Smith (2013), 'Instructor attractiveness and academic rigor: examination of student evaluations data', *Australasian Journal of Economics Education*, in press.

Mixon, F.G., Jr and K.P. Upadhyaya (2014), 'Eyes on the prize: human capital and demographic elements of economics' Nobel Prize and John Bates Clark Medal', *Briefing Notes in Economics*, forthcoming.

Moore, W.J., R. Newman and G. Turnbull (1998), 'Do academic salaries decline with seniority?', *Journal of Labor Economics*, **16**(2), 352–66.

Morling, B., M. McAuliffe, L. Cohen and T. DiLorenzo (2008), 'Efficacy of personal response systems ("clickers") in large, introductory psychology classes', *Teaching of Psychology*, **35**(1), 45–50.

Mueenuddin, D. (2007), 'The Nawabdin Electrician', *The New Yorker*, **83**(25), 72.

Murphy, J.J. (2004), 'A simple program to conduct a hand-run double auction in the classroom', *Journal of Economic Education*, **35**(2), 212.

Musgrave, R.A. (1987), 'Short of euphoria', *Journal of Economic Perspectives*, **1**(1), 59–71.

Myers, D.G. (1998), *Social Psychology*, 5th edn, New York, NY, USA: McGraw-Hill.

Myers, S.C., M.A. Nelson and R.W. Stratton (2011), 'Assessment of the undergraduate economics major: a national survey', *Journal of Economic Education*, **42**(2), 195–9.

NBER (National Bureau of Economic Research) (2010), *Report of the Business Cycle Dating Committee*, available at http://www.nber.org/cycles/sept2010.html (accessed 12 March 2013).

Nowell, C. and R.M. Alston (2007), 'I thought I got an A! Overconfidence across the economics curriculum', *Journal of Economic Education*, **38**(2), 131–42.

Nowell, C. and D. Laufer (1997), 'Undergraduate student cheating in the fields of business and economics', *Journal of Economic Education*, **28**(1), 3–12.

Oates, J.C. (ed.) (1992), *The Oxford Book of American Short Stories*, New York, NY, USA: Oxford University Press.

Oaxaca, R. (1973), 'Male-female wage differentials in urban labor markets', *International Economic Review*, **14**(3), 693–709.

Okoye, I. (2011), 'Attracting economics majors', *American Journal of Business Education*, **4**(8), 25–30.

O'Sullivan, A., S.M. Sheffrin and S.J. Perez (2012), *Economics: Principles, Applications, and Tools*, Boston, MA, USA: Prentice Hall.
Owens, M.F. (2008), 'The search for an economics job with a teaching focus', *Journal for Economic Educators*, **8**(2), 7–27.
Oxoby, R.J. (2009), 'On the efficiency of AC/DC: Bon Scott versus Brian Johnson', *Economic Inquiry*, **47**(3), 598–602.
Pannell, D.J. (2002), 'Prose, psychopaths and persistence: personal perspectives on publishing', *Canadian Journal of Agricultural Economics*, **50**(2), 101–16.
Parkin, M. (2012), *Economics*, Boston, MA, USA: Addison-Wesley.
Pashler, H., M. McDaniel, D. Rohrer and R. Bjork (2008), 'Learning styles: concepts and evidence', *Psychological Science in the Public Interest*, **9**(3), 105–19.
Pestieau, P., U. Possen and S. Slutsky (1994), 'Optimal differential taxes and penalties', *Public Finance/Finances Publiques*, **49**(1), 15–27.
Pfann, G.A., J.E. Biddle, D.S. Hamermesh and C.M. Bosman (2000), 'Business success and businesses' beauty capital', *Economics Letters*, **67**(2), 201–7.
Pigou, A.C. (1932), *The Economics of Welfare*, London, UK: Macmillan and Co.
Poulter, M. (2010), 'Copyright and licensing your materials', available at http://www.economicsnetwork.ac.uk/themes/licensing.htm (accessed 15 March 2013).
Powell, B. (2007), 'A taste of protection: Coca-Cola in the classroom', *Journal of Private Enterprise*, **23**(1), 154–8.
Pozo, S. (1996), *Exploring the Underground Economy*, Kalamazoo, MI, USA: Upjohn Publishing.
Proulx, A. (2003), 'What kind of furniture would Jesus pick?', *The New Yorker*, **80**(29), 126–37.
Pyle, D.J. (1989), *Tax Evasion and the Black Economy*, New York, NY, USA: St Martin's Press.
Pyne, D. (2007), 'Does the choice of introductory microeconomics textbook matter?', *Journal of Economic Education*, **38**(2), 279–96.
Ramsett, D.E., J.D. Johnson and C. Adams (1973), 'Some evidence on the value of instructors in teaching economic principles', *Journal of Economic Education*, **5**(1), 57–62.
Rask, K.N. and E.M. Bailey (2002), 'Are faculty role models? Evidence from major choice in an undergraduate institution', *Journal of Economic Education*, **33**(2), 99–124.
Reay, N.W., L. Pengfei and L. Bao (2008), 'Testing a new voting machine question methodology', *American Journal of Physics*, **76**(2), 171–8.

Roback, J. (1985), 'The economic thought of George Orwell', *American Economic Review*, **75**(2), 127–32.

Roth, A.E. (1995), 'Introduction to experimental economics', in J.H. Kagel and A.E. Roth (eds), *The Handbook of Experimental Economics*, Princeton, NJ, USA: Princeton University Press, pp. 3–110.

Round, D.K. and M.P. Shanahan (2010), 'The economics degree in Australia: down but not out?', *Journal of Economic Education*, **41**(4), 425–35.

Ruder, P.J. (2010), 'Teaching economics with short stories', *Australasian Journal of Economics Education*, **7**(1), 20–30.

Ruder, P.J. (2013), 'Economics in short stories', available at https://sites.google.com/a/ruders.org/economics-in-short-stories/home.

Salemi, M. (2009), 'Clickenomics: using a classroom response system to increase student engagement in a large-enrollment principles of economics course', *Journal of Economic Education*, **40**(4), 385–404.

Salemi, M. and J.J. Siegfried (1999), 'The state of economic education', *American Economic Review*, **89**(2), 355–61.

Salomon, G. (1979), *Interaction of Media, Cognition and Learning: An Exploration of How Symbolic Forms Cultivate Mental Skills and Affect Knowledge Acquisition*, San Francisco, CA, USA: Jossey-Bass.

Salter, S.P., F.G. Mixon, Jr and E.W. King (2012), 'Broker beauty and boon: a study of physical attractiveness and its effect on real estate brokers' income and productivity', *Applied Financial Economics*, **22**(10), 811–25.

Samuelson, P. and W.D. Nordhaus (1989), *Economics*, 13th edn, New York, NY, USA: McGraw-Hill.

Saunders, P. (1971), 'The lasting effects of elementary economics courses: some preliminary results', *American Economic Review*, **61**(2), 242–8.

Saunders, P. (1980), 'The lasting effects of elementary economics courses', *Journal of Economic Education*, **12**(1), 1–14.

Scahill, E.M. (1998), 'A Connecticut yankee in Estonia', *Journal of Economic Education*, **29**(4), 340–7.

Sexton, R. (2006), 'Using short movie and television clips in the economics principles class', *Journal of Economic Education*, **37**(4), 406–17.

Siegfried, J.J. (2001), 'Principles for a successful undergraduate economics honors program', *Journal of Economic Education*, **32**(2), 169–77.

Siegfried, J.J. (2010), 'Trends in undergraduate economics degrees, 1991–2009', *Journal of Economic Education*, **41**(3), 326–30.

Siegfried, J.J. and B. Bidani (1992), 'Differences between economics programs located in liberal arts colleges and in business schools', *Journal of Economic Education*, **23**(2), 181–8.

Siegfried, J.J. and J.E. Raymond (1984), 'A profile of senior economics majors in the United States', *American Economic Review*, **74**(2), 19–25.

Siegfried, J.J. and A.R. Sanderson (2003), 'Keeping economics from becoming a sexy social science', *Southern Economic Journal*, **70**(1), 209–14.

Siegfried, J. and K. White (1973), 'Financial rewards to research and teaching: a case study of academic economists', *American Economic Review*, **63**(2), 309–15.

Siegfried, J.J., R.L. Bartlett, W.L. Hansen, A.C. Kelley, D.N. McCloskey and T.H. Tietenberg (1991), 'The status and prospects of the economics major', *Journal of Economic Education*, **22**(3), 197–224.

Sloman, J. and D. Garratt (2010), *Essentials of Economics*, 5th edn, Harlow, UK: FT Prentice Hall.

Sloman, J. and A. Wride (2009), *Economics*, 7th edn, Harlow, UK: FT Prentice Hall.

Smith, G.W. (2008), 'Japan's Phillips Curve looks like Japan', *Journal of Money, Credit, and Banking*, **40**(6), 1325–6.

Smith, K. (2005), 'Getting econometrics students to evaluate student evaluations', in F.G. Mixon, Jr (ed.), *Shaping the Learning Curve: Essays on Economic Education*, New York, NY, USA: *i*Universe, pp. 15–25.

Snowden, B. (2004), 'Outside the mainstream: an interview with Axel Leijonhufvud', *Macroeconomic Dynamics*, **8**(1), 117–45.

Snower, D.J. (1982), 'Macroeconomic policy and the optimal destruction of vampires', *Journal of Political Economy*, **90**(3), 647–55.

Sobel, R. and J.C. Hall (2007), 'Can you hear me in the back? Using walkie talkies to improve large section instruction', *Journal of Private Enterprise*, **23**(1), 157–64.

Spicer, M.W. and J.E. Thomas (1982), 'Audit probabilities and the tax-evasion decision: an experimental approach', *Journal of Economic Psychology*, **2**(2), 241–5.

Spraggon, J.M. and R.J. Oxoby (2009), 'Game theory for playing games: sophistication in a negative-externality experiment', *Economic Inquiry*, **47**(3), 467–81.

Staff (2011), *Oracle CEO Larry Ellison Settles Tree-trimming Dispute with Neighbors*, available at http://www.hollywoodreporter.com/news/oracle-ceo-larry-ellison-settles-193984 (accessed 13 February 2013).

Stigler, G.J. (1963), 'Elementary economic education', *American Economic Review*, **53**(2), 653–9.

Stigler, G.J. (1977), 'The conference handbook', *Journal of Political Economy*, **85**(2), 441–3.

Stinson, T.A. and X. Zhao (2008), 'Unmet expectations: why is there such a difference between student expectations and classroom performance?', *Journal of College Teaching and Learning*, **5**(7), 33–42.

Swope, K.J. and P.M. Schmitt (2006), 'The performance of economics graduates over the entire curriculum: the determinants of success', *Journal of Economic Education*, **37**(4), 387–94.

Tanzi, V. (1982), *The Underground Economy in the United States and Abroad*, Lexington, MA, USA: Lexington Books.

Tanzi, V. (1983), 'The underground economy in the United States: annual estimates, 1930–1980', *IMF Staff Papers*, **30**(2), 283–305.

Taylor, P.A. (2009), 'Do they, or don't they? A review of evidence of economics majors' cheating', in F.G. Mixon, Jr and R.J. Cebula (eds), *Expanding Teaching and Learning Horizons in Economic Education*, New York, NY, USA: Nova Science, pp. 77–88.

Thomson, W. (2001), *A Guide for the Young Economist*, Cambridge, MA, USA: MIT Press.

Thurman, Q.C. (1991), 'Taxpayer moncompliance and general prevention: an expansion of the deterrence model', *Public Finance/Finances Publiques*, **46**(2), 289–98.

Tittle, C.R. and A.R. Rowe (1973), 'Moral appeal, sanction threat, and deviance: an experimental test', *Social Problems*, **20**(4), 488–98.

Trees, A.R. and M.H. Jackson (2007), 'The learning environment in clicker classrooms: student processes of learning and involvement in large university-level courses using student response systems', *Learning, Media, and Technology*, **32**(1), 21–40.

Twain, M. and C.D. Warner (1873), *The Gilded Age*, reprinted in 2006, New York, NY, USA: The Modern Library.

US Department of Commerce (2012), *USA Quick Facts*, available at http://quickfacts.census.gov/qfd/states/00000.html (accessed 12 March 2013).

US Department of Education, National Center for Education Statistics (2010), *Earned Degrees Conferred, 1986–87 through 2008–09 Integrated Postsecondary Education Data System,'Completions Survey' (IPEDS-C:87-99), and Fall 2000 through Fall 2009*, available at http://nces.ed.gov/programs/digest/d10/tables/dt10_329.asp (accessed 10 January 2011).

US Senate Reference (2001), *The Gilded Age*, available at http://www.senate.gov/reference/reference_item/gilded_age.htm (accessed 12 March 2013).

Vachris, M.A. and C.E. Bohanon (2012), 'Using illustrations from American novels to teach about labor markets', *Journal of Economic Education*, **43**(1), 72–82.

Van der Ark, L.A., W.H.M. Emons and K. Sijtsma (2008), 'Detecting answer copying using alternate test forms and seat locations in small-scale examinations', *Journal of Educational Measurement*, **45**(2), 99–117.

Van Rooij, M.C.J., A. Lusardi and R. Alessie (2011), 'Financial literacy and stock market participation', *Journal of Financial Economics*, **101**(2), 449–72.

Walstad, W.B. and M. Larsen (1992), *A National Survey of American Economic Literacy*, Lincoln, NE, USA: Gallup.

Walstad, W.B. and K. Rebeck (2002), 'Assessing the economic knowledge and economic opinions of adults', *Quarterly Review of Economics and Finance*, **42**(5), 921–35.

Walstad, W.B. and K. Rebeck (2005), *Financial Fitness for Life: High School Test Examiner's Manual*, New York, NY, USA: Council for Economic Education.

Walstad, W.B. and K. Rebeck (2008), 'The test of understanding of college economics', *American Economic Review: Papers and Proceedings*, **98**(2), 547–51.

Walstad, W.B. and K. Rebeck (2012), 'Economics course enrollments in U.S. high schools', *Journal of Economic Education*, **43**(3), 339–47.

Watts, M. (1998), 'Using literature and drama in undergraduate economics courses', in W.E. Becker and M. Watts (eds), *Teaching Economics to Undergraduates: Alternatives to Chalk and Talk*, Cheltenham, UK and Lyme, NH, USA Edward Elgar, pp. 185–207.

Watts, M. (2003), *The Literary Book of Economics*, Wilmington, DE, USA: Intercollegiate Studies Institute.

Watts, M. and G. Schaur (2011), 'Teaching and assessment methods in undergraduate economics: a fourth national quinquennial survey', *Journal of Economic Education*, **42**(3), 294–309.

Watts, M. and R.F. Smith (1989), 'Economics in literature and drama', *Journal of Economic Education*, **20**(3), 291–307.

Weinstein, N.D. (1980), 'Unrealistic optimism about future life events', *Journal of Personality and Social Psychology*, **39**(5), 806–20.

Welker, J. (2007), 'Making economics stick… try humor!', in J. Welker (ed.), *Economics in Plain English*, available at http://welkerswikinomics.com/blog/2007/08/18/stand-up-economist/.

Wenzel, N. (2010), 'From contract to mental model: constitutional culture as a fact of the social sciences', *Review of Austrian Economics*, **32**(1), 55–78.

Wetzel, J.N., D.M. O'Toole and E.L. Millner (1991), 'A qualitative response model of student performance on a standardized test', *Atlantic Economic Journal*, **19**(3), 8–25.

Wheelan, C. (2002), *Naked Economics: Undressing the Dismal Science*, New York, NY, USA: W.W. Norton & Company.

Whitman, G. and J.P. Dow (2013), *Economics of the Undead: Blood, Brains & Benjamins*, New York, NY, USA: Rowman & Littlefield.

Willingham, D.T. (2009), *Why Don't Students Like School?*, San Francisco, CA, USA: Jossey-Bass.

Yandle, B. (1983), 'Bootleggers and Baptists – the education of a regulatory economist', *Regulation*, **7**, May/June, 12–16.

Yang, C.W. and R.D. Raehsler (2005), 'An economic analysis on intermediate microeconomics: an ordered probit model', *Journal for Economics Educators*, **5**(3), 1–11.

Yaniv, G. (1994), 'Tax evasion and the income tax rate: a theoretical examination', *Public Finance/Finances Publiques*, **49**(1), 107–12.

Index